THE DESERT A CITY

THE DESERT A CITY

An Introduction to the Study of
Egyptian and Palestinian Monasticism
under the Christian Empire

Derwas J. Chitty

ἡ ἔρημος ἐπολίσθη ὑπὸ μοναχῶν ἐξελθόντων ἀπὸ τῶν ἰδίων
καὶ ἀπολραψαμέων τὴν ἐν τοῖς οὐρανοῖς πολιτείαν.
Vita Antonii, c. 14

ST VLADIMIR'S SEMINARY PRESS
CRESTWOOD, NEW YORK 10707
1999

To Michael Markoff

Library of Congress Cataloging-in-Publication Data

Chitty, Derwas J. (Derwas James)
   The desert a city: an introduction to the study of Egyptian
and Palestinian monasticism under the Christian Empire / by
Derwas J. Chitty.
         p.   cm.
   Originally published: Oxford: Blackwell, 1966.
   Includes bibliographical references (p. 216-222) and indexes.
   ISBN 0-913836-45-1
   1. Monasticism and religious orders—Egypt—History—Early
Church, ca. 30-600.   2. Monasticism and religious orders—
Palestine—History—Early Church, ca. 30-600.   3. Egypt—Church
history.   4. Palestine—Church history.   I. Title.
BR190.C48   1995
271'.00932—dc20   95-4143
                                                        CIP

THE DESERT A CITY

ISBN 0-913836-45-1

First Printing 1977
Second Printing 1995
Third Printing 1999

PRINTED IN THE UNITED STATES

TABLE OF CONTENTS

CONTENTS

LIST OF ILLUSTRATIONS

between pp. 96 and 97

MAPS

between pp. 96 and 97

ACKNOWLEDGMENTS, ETC.

To the genial encouragement of Professor Cuthbert Turner I owe my persistence (in 1925) in finding ways of spending the second year of a Liddon Studentship in the Middle East; to the Dominican Friars of the École Biblique de S. Étienne at Jerusalem (the kindest of hosts and instructors during that and the following year) my first introduction to the history and archaeology of the Judaean monasteries; to the generosity of New College, Oxford, at the instigation of Professor (later Sir John) Myres, the opportunity to excavate one of these in 1927-30; to Professor A. H. M. Jones, my companion in excavation in 1928, constant encouragement and help over many years; to Trinity College, Cambridge, the invitation to give the Birkbeck Lectures in 1959-60, which gave the occasion for this book; to my brother-in-law, Dr. George Kitson Clark, and my sister, Miss Lily F. Chitty, material help which made possible its publication.

I am also indebted to Dr. Timothy (Kallistos) Ware for assistance in proof-reading; to a sister of the Community of the Love of God for the spade-work on the Index, and to my wife for aid in its completion; to Mrs. Pat Russell for the production of the necessary maps; to Canon Edward Every of Jerusalem for procuring me photographs of the return of the relic of St. Sabas; to the village of Upton in Berkshire—my parish for over thirty years—for the incentive to link things of far away and long ago with my own time and place; and to Michael Markoff and his mother Nadiejda Alexandrovna for unveiling to me that warm reality of Christian life which the Eastern Orthodox Church of to-day preserves in continuity from the monks of old.

Few scholars in this or kindred fields can be without some debt to M. l'abbé Marcel Richard. But I have been particularly happy in the co-operation also of a number of other continental scholars, notably Dom Lucien Regnault, Dom Jean Gribomont, Père J.-C. Guy, S.J., and M. Antoine Guillaumont. On p. 30 I speak of the latter's confirmation of the site of the Cells. Two bouts of excavation since I wrote that, on one of many groups of ruins at Qusûr el Rubaiyât, have proved highly successful, with dated inscriptions from the eighth century, and others apparently going back to the fifth. A first account has been published by the Académie des

Inscriptions et Belles-Lettres—Comptes rendus des séances de l'année 1965, Janvier-Juin: Premiers fouilles au site des Kellia (basse-Égypte). But he has pointed out to me, what neither of us had noticed, that A. F. C. de Cosson had already visited the site and recognized it as Cellia = El Muna, describing it in an·article in the *Bulletin de la Société royale d'Archéologie d'Alexandrie*, N.S. vol. IX. 2 (1937), pp. 247–53. We should also note de Cosson's article just earlier in the same periodical (Vol. IX. 1, pp. 113–16), tracing the history of the village of Barnûgi back to the Middle Empire.

. . . . .

This is an untidy work. Three references (fortunately not important ones) I have failed to recover: and the process of indexing has revealed in the notes a large number of unnecessary repetitions, and inconsistencies in form, which it is too late to correct. But I know of no other book covering the same ground, and it seemed important to make it available as quickly as possible. Not a little original research lurks buried in the notes. The main text is an introductory sketch, and the larger questions it raises are answered only by implication, if at all. Perhaps in a later work it may be possible to take these severally and marshal the evidence in more systematic form.

. . . . .

This hope was extinguished by my husband's untimely death on February 19, 1971, the work of revealing and interpreting ancient Christian monasticism is being carried on by others, as he would wish it to be.

Here I would add a personal note. Derwas Chitty gave a copy of *The Desert a City* to George Kitson Clark 'without whose support, encouragement and aid these lectures might never have been given nor this book published'. Let me thus link together the names of two scholars, workers for truth in widely different fields both dear to me.

MARY CHITTY
July 1977

ABBREVIATIONS

A.B. (or *Anal. Boll.*) = Analecta Bollandiana.

A.C. (or *Act. Conc.*) = Acta Conciliorum, ed. Schwartz—t. I, Ephesus; t. II, Chalcedon; t. III, Contra Acephalos et Origeniastas; t. IV, Constantinople II.

A.C.W. = *Ancient Christian Writers*, the Works of the Fathers in translation, ed. J. Quasten and J. C. Plumpe.

A.M.G. = Annales du Musée Guimet.

Amm. Marc. = Ammianus Marcellinus.

A.M.S. = P. Bedjan, *Acta Martyrum et Sanctorum* (Syriac)—Paris, 1890–7.

Anacr. = *Anacreontica* of Sophronius—P.G. 87. 3, 3733–3838.

A.S. = *Acta Sanctorum* Bollandiana.

Bedjan = A.M.S. VII (Paradisus Patrum)—numbering as in Bousset.

Berol. 1624 = Codex Berolinensis 1624.

Bousset = W. Bousset, *Apophthegmata*, Tübingen, 1923.

B.Z. = *Byzantinische Zeitschrift*.

C.I. = Cyril of Jerusalem, *Catecheses Illuminandorum*.

C.I.G. = Corpus Inscriptionum Graecorum.

Coll. = Cassian, *Collationes*.

C.P. = P. Ladeuze, *Étude sur le Cénobitisme Pakhomien*, Louvain, 1898.

C.S.C.O. = Corpus Scriptorum Christianorum Orientalium.

C.S.E.L. = Corpus Scriptorum Ecclesiasticorum Latinorum.

Chr. and P. = W. Christ and M. Paranikas, *Anthologia Graeca Carminum Christianorum*—Leipzig (Teubner), 1871.

Chron. Pasch. = *Chronicon Paschale*, P.G. 92, 67–1028.

C. of S. (or Cyr. Scyth.) = Cyril of Scythopolis, ed. Schwartz, *Kyrillos von Skythopolis*, T. und U. 49. 2.

D.V.C. = Palladius, *Dialogus de Vita Chrysostomi*.

De Ob. Th. = *Narratio de obitu Theodosii Hierosolymorum et Romani monachi*, ed. Brooks, C.S.C.O., Scr. Syr., ser. 3, t. 25, pp. 18–27.

E.O. = *Échos d'Orient*.

Ehrhard = A. Ehrhard, *Überlieferung und Bestand der hagiographischen und homiletischen Literatur der griechischen Kirche*, T. und U. 50–2.

Ep. ad E. = Antiochus, *Epistula ad Eustathium*, P.G. 89.

Ep. Am. = *Epistula Ammonis* (ed. Halkin, S.P.V.G., pp. 97–121).

Ep. Ant. = *Epistulae Antonii*.

Ep. Fest. = St. Athanasius, *Festal Letters*.

Epp. R. P. = Thiel, *Epistulae Romanorum Pontificum*.

Epiph. *c. Haer.* = Epiphanius, *contra Haereses*.

Eus. = Eusebius Pamphili.

F.M. = *Histoire de l'Église depuis les origines jusqu'à nos jours*, ed. A. Fliche and V. Martin.

G. Ant., Ars., etc. = P.G. 65, 71–440, Alphabetical Gerontikon.

G.C.S. = Griechische christliche Schriftstellere.

H.E. = *Historia Ecclesiastica* (Eusebius, Socrates, etc.).

H.L. (or *Hist. Laus.*) = Palladius, *Lausiac History.*
H.M. (or *Hist. Mon.*) = *Historia Monachorum in Aegypto* (Greek).
H.M. (Lat.) = *Hist. Mon.* (Rufinus' Latin translation).
H.R. (or *Hist. Rel.*) = Theodoret, *Historia Religiosa,* P.G. 82, 1283–1496.
Hist. Aceph. = *Historia Acephala* Athanasii, P.G. 26, 1443–50.
Hist. Patr. = Severus of Ashmunein, *History of the Patriarchs of the Coptic Church,* ed. Evetts, P.O. I. pp. 99–214, 381–518, etc.

Inst. = Cassian, *Institutes.*
It. Aeth. (or *Itin. Aeth.*) = Itinerarium Aetheriae.

Jaffé-Wittenbach = *Regesta Pontificum Romanorum,* Jaffé, ed. Wittenbach, etc.
Jer. = Jerome.
J.E.H. = *Journal of Ecclesiastical History.*
J.M. = John Moschus, *Pratum Spirituale,* P.G. 87. 3, 2851–3112.
J.T.S. = *Journal of Theological Studies.*

Lib. Ors. = *Liber Orsiesii* (*Pach. Lat.,* pp. 109–47).

Mansi = Mansi, *Sacrorum Conciliorum nova et amplissima Collectio.*

N = Nau's analysis (in R.O.C. 1907–13) of Apophthegmata in MS Coislinianus 126.
N(G) = Guy's completion of the same in his Apophthegmata Patrum, pp. 64–74.
Nic. Rhac. = Nicodemus Rhacendytus' Ascetic Anthology, MS B.M. Add. 28.825.

O.C. = *Oriens Christianus.*
O.C.P. = *Orientalia Christiana Periodica.*
Or., Orr. = Oratio, Orationes.
Oros. *Hist. adv. Pag.* = Orosius, *Historia adversus Paganos,* C.S.E.L.5.

Pach. Lat. = *Pachomiana Latina,* ed. A. Boon, Louvain, 1932.
   Praef. ad Reg. = Praefatio Hieronymi (ibid., pp. 1–9).
   Praec. = Praecepta (ibid., pp. 13–52).
   Pr. et Inst. = Praecepta at Instituta (ibid., pp. 53–62).
   Pr. et Jud. = Praecepta atque Judicia (ibid., pp. 63–70).
   Pr. et Leg. = Praecepta ac Leges (ibid., pp. 71–4).
Paral. = De SS. Pachomio et Theodoro Paralipomena, S.P.V.G. pp. 122–65.
P. de J. = *Prise de Jérusalem* (Strategius: Georgian version), ed. Garitte, *C.S.C.O.,* Scr. Iber. 12.
P.E. = Paul Evergetinos, Συναγωγὴ τῶν θεοφθόγγων ῥημάτων καὶ Διδασκαλιῶν τῶν ἁγίων καὶ θεοφόρων Πατέρων, 3rd edition, Athens, 1900.
P.E.F.Q.S. = Palestine Exploration Fund Quarterly Statement.
P.G. = Migne, *Patrologia Graeca.*
P.J. = Pelagius and John, *Verba Seniorum,* P.L. 73, 851–1022.
P.L. = Migne, *Patrologia Latina.*
P.O. = *Patrologia Orientalis.*
P.P.T.S. = Palestine Pilgrims' Texts Society.

Q.R. = Quaestiones (Q.) et Responsiones (R.).

R.A.M. = *Revue d'Ascétique et de Mystique.*

R.B. = *Revue Biblique.*
Récits = *Récits du moine Anastase,* ed. Nau, *O.C.* II, pp. 58–89, and III, pp. 56–90.
R.H.E. = *Revue d'Histoire ecclésiastique.*
R.O.C. = *Revue de l'Orient Chrétien.*
R.O.L. = *Revue de l'Orient Latin.*
R.Q. = *Römische Quartalschrift.*
R.S.R. = *Revue de Sciences religieuses.*
Ruf. = Rufinus.

S.C. = *Sources Chrétiennes.*
Socr. = Socrates.
Soz. = Sozomen.
S.P.V.G. = *Sancti Pachomii Vitae Graecae,* ed. Halkin, Subsidia Hagiographica 19, Brussels, 1932.
SS. C. et J.M. = *SS. Cyri et Johannis Miracula,* P.G. 87. 3, 3423–3696.
Stein = É. Stein, *Histoire du Bas-Empire,* I. 284–476 (2nd edition in French), Paris, 1959: II. 476–565, Paris, 1949.
Theod. Lect. = Theodorus Lector, H.E., P.G. 86, 165–228.
T. und U. = Texte und Untersuchungen zur Geschichte der altkirchlichen Literatur.

V. Abr. = *Vita Abramii,* Cyr. Scyth. pp. 243–9; for Arabic version, see *B.Z.* 14 and *A.B.* 24.
V.A. = *Vita Antonii,* P.G. 26, 835–976.
V.C.S.P. = *Viés coptes de S. Pachôme,* Louvain, 1943.
V.C. S¹, B⁰, etc. = V.C.S.P., Sahidic¹, Bohairic, etc.
V. Char. = *Vita Charitonis,* ed. Garitte, Bulletin de l'Institut historique belge de Rome, 1941, pp. 5–50.
V. Cyr. = *Vita Cyriaci,* Cyr. Scyth., pp. 222–35.
V.E. = *Vita Euthymii,* Cyr. Scyth., pp. 3–85.
V. Es. = *Vita Esaiae,* ed. Brooks, C.S.C.O., Scr. Syr., Sser. 3, t. 25, pp. 1–16.
V. et R. = *Vie et Récits de l'Abbé Daniel le Scétiote,* ed. Clugnet, Paris, 1901 (reprinted from *R.O.C.* 5: Greek, Syriac and Coptic).
V.G.C. = *Vita Georgii Chozibitae,* A.B. 7, pp. 97–144, 336–59.
V. Ger. = *Vita Gerasimi,* ed. K. Koikylides, Αἱ παρὰ τὸν ᾿Ιορδάνην Λαῦραι Καλαμῶνος καὶ ἁγίου Γερασίμου, καὶ οἱ βίοι τοῦ ἁγίου Γερασίμου καὶ Κυριακοῦ τοῦ ἀναχωρητοῦ. Jerusalem, 1902.
V. Greg. = *Vita S. Gregorii Papae,* P.L. 75.
V. Hil. = *Vita Hilarionis* (Jerome), P.L. 23.
V. J. El. = *Vita S. Johannis Eleemosynarii.*
V.J.H. = *Vita Johannis Hesychastae,* Cyr. Scyth., pp. 201–22.
V.M.J. = *Vitae Melaniae Junioris,* ed. Gorce, *Vie de Ste. Melanie,* S.C. 90.
V.P.C. = *V.C.S.P.*
V.P.G.¹ = *S.P.V.G.,* Vita Prima.
V. Petr. Ib. = *Vita Petri Iberitae,* ed. Raabe, *Petrus der Iberer,* Leipzig, 1895.
V. Porph. = Marcus Diaconus, *Vita S. Porphyrii Gazensis,* edd. Grégoire and Kugener, *Vie de Porphyre,* Paris, 1930.
V.S. = *Vita Sabae,* Cyr. Scyth., pp. 85–200.
V. Sev. = *Vita Severi* (Zacharias of Mitylene), P.O. II, 1–115.
V. Theod. Syk. = *Vita Theodori Sykeotae.*

V. Theod. = *Vita Theodosii Coenobiarchae.*

V. Th. (C.S.) = *V. Theod.*, Cyr. Scyth., pp. 235–41.

V. Th. (Th. P.) = *V. Theod.* by Theodore of Petra, ed. Usener, *Der heilige Theodosius*, Leipzig (Teubner), 1890.

V. Theogn. (C.S.) = *Vita Theognii*, Cyr. Scyth., pp. 241–3.

V. Theogn. (P.E.) = *Vita Theognii*, by Paul of Elousa, *A.B.* 10.

Wilcken = Grundzüge und Chrestomathie der Papyruskunde, von L. Mitteis und U. Wilcken. Erste Band: historische Teil. Zweite Halfte: Chrestomathie, von Ulrich Wilcken. Teubner, 1912.

Zach. Mit. *Chr.* = Hamilton and Brooks, *The Syriac Chronicle known as that of Zachariah of Mitylene* (translation), London, 1899.

Zoega = G. Zoega, *Catalogus Codicum Copticorum MSS qui in Museo Borgiano Velitris asservantur*, Rome, 1810.

Zos. = Zosimas (Abba), ed. Avgoustinos, Τοῦ ὁσίου πατρὸς ἡμῶν ᾽Αββᾶ Ζωσιμᾶ κεφάλαια πάνυ ὠφέλιμα, Jerusalem, 1913 (less complete in P.G. 78, 1680–1701).

PROLOGUE

THE heat of an October afternoon in 1925, in the deep gorge of the Wadi Qelt in the mountains behind Jericho: the monastery of Choziba hanging, baked in the sun, on the foot of the northern cliff: and in its church (the windows had been smashed and the woodwork burnt by the retreating Turks in 1917) two spare and shabby Greek lay monks chanting their office on and on with its interminable, tinny, nasal, gabbled *Kyrie eleisons*.

A young student, fresh from Oxford, having his first taste of Greek monasticism, was oppressed with a strange desolation. Could this be Reality? But if not—how dreadful! For most of our ways of life some justification would remain even if the faith on which we believe them to be based were disproved and overthrown. These two peasants—not particularly good monks—were devoted to a life which would be wholly meaningless and outrageous if God were not real, nor the Christian Faith true.

So in his first week in Palestine that student was faced with the question that can never be set aside, and found a subject of research sufficient for more than a lifetime. How had these monasteries first come to be? What first brought men to this life? And through what vicissitudes had it reached its present condition? In the two years that followed, he came increasingly under the spell of that Wilderness, scrambling over its stark ridges and valleys until, from the moonlike monotony which seems to mark our first view of it from Olivet, each turn of it began to have for him its own character. His constant companion on his journeys was a young Russian exile with the faith of the old monks in his bones.

For three more years he was able to return at intervals to continue his explorations and to conduct excavations (somewhat amateur, for his own part in them) in one of the principal ruins—the monastery of St. Euthymius. Then, unexpectedly, he found himself settled back in England. But what he had been studying in its solid reality—its skies, its rocks, its ruins, and its living inheritors—he could now continue to study in books and manuscripts, building up and filling in, as his time and ability would allow, the story of the monasteries and their early occupants.

These lectures are the result. They do not claim to be more than an introduction. Their omissions are innumerable. They are limited

xv

roughly to the first three centuries of monastic history, and to Egypt and Palestine, leaving aside both Syria and Asia Minor, and dealing in Egypt only with what was to form part of the heritage handed on through the ages in the monasticism of Chalcedonian Orthodoxy: Shenuti, for instance, is not mentioned. Nor have I done more than hint at the great questions to be raised, and the answers to them, concerning the prehistory of Christian monasticism in the Jewish and Pagan world, or the reasons for its prodigious flowering in the centuries of which I write. I have simply tried to tell the story, very incompletely, but with sufficient signposts, I hope, to guide others into research which one day should make these lectures indeed seem child's play. At the moment, even such an introduction as this is sadly needed.

Of one thing we can be certain. This making a City of the Wilderness was no mere flight, nor a rejection of matter as evil (else why did they show such aesthetic sense in placing their retreats, and such love for all God's animal creation?). It was rooted in a stark realism of faith in God and acceptance of the battle which is not against flesh and blood, but against principalities, against powers, against the world-rulers of this darkness, against the spiritual things of wickedness in the heavenly places.

Has it not its challenge for to-day?

THE DESERT A CITY

I

THE CALL

THE martyrdom of Peter the Pope of Alexandria, which we would date on 25th November, A.D. 312, set the seal on the last great persecution.[1] Constantine had already entered Rome victorious: and soon Maximin Daia, who was then in control in Egypt, grudgingly conformed to the policy of the other emperors. Within a few months Maximin was dead, having first lost Asia Minor and his army in battle with Licinius.

Three events in that vital year, A.D. 313, set the stage for us. At Alexandria, as the story goes, the new Pope Alexander (Peter's immediate successor, Achillas, had survived only five months) was looking out onto the beach on the anniversary of Peter's martyrdom when he saw some boys playing at church: he was struck with the manner of an elder boy playing the part of bishop, and took him into his household.[2] In Middle Egypt, an ageing ascetic (he was already in his sixties), fleeing from fame, was waiting by the Nile in hopes of a ship to take him to regions where he was unknown, when the Spirit moved him to go with an Arab caravan three days' journey into the wilderness, to a lonely oasis at a mountain's foot towards the Red Sea.[3] In Upper Egypt, a young conscript, released from the army by the defeat of Maximin, came to seek baptism at Chenoboscia.[4]

Athanasius, Antony, Pachomius—bishop and theologian; anchorite; coenobitic abbot. Sailing up to the Thebaid near the beginning of his episcopate, Athanasius was watched from the shore by Pachomius hidden among the crowd of his monks:[5] and he held converse with Antony at least once, when Antony came down to Alexandria in A.D. 338.[6] Pachomius and Antony never met. But the mutual confidence of the three was momentous for their generation in Egypt, and for the universal Church ever since. To it primarily, under God, we owe the integration of monasticism into the Church organism.

1

Pachomius' disciples remembered his saying: 'In our generation in Egypt I see three chapter-heads given increase by God for profit of all who understand—the bishop Athanasius, Christ's champion for the Faith even unto death; and the holy Abba Antony, perfect pattern of the anchoretic life; and this Community, which is the type for all who desire to gather souls according to God, to take care of them until they be made perfect'.[7]

Athanasius may not appear directly our concern. But his conflict could never be far from the minds or absent from the prayers of the monks in their retreat, who knew that Christ reigned on the bishop's throne in Alexandria in the person of its occupant.[8] And when political necessity drove him at last to share their long quiet, he occupied himself with giving us, in his *Life of St. Antony* recently dead, the first great manifesto of the monastic ideal—a classic of the spiritual life which was exerting its influence over the Christian world within a very few years of its writing.[9]

.   .   .   .   .

It is salutary to remember, when we think of monasticism as flowering with the conversion of the Empire, that about half the ascetic life of Athanasius' hero was completed when he went on into the Interior Desert in A.D. 313. He was born (*c.* A.D. 251) under Decius: and it was under Aurelian, during a kind of false dawn of the Church's peace, that, as an orphan lad of about twenty, he heard in the Sunday Gospel in church the words that give the key to his life's aim: 'If thou wilt be *perfect*, go and sell all that thou hast and give to the poor, and come and follow Me'.[10]

Obeying this, but keeping a little of the money from the sale to provide for his sister, he heard once more the Gospel: 'Take no thought for the morrow'. So he gave away the rest of the money, entrusted his sister to a community of virgins—a 'parthenon'—and betook himself, as one might say, to the pigsty or cowshed at the bottom of the garden of his old home.

He was not the first in the field. There was an old solitary in the neighbourhood, and there were others farther off, to whom he could look for advice. But 'there was not yet in Egypt this continuous chain of monasteries: and, indeed, none knew the distant desert; but each of those who desired to give heed to themselves would practise his asceticism in solitude not far from his own village'.

We have, then, the picture of young Antony at this stage as one of the σπουδαῖοι—'devotees'—a word which continues to be used throughout our period of men devoted to the full Christian life with little, perhaps, to mark outwardly any sharp line between them and the rest of the Christian community. He keeps to his place save when going out to learn from older 'devotees', humbly gathering from many examples the diverse ingredients of Christian perfection. Unlettered, he is persistent in the full round of the Church's worship, and so attentive to the readings of Scripture that his memory serves him instead of books. He is assiduous in the work of his hands, to provide for himself and for those in need—no doubt that monotonous work, the making of rope, mats, baskets and sandals, from palm-blades and rushes, which became the staple industry of the monks because it fitted best with the duty of unceasing prayer. It is a way of life that must have been known in the Church from the beginning. It is noticeable that Athanasius does not use the word 'monk' with reference to Antony or the other ascetics at this stage: and, while Antony shows true subjection to his teachers, there is no suggestion of any formal acceptance of absolute obedience to one spiritual father.[11]

The earnest prayer of the young man is for purity of heart:[12] and it has to be remembered that in Coptic a single word (ϱHT) does duty for 'heart' and 'mind'. He is gradually casting out the temptations of his own thoughts, until the demons, expelled from within, begin to attack him from without, even as Satan in the wilderness attacked the Lord into whom he could find no entry.[13] This stage of training comes to its climax when Antony goes out into one of the tombs near the village and shuts himself in, to be so assaulted that his friend finds him unconscious, and carries him to the village church believing him to be dead—but he wakes up in the night and insists on being taken back to the tomb, where he challenges the demons' attack and they cannot penetrate his defence.[14] Then at last his urgent prayer is answered, and the quiet light of the Christ disperses the demonic fantasies. Complaining, 'Where wast Thou? Why didst Thou not appear from the beginning to cease my pains?' he hears the reply, 'Antony, I was here: but I was waiting to see thy contest'.[15]

It is at this point that the pioneer begins to break new ground, his old ascetic master refusing to go with him into the desert—'for as yet there was no such custom'. Antony is now about thirty-five—which brings us to the beginning of the reign of Diocletian and Maximian. Alone he crosses the Nile, and shuts himself in for twenty years of solitude in a deserted fort on the confines of the desert, where bread is brought to him twice a year. He enters this dark fort as an ἄδυτον.[16] And when after twenty years his friends break down the gate and he comes forth, he does so 'as from some inmost shrine, initiate into the mysteries and God-borne'—ὥσπερ ἔκ τινος ἀδύτου μεμυσταγωγημένος καὶ θεοφορούμενος.[17]

Of course Athanasius in writing this has his eye on the pagan world. Here is the true initiate of the mysteries, who in achieving his Gospel vocation to become τέλειος—'perfect'—is achieving an ideal which the pagan can understand—the very word is common to Calvary and Eleusis. And while, primarily, Antony looked back to Elijah for his prototype, his way of life had also its *praeparatio* in Greek and Egyptian philosophy and religion—Neo-Platonist, Pythagorean, Stoic, Cynic, etc. But Athanasius at once draws a distinctively Christian picture in this respect—Antony's bodily condition is not deteriorated but improved by his strange training. His friends marvel to see his body neither grown fat from lack of exercise, nor dried up from fasting and fighting with the demons. Physically and in disposition of soul he is 'all balanced, as one governed by reason and standing in his natural condition'—ὅλος ἦν ἴσος, ὡς ὑπὸ τοῦ λόγου κυβερνώμενος καὶ ἐν τῷ κατὰ φύσιν ἑστώς.[18]

We are reminded how Porphyry's Life of Plotinus starts off in the first sentence by describing Plotinus as like a man ashamed of being in a body.[19] The contrast is quite clear. Against all types of dualism, pagan or para-Christian, Antony's perfection is shown reflected in his bodily condition, retained right up to his death fifty years later, when he was still sound in all his senses and vigorous in his limbs, with even his teeth complete in number, though worn down to the gums.[20] A dualism which regards matter as evil has been typical of most ascetic religions, and has been a besetting temptation also to the Christian. Hints of it will be constantly turning up in our path. About this very time, at Leontopolis in the Delta, Hierax was treating marriage as an Old Testament condition, and denying the resurrection of the body.[21] But the central teaching of the monks is free from this, even in the extremes of ascetic practice.

Note, too, how we see Antony's perfection as the return to man's *natural* condition. This is the constant teaching of East Christian ascetics. Their aim is the recovery of Adam's condition before the Fall. That is accepted as man's true nature, man's fallen condition being παρὰ φύσιν—'*un*natural'. We of the West have to revise our ideas inherited from an Augustinianism which Augustine would have disowned,[22] to understand the mind of the Greek. In passing we might note, what the mistranslation of ψυχικός ('animal') as 'natural' in both A.V. and R.V. in I Corinthians xv has obscured for us, that St. Paul's use of the term φύσις ('nature') is normally accordant with its later patristic use. Only once—'by nature children of wrath' (τέκνα φύσει ὀργῆς, Eph. ii. 3)—does he seem to use it in a pejorative sense.

We may ask how far the *Vita* gives us a picture of the real Antony, how far a very active bishop's idealized picture of what a contemplative monk should be. To some extent the question is irrelevant—what is certain is that through succeeding centuries this has continued to be the pattern of the true anchorite. At the same time we must remember that Athanasius was depicting a person whom he himself had seen, and whom some of his readers must have seen also. It is reasonable to suppose that he is in his main outline describing the man as he was known to his contemporaries.

Not unnaturally, the bishop's attention is turned to the power that begins to spread from Antony at this point—healing the sick, casting out demons, and with the grace of speech comforting the sorrowful, reconciling those at variance, and urging all to put nothing in the world before the love of Christ. It is now that his words 'persuaded many to choose the solitary life; and so henceforth there arose monasteries even in the mountains, and the desert was made a city by monks coming out from their own and enrolling themselves in the heavenly citizenship'.[23]

The words 'monk' and 'monastery' are here used for the first time in the *Vita* in direct reference to the events described. And it is at this point that Athanasius introduces Antony's long discourse to the monks which occupies more than a quarter of the whole work.[24] We are, in fact, being shown monasticism becoming an institution before the peace of the Church—for the implied date, c. A.D. 306, takes us into the beginnings of the last great persecution. Many 'monasteries' begin to people the mountains in the neighbourhood of Antony's own 'monastery', all looking to him as their 'father'. There is no mention of formal rules or vows, or even of common worship: and the word 'monastery' throughout the *Vita* should probably be understood in the strict etymological sense—a solitary cell, not an abode of a group of monks.

As the persecution grew, and Christians were being arrested and taken down to Alexandria, Antony left his monastery and followed in their train, to serve and encourage them, exposing himself to

arrest, but never drawing it upon himself. His support to the con-
fessors in court led the judge to give orders that none of the monks
should appear there—surely this must have been the first official
mention of a monk as such in public life.[25]

When Peter had been martyred, and the persecution was ended,
Antony returned to his monastery.[26] But the new freedom of the
Church meant less quiet for him. It is to some purpose that Athanasius introduces an army officer as the first person to come worrying
him, frustrating his plans for solitude, after his return. Government
officials had no fear now in seeking the Christian saint, and the
crowds took note and followed.[27] At the same time, a large proportion of the monks in Antony's own close neighbourhood took the
Meletian side in the schism which had arisen (as schisms so often do)
during the persecution and was to persist for centuries after it.[28] Very
quickly Antony was seeking a hiding-place—and his Saracen caravan
brought him to his Interior Mountain, and seeing the place, he
loved it.[29]

Note this love for the place. Throughout our records we find a
contrast. On the one side, the desert is represented as the natural
domain of the demons, to which they have retreated on being driven
out of the cities by the triumph of the Church, and into which the
heroes of the faith will pursue them. Is it fair to suggest that, while
the great hermits were largely country folk, the writers of our
records were more often townsfolk, with always something of the
townsman's fear of the lonely, unsheltered places? But they cannot
hide the fact that the saints themselves, while quite alive to this
aspect, had at the same time a positive love for the stark beauty of
their wildernesses. Antony was to compare a monk out of the desert
to a fish out of water.[30] And when a philosopher asked him how he
could endure without books his long solitude, he would point to
the mountainous wilderness around him: 'My book, O philosopher,
is the nature of created things, and it is present when I will, for me
to read the words of God'.[31]

For St. Athanasius, Antony was the first eremite. But Jerome tells
the story he claims to have heard from Antony's disciples, that there
was at least one before him—that Antony when ninety years old
(therefore about A.D. 341) had been guided by God to go still farther
into the desert and find one Paul of Thebes, who had fled there as
a young man from the persecution of Decius, and had been there
ever since.[32] Certainly this was early believed to have been one of
the origins of the anchoretic life—Christians fleeing into the deserts

from persecution, tasting the sweetness of that solitude, and remaining in it or returning to it when the Peace of the Church came.[33] It has been suggested, but on slender grounds, that Chaeremon, the Bishop of Nilopolis at the mouth of the Faiyum (so not far from Antony's home), who disappeared with his wife into the desert at the time of the Decian persecution, may have been such an early anchorite.[34] But *anachoresis* was in the air in the third century in Egypt—men, sometimes whole communities, withdrawing into deserts or swamps to escape from the intolerable burden of taxation and the public liturgies.[35] The Christians just had another reason for the same course of action. It might be that some of the stranger ascetic practices like the wearing of chains could reflect a time when the fugitives were going into training for martyrdom.[36]

But the Peace of the Church brought an extra incentive to the ideal of monastic renunciation. Pagan and Christian alike had been inspired by the example of the martyrs. In the new worldly security of the Church, the Christian would seek to recover the old martyr spirit; while the pagan, brought to the Faith by what he had seen of the life and death of Christians in time of persecution, would seek a way of not less absolute devotion to Christ.[37]

And this brings us to the third of the great trio.

Pachomius was a pagan boy in the Thebaid—at Latopolis (Esneh) if the Coptic sources are correct.[38] Conscripted at the age of twenty for Maximin's last war against Licinius,[39] he was being taken with the other conscripts down the Nile. They were shut up for the night in the prison at Luxor—somewhere, we may suppose, in the legionary camp which enveloped a large portion of the ancient Egyptian temple. The Christians of the place came with food and drink to comfort the poor lads. Pachomius, asking what it meant, was told that Christians were merciful to strangers and to all men. Again he asked, 'What would a Christian be?' and was told, 'They are men who bear the name of Christ, the only-begotten Son of God, and do all good to all men, hoping in Him who made heaven and earth and us men'. Hearing of such grace, his heart was fired with fear of God and with joy. And withdrawing apart in the prison, he stretched out his hands to heaven to pray and say, 'O God, the Maker of heaven and earth, if indeed Thou wilt visit my abasement, since I do not know Thee, the only true God, and wilt release me from this affliction, I will serve Thy will truly all the days of my life: and loving all men, I will serve them according to Thy commandment'.

Within a few months, Maximin was defeated and dead, and Pachomius, released from the army, was back in the Thebaid seeking baptism at the village of Chenoboscia—the Goose-Pastures— the same near which the recent momentous find of Gnostic documents was made.[40]

The Coptic Lives, enlarging on the Greek, make Pachomius spend a short time before his baptism, and three years after it, practising an ascetic life without being properly a monk at a small temple of Sarapis beside the river.[41] Chronologically, three years cannot be allowed for this, and doubt may be cast on the whole story—except that there was probably such a temple of Sarapis, which was later used as a Pachomian monastery and sought early credentials. But the first appearance of the Coptic story in Amélineau's publications led some writers to remarkable speculations.[42] One even wrote of Pachomius as a priest of Sarapis carried off by the villagers and baptized against his will![43] Certainly the thread is too tenuous for any conclusions about links between recluses—κάτοχοι—of Sarapis and Christian monks.

But we learn from the Letter of Ammon[44]—one of our most reliable accounts of Pachomius as he was remembered by his successors and described to the writer about A.D. 352–5—that in the months that followed the saint's baptism, as soon as he decided on the solitary life, he was solicited by other sects—Meletians and Marcionites are named—and was reassured by a dream (of which another version is given in the Greek *Vita Prima* at a later point in the story) that the truth was with the church in which he had been baptized, and with the Archbishop of Alexandria, Alexander, in whom Christ reigned. The recent finds do at least bear out the impression this gives of Chenoboscia as a place of varied activity of religious thought and life—a village, but surely not the almost deserted village of the Coptic sources.[45] Pachomius' coming there for his baptism is made a little more intelligible.

I am relying in the main, for the life of Pachomius, on the Greek *Vita Prima*, which seems to have been written in Greek by members of the community who had known Pachomius' immediate successors, but not Pachomius himself, and who used some written material (presumably Coptic) and much oral tradition, perhaps about A.D. 390. Though its accounts may be coloured by the conditions of that time, it has a number of traits which suggest the thought-world of an earlier generation: and when these appear, we are doubly justified in relying on it within reasonable limits. The surviving Coptic

Lives are far more highly coloured by later conditions, and seem in general to be at least one step farther from the original sources, though from time to time they add details and anecdotes which suggest genuine tradition tapped at a later stage.

Wishing to become a monk,[46] Pachomius went to the old anchorite Palamon—the man of God and imitator of the saints—and sought to withdraw (ἀναχωρεῖν) with him. Palamon started by telling him that he could not do it—'for this work of God is no simple matter'. He outlined his practice—daily fasts in summer, food every other day in winter; nothing but bread and salt—no custom of oil or wine; vigils, 'as I was taught', always half the night, often the whole night, in prayer and meditation on the Word of God. When Pachomius still insisted that he believed with the help of God and of Palamon's prayers he would endure all he had told him, Palamon opened the door, led him in, and (apparently at once) clothed him in the monk's habit—the σχῆμα.

It may seem surprising to hear already of the *schema*. But confirmation is found in the Meletian papyri published by Idris Bell from the 330s, in which the λεβίτων—the sleeveless or short-sleeved tunic which is one element in the *schema*—already figures in the garb of Meletian monks,[47] in a region not very far up the river from that of St. Antony's 'Outer Mountain'. Bell's Meletians may well have been Antony's disciples in the days before the schism crystallized. But seven years (A.D. 306–13) seems a short time for the *schema* to spread right up the Nile to Chenoboscia. It sounds as if the monastic habit went back even before Antony.

Bell's papyri show other things common to Catholics and Meletians from the time before the Schism—the term μοναχός[48] itself; the word μονή ('station' or 'lodge') for a monastery,[49] whether a solitary cell or a communal abode; and probably the term ἄππα[50] for a leading monk (*not* necessarily, as Bell assumes,[51] a priest)—it occurs in this form in Greek as well as in Coptic. It is, of course, the Semitic 'Abba', and its appearance in monastic Egypt at this date does seem remarkable. We may note in passing that its occurrence in the *Vita Prima Pachomii* is limited to events in the 330s and after:[52] but this may only mean that earlier than that Pachomius would have been too young to be called Abba.

Pachomius was to hand on to his disciples in their more personal training the tradition as to how to keep vigils which Palamon had inherited and handed on to him.[53] His training with Palamon is essentially that of a solitary. And although we have the impression of a variety of conditions among monks at this time—sometimes an elder man and one disciple, sometimes clusters of cells close together, sometimes some rudimentary form of common organization—the aim is the Antonian aim. But whatever his training, we are not to forget the occasion of Pachomius' conversion, and his first promise to serve the will of God, and to serve and love men.

He would go out into the thorny wilderness to collect wood— would endure the thorns remembering the nails in the hands and feet of the Saviour upon the Cross, and would stand there in the wilderness to pray.[54] One day, wandering farther than usual, he came to a deserted village called Tabennesis, and lingering in prayer he heard a voice telling him, 'Stay here and make a monastery: for many will come to thee to become monks'. Assured that the voice was holy, he returned and persuaded Palamon, who came and helped him to build a cabin, or little lodge—μονή—then went back to his own place. They took it in turns to visit each other until, quite soon, Palamon died.[55] Pachomius was joined by his elder brother John. But there was some disagreement—John with the anchorite's aim wanted to keep the place small, while Pachomius was already wanting to extend it with a view to the numbers who would come.[56]

In all this, the writer of the *Vita Prima* is clearly trying to piece together into a consecutive history fragments of tradition handed down without the connecting links. It is not surprising that he leaves us asking a lot of questions as to those links, to which we cannot expect an answer. What he does go on to give us is an account of Pachomius' spiritual warfare which tallies in outline with that of Antony (even his language occasionally proves his indebtedness to the *Vita Antonii*): first there is the inner conflict with his own thoughts, then the stage of demonic onslaught from without, then the victorious growth, in which the wonder-working stage of perfect faith gradually gives place to the calm of perfect knowledge, wherein Pachomius is 'as seeing the Invisible God in purity of heart as in a mirror'.[57]

It is then that the writer brings us to the historic climax: 'After this, when he was on an island with brethren cutting rushes for mats, and was himself keeping vigil alone in prayer to be taught the perfect will of God, an angel appeared to him from the Lord' (this is the first direct vision) 'saying, "The will of God is to minister to the race of men, to reconcile them to Him"'.[58]

So, where Antony seeks to *be* perfect, Pachomius seeks to learn and to do God's perfect *will*.

This vision cannot have taken place later than A.D. 320. To put it much earlier would involve leaving an impossibly short time for Pachomius' training under Palamon and his own beginnings at Tabennesis. What follows belongs to the next lecture. But here we must note how the coenobitic life which he was about to create was rooted in the training of the solitary, and took over its language—so effectively that very soon the terms 'monk' and 'monastery' were beginning to be used, in spite of their etymological meaning, for the coenobite and his convent by contrast with the anchorite and his cell or cave.

. . . . .

Not so very long before or after our crucial year, A.D. 313, a rich young man, an orphan, in the Delta region, compelled by his uncle to marry, spent his wedding night persuading his bride that they should not consummate their marriage, but devote themselves to a life of chastity. She consented, but made the condition that they should share the house as brother and sister. This they did for eighteen years, earning their livelihood by the cultivation of balsam, until at last she herself came to recognize the excellence of the solitary way, and he left her in the house and went on to build himself two domed cells (θόλοι) in the Mountain of Nitria, coming back to visit his wife twice a year. This cannot have been much later than A.D. 330, as Amoun lived on for twenty-two years in his desert, and when he died Antony, who himself died in A.D. 356, saw his soul being conducted to heaven.[59]

Amoun's settlement was on the edge of the Western Desert where it forms a low promontory northward into the Delta country near the village of Pernoudj, or Nitria, about nine miles south-west of the town of Damanhur (Hermopolis Parva), under whose bishop it came. The site is identified by the Arabic name of El-Barnugi still in use. The geographical position and the story of the saint fit well with the subsequent history of Nitria, which was the gateway to the desert—the meeting-place with the world. Here first the monastic community was fitted into the parochial system of the diocese, with its own priests and other clergy. Here too the anchoretic and coenobitic paths are not so sharply distinct and independent of each other as they are with Antony and Pachomius. The geographical point was completely obscured until Evelyn White clarified the real position of Nitria in his *History of the Monasteries of Nitria and of Scetis* published in 1932. Scholars have been surprisingly slow in appreciating the implications of his work.[60]

Close to Barnugi there are natron lakes which were exploited commercially in classical times. But forty miles to the south across the desert, far more extensive natron deposits are found in the long depression known to-day as the Wadi-el-Natrun, where a Salt and Soda Company still carries on the ancient industry. Here is the name, and here survive four famous monasteries, distributed over some thirteen miles of the waste land. No monasteries survive at or near Barnugi; and it has not even now, to the best of my knowledge, been properly explored for monastic remains. For anyone who did not know Coptic, the name seemed to bear no connection with Nitria. It was not unnatural that the identity of Nitria with the Wadi-el-Natrun should be taken for granted—though this made complete hay of the topographical details given in the *Lausiac History*. Actually, the Wadi-el-Natrun is the Desert of Scetis, and Nitria, as Palladius tells us, is forty miles away, at a point approachable in his day by boat from Alexandria![61] The term 'Scetis' is sometimes used in our sources to cover Nitria as well. But the term 'Nitria' is *never* used to cover Scetis. To Scetis, in the narrower sense, let us now turn.[62]

The natural approach to Scetis is not from Nitria, forty miles away across the desert to the north (though naturally monks often travelled this way between the two centres), but from the nearest point on the Canopic branch of the Nile at Terenuthis, little more than twenty miles away.[63] The site of Terenuthis seems to be marked by the ruins of Kom Abu Billu, a mile or so from Tarraneh which preserves the name. It was from Tarraneh that expeditions used to set out by camel for the gathering of natron in the Wadi-el-Natrun before the days of railways.[64] The Salt & Soda Company's railway starts from a point about five miles farther south. In Roman times the industry was a state monopoly, with an office in Alexandria, but its working headquarters at Terenuthis.[65] A fifth-century *apophthegm* tells how a brother Martyrius brought back to his cell a piece of natron he had found dropped from a camel on its way up to Terenuthis: the Abba Agathon insisted on his restoring it to where he had found it, a distance of twelve miles.[66] Smugglers in that remote desert must always have been a problem for the authorities. A papyrus letter dated A.D. 346 from the agent in Terenuthis calls for the arrest of them and their camels if caught in the Faiyum or elsewhere.[67] They would, of course, have an intimate knowledge of the wadi itself, and of secret routes for their camels across the desert to unexpected outlets. More particularly, they would know every well and the character of its water, and every point where an ascetic might conceivably instal himself. And the day might come when they themselves would find that call of the desert.

About the year A.D. 330, the thirty-year-old Macarius settled in Scetis, where he died sixty years later.[68] He used to tell how he had started his ascetic career in a village in Egypt, moved to another village to escape enrolment in the clergy, was there accused of being responsible for a girl's pregnancy, accepted the responsibility, and set to work to provide for the girl, until in protracted labour she confessed that he was innocent: the villagers turning from vituperation to effusive honour, he fled away and came to Scetis.[69] But there is another anecdote which suggests the reason why he chose Scetis for his retreat. 'They used to tell of the Abba Macarius that if a brother came to him with fear, as to a holy and great old man, he would say nothing to him. But if any of the brethren said to him, as if setting him at nought, "Abba, when you were a camel-man, and used to steal the natron and sell it, didn't the wardens beat you?"—if anyone said this to him, he would gladly talk to him on whatever he asked.'[70]

Nitria is the gateway of the Egyptian desert. Scetis is its citadel, with a stark abased remoteness (three of its surviving monasteries are set below sea-level) that even a motor-road from Alexandria to Cairo passing within sight along the low scarp to the north cannot really destroy.

. . . . .

Let us turn to Palestinian origins. Jerome says it all began with Hilarion,[71] a native of the village of Thavatha (this is not the last we shall hear of that name), some five miles from Gaza. Born, apparently, about A.D. 293, he was sent to school in Alexandria, but was attracted to the fame of St. Antony (who can only recently have emerged from his 'inmost shrine') and spent a few months with him before returning, still only a boy of fifteen, to his Palestinian home, where his parents had died. He gave away his inheritance, and settled down to a solitary life on the Egyptian model in a hut near the seashore seven miles south-east from Maiuma, the port of Gaza. After he had spent twenty-two years in solitude there, others began to join him, and monasteries started to spring up throughout the land: this, once more, would be about A.D. 330. Jerome is a very good storyteller, and we cannot put too much reliance on the details of the life he gives us. But Hilarion is certainly a historical figure. Jerome probably got the substance of his tale from Epiphanius, another Palestinian, who had also learnt his monasticism in Egypt, and seems to have been in some measure Hilarion's pupil. Epiphanius' monastery, at Besandûk near Eleutheropolis, in the foothills half-way between Gaza and Jerusalem, must have been among these early foundations. From thence Epiphanius was taken in A.D. 367 to be Bishop of Salamis in Cyprus.[72] Hilarion, Jerome tells us, fled from popularity in Palestine in the year of St. Antony's death (A.D. 356), never to return there alive.

Gaza and Eleutheropolis continue to be important centres of monastic life throughout our period, and retain their Egyptian links. But the wilderness which looks towards Jerusalem has its own history, and pre-history, which Jerome apparently ignores. Towards the end of the second century, the aged Bishop Narcissus had fled from calumny to spend some years in it.[73] Later we have a tradition of fugitives from persecution developing an anchoretic life in the caves of Calamon near the Dead Sea.[74] The Wilderness of Judaea is in itself a call to such a life. Its memories take us back to Elijah, Elisha, and St. John the Baptist—recognized from the *Vita Pachomii*[75] onwards as the prototypes of the monks—and to our Lord's own temptation. The Qumrân finds, and what we read of the Essenes there or elsewhere in the same wilderness, show how the Jews had already been drawn towards something of the same sort. And while we have no reason to suppose any kind of continuity between the Essenes and Christian monasticism, it is difficult to imagine that land remaining for any long period without its ascetics.

Jerusalem, at the head of the wilderness, conjures up another element in the monastic vocation—that of ξενιτεία, or physical exile. It is to Jerusalem first that those look who have heard the call of Abraham: 'Get thee out of thy country, and from thy kindred, and from thy father's house, unto a land that I will show thee'. Twice at least that verse is actually quoted in the biographies of the Judaean monks.[76] It could well have been in every one of them.

The deep ravine which runs from south of Bethlehem under the western flank of Jebel Fureidîs—the artificial mountain in which Herod was buried—its sides riddled with limestone caverns, one of which was popularly known in recent times as the Cave of Adullam—is still called the Wadi Khureitûn, or the Wadi'l Mu'allak, while ruins on its western lip are the Khirbet Khureitûn. This is the Lavra of St. Chariton, which was still in use as a monastery at least as late as the twelfth century;[77] while Mu'allak Khureitûn exactly represents κρεμαστὸν Χαρίτωνος—the hanging cave of Chariton—of which we read in that saint's life,[78] perhaps written by a sixth-century monk of the Lavra, which was known as the Old Lavra, or Souka—the Syriac Shouqa, equivalent to the Arabic Sûq (market or bazaar), of which the Greek λαύρα is clearly intended to be a translation.

The writer was spurred by the monastic biographies of Cyril of Scythopolis—one of them written actually before the death of its hero[79]—to write the life of the man who was believed to have established monasticism in the Judaean wilderness a century before Cyril's earliest great saint, Euthymius, arrived there. Chariton, it was said, had been a confessor under Aurelian at Iconium, whence he had come on pilgrimage to Jerusalem, and established his first monastery in a robber's cave at 'Ain Fara (the one plentiful perennial spring in the Judaean wilderness, about seven miles north-east of Jerusalem beyond Anathoth) before the Peace of the Church, subsequently founding two other lavras, at Douka on the cliffs above Old Jericho, and in the wadi which, as we have seen, still bears his name. The life is, of course, very late, and its dating may well have been prompted by a desire to show Chariton as earlier than Antony. But we have independent evidence for the existence of all his three lavras in the fourth century. Douka is mentioned in the *Lausiac History* of Palladius as the abode of a monk Elpidius,[80] also mentioned in the *Life of St. Chariton* (probably here dependent on Palladius).[81] Souka may well be the monastery in the Tekoa region where a massacre of monks by Arabs is recorded by Cassian.[82] And at Fara, as we shall see later, Euthymius spent the first five years (A.D. 406–11) of his monastic life in Palestine.[83]

These cave assemblages would have been congenial to the Anatolian: and Chariton was the first of many from those countries to settle in the Judaean wilderness. Their monasticism was in its origins independent of Egypt. The word *lavra* does not occur in the fourth-century Egyptian records, and its monastic use seems to originate in Palestine. The organization it connotes is a row or cluster of solitary cells round a common centre, including a church and a bakehouse, where the ascetics would assemble for Saturdays and Sundays, spending the rest of the week in their cells. The meaning of the word *lavra* in this context might seem obscure. Perhaps the sense of 'market' which comes instantly to mind when we connect it with the Arabic '*sûq*' is not inappropriate. Here the ascetics brought together their produce on Saturday mornings, worshipped and fed together, and transacted any necessary business, taking back with them to their cells on Sunday evenings bread, water, and raw material for their handiwork for the coming week. But both *lavra* and *sûq* suggest not so much an open forum as a street with shops opening onto it. And perhaps this fits better with the usual geographical character of Chariton's lavras—caves or cells opening out onto a path running along the side of a ravine.

      .   .   .   .   .

Let us look once more at Antony, established in his distant oasis. The Arabs with whom he had travelled thither would bring him bread from time to time: and his disciples soon discovered him. But he did not wish to be dependent on these. He sowed a little grain in a fertile patch, enough to provide himself with bread, and persuaded the animals not to ravage his garden or disturb his peace.[84] Already we have the picture, constant throughout our monastic documents, of a relationship with animals which marks the recovery of the condition of Adam before the Fall.

His monks in the Outer Mountain, Pispir by the Nile, kept in frequent contact with him, and a few importunate inquirers would pass through to visit him in his Interior Mountain. But it was a journey fraught with dangers for the inexperienced: and he was soon persuaded to come down from time to time to Pispir, where there was presently a fairly constant stream of visitors—ecclesiastics, monks, and men of the world—seeking his advice, his consolation, and his healing power.[85] Palladius tells how Cronius, later the Priest of Nitria, came thither at the beginning of his monastic career, and had to wait five days, being told that Antony would come sometimes at twenty days' intervals, sometimes ten days', sometimes five.[86] It has even been suggested that the Interior Mountain, as a particular place, was invented by Athanasius, and that Antony spent the times away from Pispir as a simple desert wanderer or 'grazer' (βόσκος).[87] There is no sufficient ground for supposing this: the Interior Mountain is quite well authenticated independently of St. Athanasius. But neither need we suppose that he spent the whole of his time between it and Pispir. There is always a freedom of movement in Antony that belongs to the pioneer—and to one who had come through to be able to say, 'I no longer fear God: I love Him'.[88]

NOTES TO CHAPTER I

[1] Eusebius, *H.E.* VII, 32, 31. The date is commonly given as A.D. 311. But Lawlor and Oulton (Vol. II, pp. 264–5) give strong reasons for interpreting Eusebius' dates to mean A.D. 312. The earlier date would mark the beginning, not the end, of the last bout of Maximin's persecution, and would not account for the title of the 'Seal of the Martyrs' commonly given to Peter. The story that Telfer (*Anal. Boll.* LXVII, 117–30) finds lying behind the *Passio S. Petri* suggests that his execution was an individual act when Christian rejoicing at the end of persecution looked too like sedition.

[2] Rufinus, *H.E.* I. 14.

[3] Athanasius, *Vita Antonii*, c. 49 (*P.G.* 26, 913B–916A).

[4] *Vita Prima Pachomii* (=G¹), c. 5 (Halkin, *S. Pachomii Vitae Graecae*, p. 4).

[5] Ibid. c. 30.

[6] *V.A.* cc. 69–71 (941A–944A).

[7] *V.P.* G¹ c. 136 (p. 86, 3–9).

[8] Ibid. c. 31 (in MS. Athen., 1015; cf. *Vita Altera* c. 27); c. 94 (p. 63, 14–18); *Epistula Ammonis*, c. 12 (p. 103. 23–4).

[9] In *V.A.* c. 82, Athanasius speaks of Antony's vision of mules fouling the altar as a prophecy of 'what the Arians are *now* doing irrationally like the beasts'. This suits best the years when he was in hiding in Egypt under Constantius—A.D. 356–61.

[10] *V.A.* c. 2.

[11] Ibid. cc. 3–4.

[12] Ibid. c. 7 (853B).

[13] Ibid. cc. 6–7.

[14] Ibid. cc. 8–9.

[15] Ibid. c. 10.

[16] Ibid. cc. 11–12.

[17] Ibid. c. 14 (864C).

[18] Ibid. (865A).

[19] Porphyry, *Vita Plotini*, c. 1.

[20] *V.A.* c. 93 (973AB).

[21] Epiphanius, c. *Haeres.*, LXVII. 1 (709–10).

[22] Augustine, *De Natura Boni*, I: *De Civitate Dei*, XII. iii: *Enchiridion ad Laurentium*, IV. 12–15; *Opus imperfectum contra Julianum*, III. 206. I am indebted for these references to Mr. Gerald Bonner.

[23] *V.A.* c. 14 (865AB).

[24] Ibid. cc. 16–43 (868A–908A).

[25] Ibid. c. 46: probably the last bout of the persecution.

[26] Ibid. c. 47.

[27] Ibid. c. 48.

[28] The papyri edited by H. Idris Bell (*Jews and Christians in Egypt*) show Meletian monks in the neighbourhood of Antony's retreat.

[29] *V.A.* c. 50 (916A).

[30] G (Alphabetical Apophthegmata, *P.G.* LXV), Antony 10.

[31] Evagrius Ponticus, *Practica ad Anatolinm* 92 (*P.G.* XL, 1249B).

[32] Jerome, *Vita Pauli* (*P.L.* 23, 17–30).

[33] Sozomen, *H.E.* I. 12. 11.

[34] Dionys. Alex., *Ep. ad Fab.*, ap. Eus. *H.E.* VI. 42.

[35] Cf. Rostovtzev, *Social and Economic History of the Roman Empire*, especially pp. 578–9 n. 50 to p. 274) and 599 (n. 15 to p. 357).

[36] Wearing of chains seems at first to have been almost confined to Syria (see Theodoret, *Hist. Rel.*, passim). But it was found occasionally in Egypt (cf. *Annales du Musée Guimet*, XXX. 35, for the discovery of the body of Sarapion), and disapproved of there (cf. *Historia Monachorum*, c. 8. 59). I know of no valid instance in Palestine.

[37] *V.P.* G¹ c. 1.

[38] Lefort, *Vies Coptes de S. Pachôme*, p. 54. 5 (S³), 80. 6 (B⁰).

[39] *V.P.* G¹ c. 4. The Lives make Constantine the Emperor for whom Pachomius was conscripted. But he was not in control of Egypt until the final defeat of Licinius in A.D. 324. The only occasion for conscription which fits in with the dates is, in fact, Maximin's war against Licinius—A.D. 312–13: and this also explains the short duration of Pachomius' service. Naturally the writer of the Life (all the Lives are here clearly based on the *Vita Prima*) would wish to draw a veil over Pachomius' service under the persecutor Maximin.

[40] *V.P.* G^1 c. 5. For the Chenoboscia finds see Doresse, *Les livres secrets des gnostiques d'Égypte* (Paris, Librairie Plon, 1958).

[41] *Vies Coptes*, pp. 83 (B^0 c. 8) and 247 (S^5 c. 51).

[42] Grützmacher, *Pachomius und das älteste Klösterleben* (1896), pp. 39–43; Revillout in *Revue Égyptologique* I (1880), p. 160.

[43] Reference mislaid: cf. Amélineau, A.M.G. XVII, p. xcix, 'son baptême forcé'.

[44] *Ep. Am.* c. 12 (Halkin, p. 103); cf. G^1 c. 102.

[45] *Vies Coptes*, p. 83 (B^0 c. 8).

[46] *V.P.* G^1 c. 6.

[47] Bell, *Jews and Christians*, papyri 1920. 11, and 1922. 5 and 11.

[48] Ibid. 1913. 2, 9, 10,15; 1914. 20 and 23.

[49] Ibid. 1913. 2, 9, 13–15; 1914. 16, 21; 1917.12, 21, 24.

[50] Ibid. 1914, 1917, 1918, 1919 in Greek; 1921, 1922 in Coptic.

[51] Ibid. pp. 43 and 45.

[52] First in c. 61 (Halkin, p. 41. 27).

[53] *V.P.* G^1 cc. 6 (4. 30) and 60 (41. 7).

[54] Ibid. c. 11.

[55] Ibid. cc. 12–13.

[56] Ibid. cc. 14–15.

[57] Ibid. cc. 17–22.

[58] Ibid. c. 23.

[59] *Hist. Laus.* c. 8; *Hist. Mon.* c. 22 (ed. Festugiere); *V.A.* c. 60; Socr. *H.E.* IV. 23.

[60] P. Peeters, reviewing Evelyn White's book critically in *A.B.* LI (1933), pp. 152–7, adds towards the end (p. 156), 'Ses discussions topographiques importent presque toujours la conviction', but does not mention their revolutionary importance. De Labriolle, in his chapter on 'Les débuts du monachisme' in Fliche et Martin, *Histoire de l'Église*, vol. III (1936), shows (p. 302, n. 10) that he had read this review, but not the book, though he mentions it in his bibliography: he repeats the old error—'le désert de Scété, entre les montagnes de Nitrie et le Nil'. So again in 1945, Murphy (*Rufinus of Aquileia*, p. 58): 'The Valley of Nitria lies almost due south of Alexandria, at a distance of some sixty miles. . . .' He actually refers in a footnote here, and again elsewhere, to other passages in Evelyn White's book—but not to the relevant chapter, which he cannot have read. Draguet in 1949 (*Les Pères du Désret*, p. xvii, n. 2) states White's conclusion, without committing himself to it as against Butler's account in *Lausiac History*, II. 189. Fortunately Butler himself, reviewing White's book in the *Downside Review* (vol. LI, no. 145, Jan. 1933), welcomed his identifications of Nitria and Scetis as final. So also A. de Cosson, *Mareotis* (1935), and E. R. Hardy, *Christian Egypt* (1952), pp. 73 and 89–90.

[61] *H.L.* cc. 7 (24. 24–25. 5) and 26 (81. 16–17); *H.M.* (ed. Fest.) cc. 23. 1–3, 26. 11–13; *H.M.* (Lat.) c. 21, Cassian, *Coll.* VI. 1.

[62] See J.-C. Guy, *Le Centre monastique de Scété dans la litérature du Ve siècle*, O.C.P. XXX, fasc. 1 (1964).

[63] *Apophth.* G. Anoub 1, Mac. Aeg. 13, etc.

[64] See Prince Omar Toussoun, *Étude sur le Wadi Natroun* (Alexandria, 1931), pp. 8–15, for an account of the natron deposits and short history of their exploitation.

[65] Pap. Lond. II. 231 (Wilcken, *Chrestom. Pap.* 322).

[66] British Museum MS. Add. 12,170, f. 9v, in the Syriac collection (clearly translated from the Greek) of stories told by the Abba Esaias, which was the source of many apophthegmata in the published collections. G Agathon 12 is a shortened variant of the story.

[67] Cf. n. 65.

[68] *H.L.* c. 17 (43. 14–15).

[69] G Mac. Aeg. 1.

[70] G Mac. Aeg. 31.

[71] Jerome, *Vita Hilarionis* (P.L. 23, 29–54).

[72] Soz. *H.E.* VI. 32. 2–3.

[73] Eus. *H.E.* VI. 9.

[74] *Vita Charitonis*, ed. Garitte, c. 13, pp. 26. 1–4. Can this mean Qumrân? That name is quite a possible corruption of 'Calamon'' (the Reed-Bed')—see Milik in *R.B.* 60 (Oct. 1953), p. 538, n. 8. But accounts of the Qumrân 'monastery' and caves indicate in fact an abrupt end to occupation with the collapse of the Jewish revolt, and no subsequent reoccupation by Christian monks except in the case of just one building in the 'Ain Feshka complex. See

de Vaux in R.B. 60 (Jan. 1953), pp. 83–108; 65 (July 1958), pp. 405–8; 66 (April 1959), pp. 253–4 and Pl. VII; etc.
   [75] V.P. G¹ c. 2 (2.10–1); cf. V.A. c. 7(853BC).
   [76] Theodore of Petra, V. Theodosii c. 4; Paul of Elousa, V. Theognii (Anal. Boll. X) c. 5 (p. 82, l. 7).
   [77] Some of the ruins appear mediaeval, and the Russian Abbot Daniel (A.D. 1106–7) seems to be describing a living monastery when he describes the two churches (one containing the tomb of the founder) and the sepulchral cave outside with seven hundred bodies of monks, including that of St. Cyriac (see c. vii), in wonderful preservation (P.P.T.S. 6, p. 48). By the time of John of Würzburg (c. A.D. 1160–70) the bodies appear to have been recently moved to Jerusalem (P.P.T.S. 14, p. 55—but the record of their translation may be a slightly later gloss). Their preservation had already given rise to a legend, persistent among Western pilgrims through the later Middle Ages, that they had all died at one time, of grief at the death of St. Chariton. So in the fourteenth century Ludolph of Suchem (ed. Deyds, Stuttgart, 1851, c. xxxvii, p. 71). See Sir John de Mandeville (c. xix).
   [78] V. Char., c. 24, p. 34, 4–8.
   [79] Ed. E. Schwartz, Kyrillos von Skythopolis (T. und U. Bd. 49. 2). See below, cc. v to vii. The Life of John the Hesychast was written before his death.
   [80] H.L. c. 48.
   [81] V. Char., c. 21, p. 31. 5.
   [82] Cass. Coll. VI. 1.
   [83] Cyr. Scyth., V. Euthymii, cc. 6–8.
   [84] V.A. c. 50.
   [85] Ibid. cc. 54–9, 61–4.
   [86] H.L. c. 21; cf. Ruf. H.E. II. 8; H.M. c. 15; V.P. G¹ c. 120; Ep. Am. c. 29.
   [87] Reference mislaid.
   [88] G Ant. 32.

II

THE INSTITUTION

In this lecture we shall be dealing in the natural course of our story mainly with the inner form of Egyptian monasticism in the first two generations, before it has any long past of its own to look back to, and before it has felt the repercussions of its own emergence as a force in history.

Of Antony's way we spoke at the end of the last lecture. His Outer Monastery—we know little of its organization, which no doubt was very simple—appears as a kind of community of gate-keepers guarding the approach to the saint much as, later in the century, a community of monks kept the key to the approach to the three-chambered cell, on the cliffs east of Asiût, where John of Lycopolis remained enclosed for forty-eight years—they would open the approach to visitors on Saturdays and Sundays.[1]

There were other communities in Antony's neighbourhood, like that at Arsinoe in the Faiyûm to which the longest of his seven letters is addressed[2] (unlettered though he might be, he was capable of dictating letters of considerable theological and devotional interest, which at one point at least show an unexpected mark of the teaching of Origen).[3] And there were the Meletian communities nearby, in the regions of Heracleopolis and Upper Cynopolis, with their 'presidents'—προεστῶτες—and 'stewards'—οἰκονόμοι[4]—showing a degree of communal organization which, however, must not be exaggerated. There is no justification for saying, as has been done,[5] that they had already reproduced the full Pachomian system. But Cassian tells us of coenobia in his day in the Delta, claiming that their way of the common life was inherited without a break from the early days of the Church in Jerusalem, when the disciples after Pentecost 'had all things in common'.[6] And the other monasteries which appear in the *Vita Prima* of Pachomius itself, outside his own community,[7] are sufficient to warn us that his claim to be the founder of the coenobitic life may need some qualification. Nevertheless, it remains true that in some important sense Pachomius was regarded from the beginning as a pioneer.

It is characteristic of the Pachomian system that all his monasteries would seem to have been in the cultivated land near the Nile—other monasteries we have been concerned with were on the edge of the desert if not in its heart.

Before a hundred years had passed, Palladius was giving the story of a brazen tablet delivered by the angel to Pachomius at the beginning, with the rule inscribed upon it.[8] Sozomen goes further and says that the tablet was still preserved.[9] But the rule which Palladius then gives seems certainly to belong to a later stage in the development of the community, and has little direct connection with the surely genuine rule (though we cannot be sure that even this represents Pachomius' own rule unaltered) which survives in Jerome's Latin translation of a Greek version, and in fragments of the Coptic original.[10] This last bears every sign of being a gradual accretion of ad hoc rules to be fitted into a framework of daily life which is taken for granted, so that we have to infer it. That is just what we should expect from the life of the saint.

The Vita Prima gives us a fascinating picture[11] of Pachomius with his first three disciples. After examination of them and their parents, he clothes them in the habit, and leads them on to the life step by step—first to renounce all the world and their own and themselves, and to follow the Saviour who teaches thus: for this is the way of the Cross. He shows the way by example rather than precept, himself looking after all the cares of the 'station' (μονή)—preparing the table, sowing and watering the vegetables, answering the door, tending the sick—wanting his disciples to be free from care: 'Strive, brethren, to attain that whereunto ye have been called; to meditate Psalms, and the lessons from the rest of the Bible, especially the Gospel. And I myself find rest in serving God and you according to God's commandment.' His example wins their devotion: 'We used to think that all the Saints were so made by God from their mother's womb holy and unalterable, and not of their own free will, and that sinners could not live godly because that was how they were created. But now we see the goodness of God clearly in the case of this our father, that from pagan parents he is become so God-fearing, and is clad in all the commandments of God.... Let us die and live with this man; for he guides us rightly unto God.' Presently he does draw up for them a rule (ἐκανόνισεν αὐτοῖς τύπον) composed from Scripture, for balance in clothing, food, and sleep.

Others joined him, including very soon (apparently about A.D. 321) the fourteen-year-old Theodore, from Latopolis, who was destined to be his outstanding disciple.[12] Theodore was quickly followed by his mother armed with letters from bishops demanding his return, or at least the chance of seeing him. But he persuaded Pachomius not to compel him to see her—and she decided to remain in the women's convent which had already been founded by Pachomius' sister nearby: 'I shall not only see him one day among the brethren, but I too shall gain my soul'.

Numbers were grown to a hundred and went on growing. Pachomius could now depute the material cares of the community to others, and the pattern of the monastery began to take shape.[13] Buildings were of the simplest, in the sun-dried brick of the Nile Valley, no doubt plastered over. Naturally they have not survived above ground sufficiently for any archaeological account to be given without excavation—and the position of Tabennesis is actually unknown. There is a story in the so-called *Paralipomena* (a collection of vivid stories not bent on historical exactness, made probably towards the end of the century, and appended to the more faithful *Vita Prima*) of how Pachomius built a beautiful oratory with brick pillars, then found it too beautiful, and made the brethren attach ropes to the pillars and pull them askew.[14] This sounds like an attempt to explain the actual crookedness of a church the writer knew, due, in fact, to inadequate foundations, faulty material, or inexpert building.

The general plan of the monastery may be reminiscent of the military camps Pachomius would have known as a soldier. There was an enclosing wall (one of the marks of the coenobium),[15] a gate-house and guest-house,[16] a σύναξις—'assembly hall'[17]—for worship (not called an 'ecclesia' except in the *Letter of Ammon*[18]); a refectory nearby,[19] with kitchen,[20] bakehouse,[21] etc.; a hospital;[22] and a number of houses (cf. the barrack-blocks in a legionary camp) holding between twenty and forty monks each.[23] The plan of a house is never clear: but it must have included a common-room for prayer and instruction and any other communal activity of the house,[24] store-rooms,[25] and (originally) separate cells for each monk.[26] By Palladius' time, with increase of numbers, there were three monks to a cell.[27] And this is the arrangement found, for instance, in the ruins of St. Simeon's Monastery at Assuan.[28] But there the monks slept on beds, of plastered brick: in the Pachomian system they only reclined on chairs, of similar material.[29] Each house had its own house-master and second.[30] Some houses would be devoted to particular trades or services of the monastery, others to less specialized work.[31] Three houses would undertake in weekly rotation the daily routine of the monastery,[32] which had as its head or father a 'steward'—οἰκονόμος[33]—with a second in support.[34] Agriculture was undertaken outside the walls,[35] and the dead were buried in the old rock-cut tombs a few miles away,[36] where the valley meets the mountain. Commercial and other business with the outside world would be entrusted to specially approved brethren.[37]

At this early stage at least, when they needed a Eucharist (προσφορά) Pachomius would call in a priest of one of the neighbouring churches, not wishing any of the brethren to seek ordination—for ἀρχὴ λογισμοῦ φιλαρχίας ὁ κλῆρος ('the beginning of the thought of love of command is ordination').[38] At the same time he worked eagerly, at the instigation of his diocesan, the Bishop of Tentyra, for the building of a church (here the word used is ἐκκλησία) in the deserted village, for the shepherds of the neighbourhood, and would go there with the brethren on Saturdays and Sundays to act as reader until a priest was installed.[39]

It was not long before numbers grew too large for the one monastery, and a colony was formed a few miles down the river at another deserted village, Pavau or Pvoou, still known as Faou, where remains can be seen of the great stone church built a century or more after Pachomius' death. Two other monasteries already in existence soon asked to be taken into the community, to make a total of four monasteries within perhaps fifteen miles of each other, recognizing a single head and a single rule.[40] There was also the women's convent, with an elderly monk (we are not told he was a priest) set to watch over it and act as link with the men's community.[41]

This growing lay community now extended beyond the Diocese of Tentyra into that of Diospolis Parva.[42] Saprion, the Bishop of Tentyra,[43] viewed it with friendly anxiety. When the young Pope Athanasius came to visit the Thebaid in A.D. 330, Saprion laid the case before him, and begged him to ordain Pachomius 'father and priest' over all the monks in his diocese. But Pachomius got wind of the plan and hid among the brethren.[44]

About A.D. 337, Pachomius moved his headquarters to Faou, which quickly became very much the largest single monastery in the community. Theodore, now aged thirty, was appointed head of Tabennesis,[45] and was soon acting as Second to Pachomius in his care for all the monasteries.[46] In a short time the community was spreading much farther afield, to Tase in the neighbourhood of Panopolis (Akhmim), some sixty miles down the Nile.[47] About A.D. 340 a coadjutor bishop of that city, 'Arius by name but orthodox in faith', appointed to ease a situation grown difficult owing to the senility of the diocesan,[48] called in the Tabennesiotes to help him, and another monastery was founded near the city, in face of considerable active opposition,[49] and of criticism from the philosophers of the place, who seem to have thought Pachomius was bringing coals to Newcastle—'olives to Panopolis', as they put it.[50]

A landowner of Djodj in the Diospolis region, Petronius, came into the community about now with all his family property, to form another monastery, Teveu.[51] But he himself was quickly transferred to yet another foundation near Panopolis, Tismenae, to take general supervision of the three monasteries in that distant area[52]—a position which seemed to designate him, newcomer though he was, as Pachomius' intended successor, which in fact he became.[53] The monks of the first generation, in jealousy of the newcomer, turned to Theodore: but Pachomius heard of this, and deposed his beloved disciple from all authority.[54]

Pachomius also founded a women's convent across the Nile from Tismenae.[55]

Finally, a monastery of Pikhnoum was founded near Latopolis, forty miles upstream from Faou—again apparently in the face of opposition,[56] which may be linked with the arraigning of Pachomius before a synod of bishops at that city, in the autumn of A.D. 345, to answer charges concerning his powers of clairvoyancy (the *dioratic* gift). Two of the bishops there assembled (probably those of Thebes and of Latopolis itself) had been members of the Tabennesiote community before they became bishops.[57]

A few months later, on 9th May, A.D. 346, Pachomius died of the plague which was then decimating his community.[58] Petronius succeeded him, but the same plague was already upon him, and he died in July, to be succeeded by Horsiesius,[59] another newcomer to the community, who had been head of Chenoboscia.[60]

The whole community is called in the *Vita Prima* κοινόβιον (in the singular)[61] or κοινωνία.[62] This use of the term κοινόβιον (coenobium) died out very early: the Coptic Lives always replace it with κοινωνία; in Jerome's introduction to the *Rule*, and in his translations of the *Letter of Theodore* and the *Book of Horsiesius*[63] and even once in the *Paralipomena*,[64] κοινόβια is used in the plural of a number of monasteries. But it seems to be found in Cassian's account,[65] where it makes credible his numbers for the Tabennesiotes—more than five thousand brethren under one abbot. Palladius gives the total numbers of the community as seven thousand in his own day,[66] and three thousand already under Pachomius[67] (his use of the term 'archimandrite' for Pachomius seems, by the way, to be an anachronism in Egypt[68]). The numbers at Faou are given by Palladius as about thirteen hundred in his time.[69] Ammon found about six hundred assembled when he arrived there in A.D. 352.[70] The other monasteries numbered not more than two or three hundred each.[71] Pachomius, as 'head' or 'father' of the whole community, seems to have set himself clear of the more material administration. In the monastery where he was resident, he took his place as a simple member of one of the houses, under the direction of a housemaster.[72] The practical administration would be in the care of the heads (stewards) of the different monasteries under the direction of the Great Steward at Faou, where the whole community met together twice in the year, for the Paschal solemnities, and for the general audit in August, when new heads and seconds would be appointed.[73] As the community grew, it acquired two boats,[74] one of which was concerned with the sale of the monastery produce, and was in the charge of two brethren. It made a yearly journey, apparently in the autumn, to Alexandria.[75] Later, each monastery would build its own boat.[76]

Within each monastery, three weekly instructions (κατηχήσεις) would be given by the stewards—one on Saturdays and two on Sundays—and two, on Wednesdays and Fridays, by the housemasters.[77] At the end of the century, according to Palladius, the daily meal began at midday, but there were later sittings for the more ascetic.[78] It is not clear, at first sight, from the rule or the early Greek sources that this was the practice in the first generation. But closer study of the evidence suggests this rather than a single meal for the whole community following the prayers which took place at the ninth hour[79]—the normal time elsewhere in monastic Egypt. Any who wished might after prayers return to his cell and feed on bread and water.[80] An instruction would follow the meal on the appointed days.[81] But it rather seems that Pachomius himself, and Horsiesius and Theodore after him, as they would be moving about frequently from monastery to monastery, were in the habit of giving instructions on most days at this time. Sometimes it would be in the open air. Ammon gives a vivid account of such an instruction on the day when he was received as a lad of seventeen at Faou in A.D. 352—Theodore sitting under a palm-tree with the six hundred brethren gathered round him, and giving before them all a different word of Scripture to be applied to each monk who asked him.[82] The *Vita Prima*, the Coptic Lives, and the *Paralipomena* provide a number of specimens of these catecheses,[83] apparently from a collection now lost:[84] one *against Idolatry* is tacked on to the end of the *Paralipomena* in the Florentine MS.:[85] and one other survives almost whole in Coptic.[86] Those of Pachomius, especially, are marked by their intensely scriptural character; for instance, that in the *Vita Prima*, cc. 56-7, simply gives a series of scriptural quotations as heads of meditation on the central dogmas of the Faith. At the end, the leader would rise up to pray with the brethren that they might ever remember the Word of God unto salvation, and each would return to his own house in silence, meditating what he had heard, and getting it by heart.[87] In each house, a 'synaxis' of six prayers would then take place, modelled on that which had already been held in the general assembly,[88] and probably followed on Wednesdays and Fridays by the housemaster's instruction. There seems now to have been a time for conversation, strictly confined to the subject of the instruction received, before retirement to sleep.[89] Some time after midnight, the signal would be given (Jerome speaks of the 'tuba' and the Greek version of the σάλπιγξ; we should have expected just the wooden gong usual in early monasteries)[90] for the nightly Synaxis which would last until near dawn.[91]

The rule, as we have said, is no clear and ordered code laid down once and for all. Three separate small collections follow the main body of 'Precepts', which itself also, though more ordered than it appears at first reading, still gives the impression of a gradual growth. It is, as we would gather from the Life, a minimum of discipline, partly laid down for the convenience of loyal disciples, partly extorted from Pachomius for the curbing of the unruly.

It is the mitigations which reveal best the saint's humanity: 'When the signal sounds for the Synaxis by day, he who comes late for one prayer shall be admonished in the order of rebuke as above, and stand in the place of eating. But by night, he who comes after three prayers shall be admonished in the same order'[92] (Cassian, *Inst.* III. 7, shows knowledge either of this rule or of some parallels elsewhere). Some kind of sweetmeats are distributed from time to time among the brethren after the meal.[93] And when friends or relations bring presents to a brother, although everything must go through the right channels, the brother is not entirely refused a special share in them—he cannot, of course, have them all to himself.[94] Pachomius had clearly never forgotten that quality of Christian mercy which had first drawn him to the Faith.

We must note the insistence in the rule that all who enter the community must learn to read if they cannot do so already, and must learn considerable portions of Holy Scripture by heart.[95] The language, in this region of Upper Egypt four hundred miles or so from the great cosmopolitan centre of Alexandria, is naturally Coptic. The Coptic alphabet provided the saint with some kind of code, the secret of which he shared with a few of his early disciples.[96] Some letters of his, full of this code interspersed with scriptural quotations, survive in Jerome's translation.[97] We can make little of them: but one has the impression that understanding of them depended as much on a common mind in the understanding of Scripture as on having the clue to an alphabetical code. These Pachomian writings, with Antony's Letters, mark the beginnings of Coptic monastic literature: none of them are extant complete in the original.

The community soon attracted others from farther afield, and there was a house of Greek-speaking brethren at Faou, under another Theodore from Alexandria, some thirteen years before Pachomius' death. Its first inmates included two Romans and an Armenian, as well as four Alexandrians.[98] Their successors in this house were probably responsible for the Vita Prima of Pachomius and Theodore (in a single work), which, while using Coptic material no longer extant, was itself composed in Greek.[99]

Certain aspects of this early Antonian and Pachomian literature may be noted in passing. In both, there is great stress on Διάκρισις— discrimination.[100] The spiritual life is directed towards the 'acquiring of Holy Spirit'.[101] In the Letters of Antony, this is the attainment of the Spirit of Adoption,[102] and the becoming 'friends and brothers' of Jesus—John xv. 15 is quoted three times with the addition of 'brothers'.[103] In the Greek Pachomian sources, the personality of the Holy Spirit is less clear.[104] Here, too, as in the Vita Antonii but not in Antony's Letters, nor in the Coptic Catecheses of Pachomius and his successors,[105] the name of Jesus is never found apart from the title of Christ. But we note how it is said of Pachomius that 'more than the everlasting torments he feared to be estranged from the humility and sweetness of the Son of God, Our Lord Jesus Christ'.[106]

Common to all this literature is a sobriety which speaks of an early time when a paganism steeped in false miracle was very much of a present reality. The Life of Pachomius echoes that of Antony in its disallowance of any genuine demonic foreknowledge.[107] And it describes, I think, only three physical miracles—simple works of healing—wrought by the saint.[108] Pachomius' teaching here is worth quoting: 'After the manifest healings of the body, there are also spiritual healings. For if a man intellectually blind, in that he does not see the light of God because of idolatry, afterwards is guided by faith in the Lord and gains his sight, in coming to know the only true God, is not this a great healing and salvation?... One of the brethren asked me, "Tell us one of the visions you see". And I said to him, "A sinner like me does not ask God that he may see visions: for that is against His will, and is error.... Hear all the same about a great vision. If you see a man pure and humble, it is a great vision. For what is greater than such a vision, to see the Invisible God in a visible man, His temple?" '[109]

In September, A.D. 346, Zacchaeus and Theodore were taking the Tabennesiote boat down to Alexandria. Hearing that Antony was in his Outer Mountain, they moored and went up to receive his blessing. We are given his conversation with Zacchaeus when he learnt from their tears that Pachomius was dead: 'Do not weep. All you are become as Abba Pachomius. I tell you, it was a great ministry he undertook in the assemblage of so many brethren, and he goes the way of the Apostles.' Zacchaeus protests: 'You rather, father, are the light of all this world'. But Antony answers: 'I persuade you otherwise, Zacchaeus. At the beginning, when I became a monk, there was no coenobium to nourish other souls, but each of the early monks after the Persecution used to practise his asceticism alone. And afterwards your father made this good thing from the Lord. Another before him, called Aotas, wanted to obtain this ministry: and since he did not put all his heart to the endeavour, he did not achieve it. But of your father I have often heard how well he was conducting himself according to the Scriptures. Yes and indeed I have often wanted to see him in the body: but I suppose I was not worthy. Still, in the Kingdom of Heaven we see each other and all the holy Fathers—but rather, our Master and God, Jesus Christ.'[110]

It would not have been so surprising if Antony had visited him, for he showed remarkable freedom both in correspondence and in movement. It is said that in A.D. 335 he wrote to Constantine pleading for Athanasius on his first exile, and received a reply from the emperor that he could not overlook the decision of the Council of Tyre.[111] Certainly when Athanasius was returned from that exile, Antony came down to Alexandria, apparently for three days in July, A.D. 338, to demonstrate his support. Rumour may very well have represented him as falling on the Meletian or Arian side.[112] He visited Didymus the Blind,[113] and it is natural to suppose that this was also the occasion of his visit to Amoun of Nitria.[114]

We have suggested that the date of Amoun's withdrawal to Nitria may have been about A.D. 330, and was certainly not much later. The dates, so far as we know them, of his earliest companions and disciples there, fit in with this. Pambo was born about A.D. 304,[115] Benjamin about A.D. 311.[116] Macarius the Alexandrian—or 'the City man'—to be carefully distinguished from the Egyptian who founded Scetis—was baptized at the age of forty about A.D. 333.[117] Nathanael had built his cell when anchorites were still few, and in Palladius' days towards the end of the century it was empty, abandoned because it was too near civilization. About A.D. 338, Nathanael moved to a cell still nearer the village: but after three or four months there, he realized that this was a temptation of the devil, and returned to his first cell, not to leave it until his death thirty-seven years later.[118]

By A.D. 338, numbers had increased sufficiently for Amoun to be concerned to know what to do with those who wanted more complete solitude. Antony proposed that after the customary ninth-hour meal they should go out into the desert. They walked until sunset, when Antony said, 'Let us make a prayer and plant a cross here, that those who want to build may build here, so that those also who come from yonder to visit these, may taste their little snack at the ninth hour, and so come; and that those who go from here may do the same, and remain undistracted in their visits to each other'. The distance, we are told, was about twelve miles—not a bad walk for an old man of eighty-seven, between three o'clock in the afternoon and sunset.[119]

Clearly this is the record of the founding of the second Nitrian settlement of the Cells—a settlement, as it became, of some six hundred anchorites, their cells so scattered as to be out of earshot of each other; dependent on Nitria for bread, but with their own priest and church.[120] Cassian gives the distance from Nitria as only five miles,[121] Sozomen as seven,[122] Rufinus as ten,[123] and the twelve of the *Apophthegmata* may well be an exaggeration. But as the Cells were scattered over a wide area, some of them as much as three miles from the church—and Nitria also must have been a fairly widespread settlement—the apparent discrepancy need not worry us greatly.

The exact topography of the monastic Mountain of Nitria awaits elucidation. A river, or water-channel, seems to have separated it from the village, which was near enough for it to be quite usual, in early times at least, for an anchorite to have a Διακονητής—'agent'— among the villagers—a man of the world who would look after the monk's material interests, seeing that he did not lack for necessary supplies.[124] The picture in the *Historia Monachorum* of a hollow on the way, with water that had receded, and crocodiles asleep on its banks, seems consistent with this land of natron lakes.[125] There is a channel linking the Nile with Lake Mariut, which passes some four miles south of the present village of Barnugi, and there may have been another nearer the village in the fourth century.

In this region, the 'mountain' does not rise to more than four metres above sea-level—with a 'tell' rising some three metres higher. Twelve miles south of the village, just beyond the Nubariya Canal, the desert rises to eleven or even fifteen metres. Here the 1:100,000 map shows, spread over something like a six-mile stretch from east to west, a series of *Qusûr*—or 'castles'—Qasr el Waheidi, Qusûr el Rubaiyat, etc. I have no indication beyond what the map tells us as to what these are. But the word *Qasr* is often used of the kind of stone building that we may expect the cells to have been: and I strongly suspect that a visit would prove them to be the anchorites' Cells, twelve miles from Nitria and scattered out of earshot of each other, of which we have spoken. For here the truer desert has begun.

(A rapid inspection of the region by M. Antoine Guillaumont in March, 1964, discovered strong positive evidence in support of this conjecture, which it is hoped to confirm by excavation. See A. Guillaumont, *Le site des 'Cellia'*, in Revue Archéologique, 1964, tom. II (July-September), pp. 43–50.)

In Nitria, the ascetics might live alone, or in pairs, or in larger numbers. Our first and only detailed accounts are from half a century later, in Palladius and the *Historia Monachorum*:[126] but what they tell us probably holds good in general outline for the time when numbers were still comparatively small. Rufinus in his *Ecclesiastical History*[127] speaks of the numbers about A.D. 373 as three thousand or more. Palladius speaks of five thousand when he was there twenty years later. These are said in the *Historia Monachorum* to have occupied some fifty 'stations' (μοναί) of all sizes, so that if some of these had only two or three monks, others must have held several hundred. And, in fact, we read in Palladius' *Dialogue on the Life of St. John Chrysostom* of one such with 210 monks, and another with 150.[128] There was no question of being out of earshot of each other. If you stood at the centre about the ninth hour, you would hear psalmody from every station until you thought you were up in Paradise. Here at the centre was the one 'ecclesia'—the word seems to denote, as in Syria, the whole group of church-community buildings, not simply the place of worship (which in Athanasius at least is called the κυριακόν—whence our word 'church'). The whole body of monks, it seems, would assemble there on Saturdays and Sundays for common worship and a common meal. Three palm-trees stood in the compound, with whips hanging from them for punishment of monks, of robbers, and of other transgressors respectively. There were seven bakeries, to provide bread for the needs of all in Nitria and in the Cells. There was a guest-house, where visitors could stay free and at their ease for a week: after that they would be set to work in the garden, the bakeries, or the kitchen—or, if literate, on books, when they would be left in solitude until noon. Visitors would stay at the guest-house sometimes for two or three years without taking the habit. Doctors and pastry-cooks were to be found in the Mountain of Nitria, and wine was in use and on sale—a thing unthinkable with the Tabennesiotes.[129] Apart from the normal monastic rope-making, the staple industry was linen—another reminder that we are nearer the rich fields of the Delta: for we cannot imagine flax being carried thence to be worked in the Wadi-el-Natrun. It is an industry found also, as one might expect, in the Tabennesiote Community: Ammon tells of a house of twenty-two linen-weavers at Faou.[130]

Both Antony and Pachomius avoided ordination. Nitria had its clergy from very early times. Pambo, though one story at least represents him as illiterate,[131] was probably a priest before A.D. 340.[132] Certainly about A.D. 356 a letter of Theodore the Tabennesiote is addressed 'To the beloved brethren the priests and deacons and monks in the Mountain of Nitria':[133] and the *Letter of Ammon*, in which this is preserved, names four priests—Pambo and Pior, Heraclides (who seems to preside) and Hagius.[134] Already, then, we have a full complement of clergy headed by a college of priests. In Palladius' time, these last numbered eight, who formed a delibera-tive council, though celebration of the Liturgy, instruction, and administration of justice were entrusted to the senior priest alone.[135]

The Mountain of Nitria was always in close contact with its diocesan bishop at Damanhur (Hermopolis Parva), about ten miles away. Dracontius, who became bishop probably in A.D. 353-4, had himself been abbot of a monastery, though we know not where: and his immediate successors, Isidore[136] and Dioscorus,[137] had both been prominent monks in Nitria. Raised against his will to the episcopate, Dracontius started by returning to his monastery and refusing to function (it rather seems that his monks had extracted from him beforehand a promise that he would do this). We possess Athanasius' letter of sharp though friendly remonstrance,[138] pressing upon him his duty to the Church, and naming no less than seven other bishops who had been monks—among them the great Sarapion of Thmuis, who had been a disciple of Antony, and was certainly bishop by A.D. 339; and probably one of the two Tabennesiote bishops who had been at the Synod of Latopolis in A.D. 345.[139] Athanasius' letter seems to have been effective: for Dracontius was certainly functioning when he was arrested and sent into exile in A.D. 356.[140]

There was early a tendency for monks, after a period of training in coenobitic ways in Nitria, to pass on to the anchoretic life in the Cells. This is in marked contrast with the ideal of Pachomius, or of Basil, for whom the coenobium is a lifelong vocation. It is a preparation for what we shall find in Palestine in the next century. Its mind is seen in the story of a conversation between Amoun and Antony, which is to be taken probably as a contrast of ideals rather than a historical episode. 'I have more toils than you,' says Amoun, 'and why has your name been magnified among men above mine?' Antony answers, 'Because I love God more than you do'.[141]

The Cells also had their church and their priest, who was probably a member of the Nitrian chapter. But we do not know how early this goes back. When the *Letter of Ammon* speaks of an 'Isidore, priest of the anchorites in the mountain of Nitria' some time before A.D. 370, it seems probable that a priest of the Cells is meant.[142] But the first of whom we definitely know as occupying that position is Macarius the Alexandrian.[143]

Macarius, who died in A.D. 393, was then aged about a hundred.[144] He was a survival from the first adventurous generation, whose experience was to set more sober lines for their successors. In the world, in Alexandria, he had been a confectioner.[145] His conversion at the age of forty[146] seems to have been of a kind that made him eager to outstrip all others in asceticism. Hearing that the Taben-nesiotes ate no cooked food in Lent, he went without cooked food for seven years.[147] Desiring to overcome sleep, he kept himself awake for twenty days, then knew he must yield to nature's de-mands.[148] Convicting himself of vengefulness in killing a mosquito that had bitten him, he stayed naked for six months by the Marsh of Scetis, 'where the mosquitoes pierce through the hides of wild boars', and came back to his cell so swollen and disfigured that he could only be recognized by his voice.[149] Wanting, again, to prove that he was not outdone by the Tabennesiotes, he went up there disguised as an ordinary workman, and begged to be received as a monk. Having overcome Pachomius' hesitation on account of his age, he so surpassed them all in his 'fleshless' life that they all threat-ened to leave if Pachomius did not turn him out. Pachomius then realized that it was Macarius, and thanked him for having taught his disciples a lesson.[150] The story has its difficulties as history. But it is one of a number which show Pachomius not having an easy time with his disciples.[151] As Pachomius died in A.D. 346, it implies that Macarius' reputation spread very quickly after his conversion. But it also suggests that these stories belong to the earlier years of his ascetic career, and had no doubt grown by the time they reached Palladius. By that time, also, the monks had learned their lesson, and abnormal asceticism was generally discouraged.

Like others in the first generation, he was by no means confined to one place. He had four cells, one in Nitria, one at the Cells, one in Scetis, and one 'to the south-west'—whatever that may mean.[152] Mention of Scetis brings us once more to the other great Macarius, the Egyptian, who had led the way into that uncompromising utter desert about A.D. 330. Others soon began to follow him there. But for ten years at least they were without a priest. It was forty miles across the desert to Nitria—not like the well-trodden twenty miles to Terenuthis, but a path that you had to know as a natron-smuggler might know it, or run the risk of being lost in the sands. But forty miles across the desert the 'Boy-Old-Man' (παιδαριογέρων), as he was called,[153] would go to Abba Pambo's Mass.[154] The story that he told on one such occasion illustrates both the 'wanderlust' that he shared with his Alexandrian namesake, and the belief that the monastic life dated back long before his generation. Seized with a desire to go and see what lay in the desert, he fought it for five years, then went—and found an oasis with a lake and an island in it, and two naked old men, an Egyptian and a Libyan, who had been there forty years, having come from a coenobium in Egypt. They told him, 'Except a man renounce all the things of the world, he cannot be a monk'. When Macarius said he was weak, and could not do as they, they told him, 'Even if you cannot do as we do, sit in your cell and weep for your sins'. 'And so', he said, 'I told you that I have not yet become a monk: but I have seen monks. Forgive me, my brethren.'

Macarius may have felt the old men's advice pointed. For staying in his cell does not seem to have come easy to him. The stories show him constantly moving about. Yet he moves with the freedom of a king in his own domain, as a kind of embodied spirit of this desert. Once, when numbers were already growing in Scetis, he went to visit St. Antony—right over, it seems, to his Interior Mountain.[155] He told him that they had no Oblation in their place. Perhaps this means that he was becoming anxious about the needs of other monks less capable of these long desert journeys—the account of Chaeremon in his cave twelve miles from the Marsh and the water supply and forty miles from the church (surely that of Nitria) seems to go back to this time.[156] All who went to Scetis were bent on loneliness, but forty miles might be rather too much! Certainly Macarius was in the end ordained priest—perhaps in A.D. 340, when at the age of forty he attained the grace of healings and predictions.[157]

Life in Scetis would be made more practicable by the visits of the wardens and collectors of natron, who would come with their camels from Terenuthis, and act as middlemen for the anchorites' produce of rope and baskets. But the monks would also go up at harvest-time and hire themselves out to work in the fields[158] (as Scetis was below sea-level, the *Apophthegmata* are quite correct in speaking regularly of 'going *up*' from thence to Egypt). They might also from time to time take their wares up to market in the Delta.[159] There is a strange story of Macarius on one such occasion lodging in the deserted pagan temple at Terenuthis, and using a mummy for his pillow. The demons tried to play pranks on him, calling out, 'So-and-so' (a girl's name), 'come to the bath with us'— and then an answer from the pillow, 'I can't, I've got a stranger on top of me'. The old man, unperturbed, began to beat the mummy, saying, 'Get up, go off into the darkness if you can'. The demons fled away ashamed, crying out, 'Thou hast conquered us'.[160]

Once he was going up from Scetis to Nitria. His disciple, going ahead, met a pagan priest and cried out, 'Ai ai, demon, where are you running?' The pagan turned and beat him with a club, and left him half dead, then went on with the club, and met Macarius, who just said, 'Save you, save you, you weary man'. The pagan in amazement asked, 'What good did you see in me, that you talked to me like that?' 'I saw you toiling', says the old man, 'and don't you know that you are toiling in vain?' Says the priest, 'And I was pricked to the heart at your greeting, and knew that you are on God's side. But another bad monk met me and insulted me, and I beat him to death.' Taking Macarius by the feet, he said, 'I will not let you go unless you make me a monk'.[161]

While on the subject of relations with pagans, we may record the story told by Abba Olympius of the pagan priest who came down to Scetis and lodged in his cell. Seeing the monks' way of life, he asked his host, 'With this way of life, have you no visions with your God?' 'No', said the monk; and the priest replied, 'Now when we perform rites to our god, he hides nothing from us, but reveals to us his mysteries. And you with all these toils and vigils and silences and asceticisms, do you say that you have no visions? Certainly if that is so, you have evil thoughts in your hearts which separate you from your God, and that is why He does not reveal to you His mysteries.' When Olympius reported this to the old men, they wondered and said, 'Yes, that is it. For unclean thoughts separate God from a man.'[162] The story is significant in a number of ways—the pagan desire for visions, with which the Christian is not really concerned; and at the same time the humility of the monk, ready to learn his lesson from the pagan without any counter-criticism, however valid.

Macarius' original settlement is thought to have been somewhere in the region of the surviving monastery of Deir el Baramûs ('the monastery of the Roman brethren') towards the western end of the valley.[163] As numbers increased, he seems to have moved to slightly higher ground beyond a low ridge at the eastern end, near to the monastery that now bears his name.[164] By Cassian's time there were four congregations, or 'Ecclesiae',[165] in Scetis, of which the third is now represented by the twin monasteries of Abba Bshoi and of the Syrians, while the fourth, that of St. John the Short, has been deserted for a number of centuries: its site is known.[166]

.   .   .   .   .

Sailing down the Nile after their visit to Antony, Zacchaeus and Theodore reached Alexandria in time for Athanasius' great home-coming after his second exile, when the authorities and the people are said to have come out a hundred miles to meet him, on 1st October, A.D. 346.[167] His return was the signal for a great surge of religious enthusiasm, and a spurt in the outflow to the deserts.[168] Nitria and Scetis, being nearest to Alexandria, no doubt took the greater number. But up and down the Nile Valley the increase was marked (we may note that the great recluse, John of Lycopolis, seems to have taken to his cave-cell about this year).[169] Athanasius' preaching continued to encourage it. Some time in A.D. 352 he was heard by the newly-baptized, seventeen-year-old Ammon.[170] Diverted from a Theban monk suspected of heresy, whom he had first met and thought of following, Ammon was sent to Faou on the Tabennesiote boat, which had just arrived under its new crew, Theophilus and Copres, with letters for Athanasius from Theodore.

For the increase in numbers of the community, and its economic growth and prosperity (what a contrast to the deserted villages of thirty years earlier!), had proved too much for the meek Horsiesius, who before five years were out had been faced with a definite revolt from the community on the part of one monastery, and had called in Theodore to take over the reins of government—though Theodore persistently refused to regard himself as other than Horsiesius' deputy. Order was soon restored under his vigorous and sympathetic leadership. The revolted monastery was brought back.[171] The community was extended in his time to two monasteries by Hermopolis Magna (Ashmunein), a further hundred miles down the Nile. Another monastery was added at Hermonthis above Thebes, and a women's convent, Vichne, a mile from Faou.[172] The *Letter of Ammon* gives a vivid first-hand picture of the life of the community during his three years with it—though we must remember that these are the memoirs of an impressionable lad written down some forty years later. Theodore recognized in Ammon one made for an ecclesiastical career; and while intent on his education in the monastic life[173] (Ammon learned Sahidic at Faou),[174] he raised no objection when after three years the lad was discovered by a family friend, and urged to go and see his sorrowing mother—who had meanwhile become a Christian. But he told him, after seeing his parents, to go to the Mountain of Nitria.[175]

Five months after Ammon's arrival there, Antony died in his Interior Mountain, on 17th January, A.D. 356,[176] bequeathing his two goat-skin mantles, one to Athanasius, and one to Sarapion of Thmuis.[177] A month after his death, Athanasius was a fugitive.[178]

Dracontius of Damanhur was relegated to the fort of Thabubastum, north of the Bitter Lakes (where he was visited by Hilarion),[179] and a number of other monks and bishops were driven out. A hue and cry was raised for Athanasius, but he was never caught. Part of the time he was hidden by a beautiful virgin in Alexandria itself: she suffered grievously when her house was searched, but the bird had flown.[180] In A.D. 360 he was believed to be in the Thebaid, and the Duke Artemius came with a military force to invest and search Faou.[181] The monks answered with dignity, and the Duke with restraint. When the search had proved fruitless, the Duke called the monks to come and make prayer for him. But they, seeing an Arian bishop in his company, excused themselves, and left him alone at prayer in the Synaxis. Falling asleep in the heat of the day, he woke up in a fright with his nose bleeding, and came out speaking of a vision from which he had barely by God's mercy escaped with his life. Two years later, Artemius was put to death at Antioch by Julian. In spite of his Arian associations, he is still commemorated as a saint and martyr by the Orthodox Church.[182]

Theodore had been absent at the Hermopolis monasteries when Artemius came to Faou.[183] It was to Hermopolis again that he went in the spring of A.D. 363, to welcome Athanasius, who had re-appeared in Alexandria on Julian's accession, only to be banished once more from the city to the Thebaid.[184] The pageantry and enthusiasm of this reception in the spring is described so vividly in the *Vita Prima* of Pachomius as to suggest that the writer was an eye-witness. Theodore had to return to Faou for Easter, but left the Tabennesiote boat for Athanasius' use.[185] In strong contrast with this is the great Pope's own account, recorded by Ammon, of his hiding in the same Tabennesiote boat in June at Antinoe (opposite Hermopolis) in fear for his life, when Theodore, again present, and Abba Pammon of Antinoe, smiled at each other, and explained to the perplexed Athanasius that Julian was dead.[186]

Theodore watched with sorrow the growing wealth of the community in lands and boats.[187] He began to coax Horsiesius back into active leadership.[188] He himself would go out by night to the tombs in the mountains three miles away. Someone, perhaps the writer of the *Vita Prima*, followed him unobserved, and overheard his prayer at the tomb of his beloved master.[189] It was an answer to this prayer when God took him, shortly after Easter, on 27th April, A.D. 368.[190] Horsiesius returned to the helm, 'governing the brethren according to his ability: for he was a very good man, and loving to save the souls of the brethren. For God strengthened him, opening out to him the meanings of the Scriptures. And he governed the brethren long time in peace.'[191] The *Vita Prima* closes with Athanasius' letter of comfort to Horsiesius.[192]

.   .   .   .   .

Ammonas, Antony's disciple and successor at his Outer Mountain of Pispir, *may* have come thither after fourteen years in Scetis[193]— but the name, in its varying forms, is too common for any certainty. He later became a bishop,[194] and was succeeded at Pispir, according to the *Historia Monachorum*, by Pityrion.[195] But Rufinus, who visited Pispir about A.D. 373, mentions no one there except Poemen and Joseph.[196] Bishop Ammonas appears as an attractive figure in the *Apophthegmata*. He has left us a number of letters, surviving in Syriac[197] and less completely in Greek,[198] but apparently not in Coptic. They are distinguished from the *Letters of St. Antony*, with which they were early apt to be bound up, by a considerable use of apocalyptic Apocrypha of which there is no trace in Antony, and by a development of the teaching about acquiring of the Holy Spirit which may have its analogies with Messalian teaching.

Whether or no Ammonas came from Scetis to Pispir, the *Apophthegmata* tell us how after the death of Antony Sisoes, finding Scetis becoming too thickly populated, went off and found quiet in Antony's Interior Mountain.[199] We may take it that this was after the Saracen inroad there recorded by Jerome for the year A.D. 357, when Antony's disciple Sarmatas is said to have been killed.[200] Before that, if Jerome is to be believed, Hilarion had visited the Interior Mountain, and had been shown round by two other disciples of Antony, one of whom had been his interpreter.[201] Certainly when Sisoes came the Interior Mountain seems to have been deserted. Like Antony, he sometimes came thence to Pispir, the region of which is shown by another anecdote to have been still infested with Meletians.[202] In the Interior Mountain, Sisoes would receive supplies from time to time by means of a Διακονητής— 'agent'—from Pispir. But there would sometimes be delays, and once he went for ten months without seeing a man. He was beginning to pride himself on this, when he met a hunter from Paran (in the Sinai Peninsula) who had seen no man for eleven months.[203] Long afterwards, asked how he could have left Scetis, where he had been with Abba Or (Or is known to us as a Nitriote, so Scetis may be here used in its wider sense), Sisoes explained that he had found Scetis becoming too crowded, and heard Antony was dead, 'and I came and found things quiet here, and settled here a little time'. When asked how long, he answered, 'Seventy-two years'.[204]

NOTES TO CHAPTER II

[1] *H.L.* c. 35; cf. *H.M.* c. 1 (in the Greek and in Rufinus' version).
[2] *V.A.* c. 15; Ant. *Ep.* IV (ed. Garitte).
[3] *Ep.* IV. 56–7. 'Etenim ex una sunt illi omnes cognoscibili essentia; et *ex fuga eorum a Deo* multa diversitas facta est inter eos propter varietatem operationis eorum; propter hoc etiam omnia haec nomina imposita sunt eis propter unamquamque operationem eorum; propter hoc quidam ex eis vocati sunt archangeli . . .' (Garitte's translation from the Georgian).
[4] Bell, *Jews and Christians*, pap. 1913.
[5] See Holl, *Gesammelte Aufsätze* II (1928), pp. 292–7; Heussi, *Ursprung des Mönchtums*, pp. 129–31. I have mislaid another reference.
[6] Cass. *Coll.* XVIII. 5 (Piamun of Diolcus).
[7] *V.P. G*[1] cc. 33–4, 42, etc.
[8] *H.L.* c. 32 (88–9).
[9] Soz. *H.E.* III. 14. 9.
[10] *Pachomiana Latina* (ed. Boon), pp. 3–74, 155–68.
[11] *V.P. G*[1] cc. 24–5.
[12] Ibid. cc. 26 and 35–7.
[13] Ibid. c. 28.
[14] *V.P. Paral.* XIII (c. 32).
[15] *V.P. G*[1] cc. 42 (26. 14) and 81 (54. 21 and 25); *Pach. Lat.*, *Praecepta* 84: cf. Cyr. Scyth., *V. Euthymii*, c. 43 (ed. Schwartz, p. 64. 17).
[16] *V.P. G*[1] cc. 28 (18. 13–16), 40 (24. 24–5): *Praecepta* 50–2.
[17] *V.P. G*[1] cc. 70 (48. 10), 88 (59. 15, 17, 23), 131 (83. 16), 136 (86. 28, 87. 6, 11), 144 (90. 27), 147 (93. 16, 17): *Paral.* IX (c. 17, p. 140, 12–13): *Praecepta* 3, 91, 100, 132.
[18] *Ep. Am.* cc. 10 (101. 32), 14 (104. 12, 15), 22 (111. 9).
[19] *V.P. G*[1] c. 144 (90. 27): *Praec.* 28, 43, 91, 135: *Praec. et Inst.* 6, 8: *Ep. Am.* cc. 10 (101. 31), 20 (109. 11).
[20] *Paral.* VII, cc. 15–16 (138. 19, 139. 4, 8): *Praec.* 41, 80.
[21] *V.P. G*[1] cc. 89 (60. 12, 18), 121 (78. 27): *Praec.* 116, 117.
[22] *V.P. G*[1] cc. 18 (18. 10–12), 84 (57. 4–8): *Paral.* VIII, c. 16 (140. 2–3): *Praec.* 40, 42, 43, 45, 53, 54: *P. et Jud.* 5.
[23] *V.P. G*[1] cc. 28, 58–9, 94–5, 110, 121: *Ep. Am.* cc. 19, 26: Jerome, *Praef. ad. Reg.* cc. 2 and 6: *Praec.* 13, 15, 19, 24, 26, 31–2, 38, 49, 59, 65–6, 81, 83, 85, 99, 137: *Praec. et Inst.* 17: *Liber Orsiesii* cc. 15, 18, etc. *Paralipomena* and Cassian are silent about the house system: and although it might seem to be implied in Palladius' account of the numbers occupied in different trades at the Panopolis monastery, elsewhere in the same chapter he suggests a rather different picture—ποίησον Δὲ κέλλας Διαφόρους ἐν τῇ αὐλῇ, καὶ τρεῖς κατὰ κέλλαν μενέτωσαν. But the evidence of the *Vita Prima*, Jerome, and the Rule is conclusive.
[24] *V.P. G*[1] cc. 28 (19. 4–5), 58 (40. 14–16), 110 (72. 1): *Praec.* 19, 20, 115, 122: *Pr. et Inst.* 14–15: *Pr. et Leges* 5.
[25] *V.P. G*[1] cc. 59 (40. 22), 110 (72. 2–3): *Praec.* 38, 41, 65, 70: *Pr. et L.* 15: *Lib. Ors.* c. 26.
[26] *V.P. G*[1] cc. 59 (40. 20), 69 (47. 10), 74 (50. 2), 105 (68. 37), 144 (91. 1): *Ep. Am.* cc. 24 (112. 35), 26 (114. 2–4): *Paral.* I, c. 1 (123. 6, 10), IV, c. 7 (130. 25, 131. 10, 17), IX, c. 27 (154. 15), XII, c. 29 (156. 26), XV, c. 34 (159. 11): *Praef. ad Reg.* c. 4 (6. 7): *Praec.* 3, 19, 43, 78–9, 81, 89, 107, 112, 114, 126: *Pr. et L.* 2.
[27] *H.L.* c. 32 (89. 5—τρεῖς κατὰ κέλλαν μενέτωσαν).
[28] U. Monneret de Villard, *Il Monastero di San Simeone presso Aswan*, 1927.
[29] *V.P. G*[1] cc. 14 (9. 19–26), 79 (53. 21: in c. 144, p. 91. 1, καθισμάτιον may have a different meaning): *Paral.* XII, c. 29–30 (156. 27, 38): *Praec.* 87, 88: *H.L.* c. 32 (89. 7: θρόνους οἰκοδομητοὺς ὑπτιωτέρους).

[30] *V.P. G¹* cc. 28, 54, 59, 95, 110, 121–2, 134, 147: *Ep. Am.* cc. 7, 19: *Praef. ad Reg.* cc. 2 and 6: *Praec.* 1, 15–16, 19–21, 26–7, 30–1, 38, 40–2, 47, 53–4, 58–9, 69–70, 79, 81–2, 84, 96, 101, 104–6, 115, 133, 137: *Pr. et Inst.* 11, 13, 15–18: *Pr. et Jud.* 11, 13: *Pr. et L.* 1, 5–6, 9, 12, 14–15: *Epist. Pach.* IV, VI, VII: *Ep. Theod.* (106. 8): *Lib. Ors.* cc. 7, 9, 11, 15, 18, 24.
[31] *V.P. G¹* cc. 28, 84, 95, 121: *Ep. Am.* cc. 7, 19: *Praef. ad Reg.* c. 6.
[32] *V.P. G¹* cc. 28, 86, 145: *Praef. ad Reg.* c. 2: *Praec.* 12–13, 15, 27, 64, 66, 111, 124, 129.
[33] *V.P. G¹* cc. 28 (τοῦ μεγάλου οἰκονόμου ἤτοι τοῦ πατρὸς τῆς μονῆς), 54, 59, 61, 74, 78, 81, 110: *Praef. ad Reg.* cc. 2, 6–8; *Praec.* 49, 51, 53–5, 58, 81, 107, 111, 118–19, 143: *Pr. et Inst.* 5, 10, 11, 13, 17: *Pr. et Jud.* 13: *Pr. et L.* 4, 14: *Ep. Pach.* I–IV, VI: *Ep. Theod.* (106. 7). The οἰκονόμος of Faou had general supervision of the whole community, but was not identical with its Head—Pachomius, Orsiesius, or Theodore: *V.P. G¹* cc. 83, 114, 122, 124, 134, 138: *Praef. ad Reg.* c. 7.
[34] *V.P. G¹* cc. 28 (18. 3, 29), 54 (37. 3), 134 (84. 22), 149 (94. 24): *H.L.* c. 32 (94. 2: Aphthonius). Draguet (*Le Muséon*, 57 (1944), p. 126; 58 (1945), pp. 41–2) denied the existence in the Tabennesiote Community of the office of Second of a Monastery. But the evidence of *V.P. G¹* and Palladius is confirmed by the *Liber Orsiesii*, where four successive sections are addressed,
    c. 13 Et vos ergo monasteriorum principes . . .
    c. 14 Sed et vos qui secundi estis monasterii . . .
    c. 15 Vos quoque praepositi domuum singularum . . .
    c. 18 Vos quoque qui secundi estis singularum domorum . . .
[35] Especially the cutting of rushes (θρύα), which were then used for plaiting ropes and mats: *V.P. G¹* cc. 23, 51, 71, 76: *Ep. Am.* c. 19: *Paral.* V, c. 9 (133. 8, 11). Commonly the rushes were harvested from islands in the Nile. For undifferentiated agricultural work, see *Praec.* 24, 58–65, 80: for harvesting of grain, *V.P. G¹* c. 106 (70. 1); of fruit, *Praec.* 76–7; gathering wood for timber, *Ep. Am.* c. 22; for fuel, ibid. c. 27: for herdsmen, *Praec.* 108: for goat-shearing, *Ep. Pach.* VIII.
[36] *V.P. G¹* cc. 32 (MS. Athen. 1015, or *V.P. G²* c. 29), 103, 116–17, 139, 146 (92. 23: εἰς τὸ ὄρος ὅπου οἱ τάφοι τῶν ἀδελφῶν ὡς ἀπὸ μιλίων τριῶν), 149: *Paral.* III, c. 6 (130. 10): *Praec.* 127–9. The tombs at the foot of the eastern face of Gebel-et-Tarif (there are Sixth-Dynasty rock-cut tombs half-way up the cliff above) are some five miles from Faou, but in other ways, in date and character, would fit well enough with the account in the Lives. In one of these tombs the momentous find of Gnostic papyri was made (Doresse, *Les livres secrets*, pp. 149–51). Is there another cemetery a little further to the east, and nearer to Faou?
[37] *V.P. G¹* cc. 28 (18. 17–19), 59 (40. 26–41. 1), 109 and 113: *Ep. Am.* cc. 2 and 29: *Paral.* IX, c. 21–3: *Praec.* 46, 56, 118, 142.
[38] *V.P. G¹* c. 27.
[39] Ibid. c. 29.
[40] Ibid. c. 54.
[41] Ibid. c. 32 (MS. Athen. 1015).
[42] *Ep. Am.* c. 2 (97. 27–98. 1: Βαῦ, ἐν τῷ ἄνω Διοσπολίτῃ νόμῳ τυγχάνοντι).
[43] *V.P. G¹* c. 29, and the Coptic Lives, call him Sarapion. But Athanasius in his letter from Rome to Sarapion of Thmuis, which follows *Ep. Fest.* XI, speaks (*P.G.* 26, 1413c) of Andronicus' succeeding his father Saprion as Bishop of Tentyra. Saprion is named among the Egyptian bishops who went to Tyre in A.D. 335, and G², supported by the Latin of Dionysius Exiguus, calls him Aprion—an easy corruption of Saprion.
[44] *V.P. G¹* c. 29.
[45] Ibid. c. 78.
[46] Ibid. cc. 91–2, 106.
[47] Ibid. c. 83: *Vies Coptes*, S⁵ c. 52—the Coptic Lives have important information in these chapters.
[48] Athanasius, *Ep. Fest.* XIX, for A.D. 347, gives (*P.G.* 26, 1430b) the names of all bishops appointed since his exile in A.D. 339. It is here that we learn that 'In Panopolis, because Artemidorus desired it on account of his old age and infirmity of body, Arius is appointed as coadjutor with him'. Artemidorus was at Tyre in A.D. 335. Several bishops named Arius were at Sardica in A.D. 343.
[49] *V.P. G¹* c. 81: *V.C.* S⁵ c. 54.
[50] *V.P. G¹* c. 82: *V.C.* B⁰ c. 55.
[51] *V.P. G¹* c. 80: *V.C.* B⁰ c. 56.
[52] *V.P. G¹* c. 83: *V.C.* B⁰ c. 57. Petronius' position at Tismenae, mentioned at this point in the Coptic but not in the Greek, is confirmed by *V.P. G¹* c. 114 (75. 9).

⁵³ *V.P. G¹* cc. 114 and 117: see my article in *Studia Patristica* II, pp. 379 ff., 'A Note on the Chronology of the Pachomian Foundations'.

⁵⁴ *V.P. G¹* c. 106.

⁵⁵ *V.P. G¹* c. 134 (84. 27–8): cf. *H.L.* c. 33.

⁵⁶ *V.P. G¹* c. 83 (56. 9–10).

⁵⁷ *V.P. G¹* c. 112, where the bishops are named Philo and Mouis. The appointment of Philo to Thebes in succession to another Philo is recorded in Athanasius' Letter from Rome to Sarapion (*P.G.* 26, 1413c). The name Masis given in *Ep. Fest.* XIX (1430B) to Ammonius' successor at Latopolis is probably a corruption, easy in the Syriac, for our Mouis. Both names, Philo and Mouis, are found among the signatories at Sardica, and also among those exiled in A.D. 356. Athanasius in his letter to Dracontius speaks of Μουΐ τοῦ ἐν τῇ ἄνω Θηβαΐδι and Paul in Latopolis, as examples of monks who had become bishops. The Coptic account of the Synod of Latopolis, which survives in Amélineau's Arabic version (pp. 591–5), is inconsistent with the Greek, and less reliable.

⁵⁸ *V.P. G¹* cc. 114–16.

⁵⁹ Ibid. c. 117.

⁶⁰ Ibid. cc. 118–19.

⁶¹ *V.P. G¹* pp. 36. 19, 54. 11, 66. 32, 74. 1, 81. 4. Other passages, 11. 21, 16. 15, 17. 2, 23. 17, 25. 9, 77. 32, 78. 28, are more ambiguous: but the plural, κοινόβια, is never used in G¹.

⁶² Ibid. pp. 13. 17, 37. 6, 54. 17, 60. 12, 81. 1, 7, 84. 21, 86. 7.

⁶³ *Praef. ad Reg.* c. 1 (p. 4. 3 and 9): *Ep. Theod.* (105. 15): *Lib. Ors.* pp. 116. 16, 18, 125. 11, 142. 23.

⁶⁴ *Paral.* p. 141. 21.

⁶⁵ Cass. *Inst.* IV. 1.

⁶⁶ *H.L.* c. 32 (93. 8).

⁶⁷ Ibid. c. 7 (26. 18).

⁶⁸ In the *Lausiac History* the term 'Archimandrite' is used of Pachomius, and only once (p. 63. 21) of anyone else. But it does not occur in G¹ or the other early Greek Pachomian sources; nor in the Coptic Pachomian documents, other than the Lives, except in late titleheads (see Lefort, *Oeuvres de S. Pachôme et de ses Disciples*, C.S.C.O., scr. Copt., tom. 23 and 24). It seems to be an introduction from Syria, where the monastic enclosure was frequently called μάνδρα—a 'fold'. It occurs already in the superscription of the letter to Epiphanius, in A.D. 375, from Acacius and Paul, πρεσβυτέρων ἀρχιμανδριτῶν, τουτέστι πατέρων μοναστηρίων, of the region of Chalcis and Berrhoea (Acacius was, of course, later Bishop of Berrhoea), inviting him to write his *Panarion*. But the word seemed still to need an explanation.

⁶⁹ *H.L.* c. 32 (94. 1)—Palladius does not name Faou, but its identity is clear.

⁷⁰ *Ep. Am.* c. 2 (98. 4).

⁷¹ *H.L.* loc. cit. (94. 5–6): Palladius gives an interesting account of the monastery he visited near Panopolis—apparently Tismenae—and the women's convent on the opposite bank of the Nile (cf. *V.P. G¹* c. 134, p. 84. 27–8).

⁷² *V.P. G¹* c. 110.

⁷³ Ibid. cc. 78 (52. 26–53. 1), 83, 122, 148 (93. 24–5): *Praef. ad Reg.* cc. 7–8 (Jerome's figure of 50,000 should, of course, be divided by ten): *Ep. Pach.* V and VII: *Ep. Theod.*

⁷⁴ *V.P. G¹* c. 113 (δύο δὲ ἦσαν μόνα ὅλου τοῦ κοινοβίου). *V.C.* S⁵ cc. 53 and 54, relates how these two boats were given—by a notable of Kous (Apollonopolis) and by Bishop Arius of Panopolis. But the community must have had at least one small boat very early—cf. *V.P. G¹* cc. 60–1, 71.

⁷⁵ *V.P. G¹* cc. 109, 113, 120: *Ep. Am.* cc. 2 and 29.

⁷⁶ *V.P. G¹* c. 146 (92. 13–14). Cf. *Praec.* 118–19.

⁷⁷ *V.P. G¹* cc. 28 (19. 3–5), 77 (52. 2), 110 (72. 1), 131 (82. 35–6), 145 (92. 2): *Praec.* 20–2, 138: *Praec. et Inst.* 15: *Pr. et L.* 12.

⁷⁸ *H.L.* c. 32 (88. 10–89. 6 and 95. 6–12).

⁷⁹ Jerome, *Praef. ad Reg.* c. 5 (7. 5–13), states 'Aliis diebus comedunt qui volunt post meridiem ... Omnes pariter comedunt'. This noon meal is made certain by *Praec.* 103, of which the Coptic survives: 'Ad meridiem, quando fratres convocantur ad cibum'. The gong at noon called the brethren directly to the refectory, not to an office in the Synaxis first. So in *Praec.* 91, 100 and 102, it is assumed that the brethren may be going direct from their work or study, sometimes to the Synaxis, sometimes to the refectory: and *Praec.* 36 speaks of 'qui percutit et ad vescendum congregat fratres'. In G¹ c. 52 we find Pachomius recovering from illness, and κρούσαντος τοῦ οἰκονόμου φαγεῖν girding himself and going to the τράπεζα of the brethren in good health, and eating. In c. 69 (46. 8–11) we have still more clearly τέως ὅτε

κρούουσιν ἡμέρας εἰς τὸ φαγεῖν τοὺς ἀδελφούς, μὴ μείνης ἕως ὀψέ, ἀλλὰ ἀπελθὼν φάγε ὡς πέντε κλάσματα, καὶ τὸ Διδόμενον αὐτοῖς ἐψητὸν γεῦσαι. The meal, then, might be ἡμέρας or ὀψέ. Jerome's 'Omnes pariter comedunt', if it means the whole community ate *together*, is not true. ἡμέρας no doubt means at noon, as in Praec. 103. But what of ὀψέ? We have it again in c. 55, when Pachomius comes to Mouchonsis and ὀψὲ τῇ ὥρᾳ τοῦ γεύσασθαι ἡτοίμασαν; and in c. 84 (57. 10) of Tithoes μὴ ἀπελθὼν ὀψὲ εἰς τὴν τράπεζαν φαγεῖν. This second sitting surely followed an office in the Synaxis, after which (*Praec.* 28) the brethren might be going either to their cells or to the refectory—'Dimissa collecta singuli egredientes usque ad cellulas suas vel usque ad vescendi locum'. So in G¹ c. 40 guests are τῇ μὲν ὥρᾳ τῆς συνάξεως συνέρχεσθαι μεθ' ἡμῶν, μετὰ δὲ τὴν εὐχὴν εἰς πρέποντα καὶ ἥσυχον τόπον ὄντες ἐσθίειν καὶ ἀναπαύεσθαι. This would be the time of day when (cc. 96–7) Pachomius, visiting Tabennesi, discoursed to the brethren, then, in haste to get back to Faou, ἀναστὰς μετὰ τῶν ἀδελφῶν ηὔξατο, καὶ ἀπῆλθεν μὴ γευσάμενος. In *Paralipomena* IV, c. 7, the Origenist monks, having stayed with Pachomius until the *ninth hour*, refuse the offer of a meal, εὐξάμενοι δὲ καὶ συνταξάμενοι ἀπῆλθον: in IX, c. 17, Pachomius is described as entering with the brethren for the prayers, then, when they are completed, and ἐξελθόντων αὐτῶν ἐπὶ τὸ γεύσασθαι, remaining himself in the Synaxis and extending his prayers ἀπὸ ὥρας δεκάτης ἕως οὗ κρούωσιν τοῖς ἀδελφοῖς τὴν νυκτερινὴν λειτουργίαν—i.e. until the small hours.

It seems, then, that the Rule and the early Greek sources do confirm at least two sittings for meals, one at noon, one after an office in the Synaxis at or about the ninth hour.

⁸⁰ *V.P. G¹* c. 28 (18. 8–9): *Praef. ad Reg.* c. 5 (7. 11–3).

⁸¹ That the evening instruction was *after* the meal seems proved by *V.P. G¹* c. 77 = *V.C.* B⁰ c. 69 (Theodore to give the instruction in the customary place ὅτε ἐξέρχονται τῆς τραπέζης ὀψὲ οἱ ἀδελφοί—τῆς τραπέζης, missing in the Florentine MS., is confirmed by the Ambrosian and Athenian, the *Vita Tertia*, and the Coptic). So also *V.C.* B⁰ c. 29, and *V.P. G¹* c. 71 (48. 23–5). But in *V.P. G¹* c. 97 (65. 19) we find Pachomius, after a discourse and its concluding prayer, going off without partaking.

⁸² *Ep. Am.* cc. 2–7. That the Synaxis was not the normal place of the discourse is borne out by the language used elsewhere, e.g. *V.P. G¹* c. 77 (52. 2): ὅπου συναγόμεθα εἰς κατήχησιν κατὰ τὴν κυριακήν; *Paral.* I, c. 1 (122. 12): εἰς ὡρισμένον τόπον τῆς μονῆς.

⁸³ For Pachomius—to quote the Greek sources only—we have *V.P. G¹* cc. 47–9, 56–7, 63, 75, 96–7, 102; *Paral.* IX, cc. 19–20, XVII. cc. 37–41. For Theodore, *V.P. G¹* cc. 131, 135, 140–2; *Ep. Am.* cc. 23, 28. For Orsiesius, *V.P. G¹* cc. 118, 126.

⁸⁴ See *V.P. G¹* c. 99 (66. 3–7).

⁸⁵ *Paral.* XVII. It is to be noted that the Greek of this homily is closer to that of the *Vita Prima* than to that of the rest of the *Paralipomena*.

⁸⁶ Lefort, *Oeuvres de S. Pachôme et de ses Disciples* (C.S.C.O. 159–60, scr. Copt., 23–4), pp. 1–24: also several other fragments of Pachomius, pp. 24–30; of Theodore, pp. 37–62; and of Orsiesius, pp. 66–82.

⁸⁷ *V.P. G¹* c. 58 (40. 10–14): *Praec.* 28.

⁸⁸ *V.P. G¹* loc.cit. (40. 14): *Pr. et. Inst.* 14: *Pr. et L.* 10.

⁸⁹ *V.P. G¹* loc.cit. (40. 15–18): *Praec.* 122.

⁹⁰ *V.P. G¹* c. 61 (41. 35): *Paral.* IX, c. 17 (140. 17): *Praec.* 3, 5, 9: *Pr. et L.* 2.

⁹¹ *V.P. G¹* cc. 60–61 (41. 15–16, 35–6), 88 (59. 21), 101 (67. 22): *Paral.* IX, c. 17 (140. 17), c. 19 (143. 13–14), XII, c. 29 (156. 28), XVI, c. 35 (160. 13–14): *Praec.* 24.—*Paral.* IX, c. 19 (143. 14), X., c. 26 (154. 8), and perhaps IV., c. 7 (130. 19) show us instances of morning discourses following the nocturnal office. Cf. *Praec.* 19.

⁹² *Praec.* 9–10.

⁹³ *Praec.* 37–9: *V.P. G¹* c. 111.

⁹⁴ *Praec.* 53.

⁹⁵ *Praec.* 49, 139.

⁹⁶ *V.P. G¹* c. 99 (66. 33–6): *Praef. ad Reg.* c. 9 (8. 19–9. 5). Palladius (H.L. c. 32, 90. 4–91. 6) seems to have misinterpreted what he had heard of this.

⁹⁷ *Pach. Lat.*, pp. 77–101.

⁹⁸ *V.P. G¹* cc. 94–5 and 147 (93. 13): also *Ep. Am.* c. 7 where the number in the house is put at about twenty).

⁹⁹ *V.P. G¹* c. 99: *V.C.* B⁰ c. 196 (p. 216. 16–26); S⁵ᵇ, p. 341. 8–16; S²¹ p. 389. 27–8. See Ladeuze, *C.P.*, pp. 32 ff., Lefort, *V.C.S.P.* XI–XII, Halkin, *S.P.V.G.*, p. 90.

¹⁰⁰ Χάρισμα διακρίσεως πνευμάτων, *V.A.* 876ʙ, 900ᴀ, 965ʙ: δοθεῖσαν χάριν εἰς τὴν διάκρισιν τῶν πνευμάτων, *V.A.* 908ᴀ: 'cor scientiae et spiritum discretionis', *Ep. Ant.* IV. 29 (cf. I. 66).

Διάκρισις πνεύματος, V.P. G¹ 34. 5, 51. 17, 22, 58. 24, 64. 30, 73. 22 (Δ.πνεύματος ἁγίου): Διακρίνω 6. 18, 8. 6, 35. 16, 58. 24, 64. 2, 73. 18: ἐὰν μὴ ἀκρότατος Διακριτικὸς εὑρεθῇ 85. 19.

101 Τί πλεῖον τοῦ ἔχειν πνεῦμα ἅγιον; V.P. G¹ 85. 2.

102 Ep. Ant. II. 7, 27, 29: VI. 31.

103 Ibid. II. 27, VI. 30, VII. 9.

104 Apart from a quotation of the baptismal formula (1. 13), the Vita Prima has only three (31. 17, 50. 14, 88. 10) unambiguous references to God the Holy Spirit—though the adjective is not expressed. On other occasions, where the adjective is expressed, the article is commonly absent (33. 7, 73. 22, 85. 2), and we should translate 'holy spirit', or 'a holy spirit'; or, if it is present, it may still mean the particular holy spirit dwelling in a man, rather than God the Holy Spirit (42. 3, 69. 6, 76. 32). In 58. 24–5 we have 'the discernment of the spirit, to distinguish the wicked spirits from the holy': and as an example of this, we have in 48. 7–9 the case of two monks requited, one with the spirit of obedience and power, the other with the spirit of unbelief.

Paralipomena has, apart from the baptismal formula (155. 17), only two references to the Holy Spirit—but both of them explicit and unambiguous (123. 23, 147. 9): it has also a reference to 'spirit-bearing men' (153. 19).

The Letter of Ammon exhibits a more developed pneumatology, in which the personality of the Holy Spirit is clearly marked (101. 30, 103. 34, 104. 1, 110. 34, 111. 28).

The Coptic Catechesis of Pachomius published by Lefort in C.S.C.O., Vols. 159–60, has four explicit references to the 'Spirit of God' (10. 27, 10. 31, 23. 25, 24. 5), one to the 'Spirit of Jesus' (23. 17). A reference (6. 31) to the 'language of the Spirit' reminds us of the 'secret language of the Spirit' of V.P. G¹ c. 99 (66. 35): and 'lest the Spirit of God withdraw from thee' (10. 31) lessens the ambiguity of V.P. G¹ 76. 32, ὅσον ὅσον τὸ ἅγιον πνεῦμα ἀπ' αὐτῆς (τῆς ψυχῆς) ἀναχωρεῖ. Another excerpt attributed to Pachomius (26. 24) speaks of the devil retiring when he sees that the Holy Spirit is in a man. The Catecheses attributed to Theodore and Horsiesius, published in the same volumes, indicate in regard to the Holy Spirit a number of themes which become typical of the Coptic Lives. These last belong to a later stage in pneumatology.

105 Ep. Ant. II. 27, III. 35, IV. 16, 108, V. 34, 39, 45, VI. 16, 26, 29, 30, 37, 43, VII. 9. The name of Jesus alone similarly occurs six times in the Coptic Catechesis of Pachomius, once in those of Theodore, and twice in those of Horsiesius.

106 V.P. G¹ c. 110 (72. 4–7).

107 V.A. cc. 31–5 (889–93): V.P. G¹ c. 3 (3. 3–11).

108 V.P. G¹ cc. 41, 43, 44.

109 Ibid. cc. 47–8.

110 Ibid. c. 120. The Coptic account of this voyage and visit (V.C. S⁵ cc. 119–23) differs considerably from the Greek. But in spite of some interesting details, it bears clear evidence of its secondary character, and historical unreliability where it conflicts with the Greek.

111 Soz. H.E. II. 31.

112 V.A. cc. 69–71.

113 Ruf. H.E. XI. 7; Socr. H.E. IV. 25; Soz. H.E. III. 15; H.L. c. 4 (20. 6–12).

114 G Ant. 34. Amoun also visited Antony, apparently several times—G Am. Nitr. 1; V.A. c. 60 (where the distance from Nitria to St. Antony's Mountain—apparently the Interior Mountain—is given as thirteen days' journey).

115 H.L. c. 10, and Butler's Note 18. If he died while Melania was in Nitria, A.D. 374, at the age of seventy, he would have been born in A.D. 304.

116 H.L. c. 12. Benjamin was eighty when he died, which was after Palladius' arrival at the Cells, and before Dioscorus' consecration as Bishop of Damanhur—therefore about A.D. 391; which places his birth about A.D. 311. An Apophthegm (G Benj. 2) calls him Priest of the Cells.

117 H.L. c. 18: H.M. (Gr.) c. 23, (Lat.) c. 29. He died, nearly a hundred years old, A.D. 393, having been baptized sixty years before (H.L. 58. 3–4).

118 H.L. c. 46. He died fifteen years before Palladius' arrival, therefore about A.D. 375. Thirty-seven years before that takes us back to A.D. 338.

119 G Ant. 34.

120 H.M. (Lat.) c. 22: H.L. cc. 7 (25. 8–9), 18 (47. 22–4), 38 (120. 7–8).

121 Cass. Coll. VI. 1.

122 Soz. H.E. VI. 31.

123 H.M. (Lat.) c. 22.

124 Verba Seniorum, P.J. XIV. 16 (= Nau 293).

[125] *H.M.* (Gr.) c. 26. 11–13.

[126] *H.L.* c. 7: *H.M.* (Gr.) c. 20, (Lat.) c. 21.

[127] Ruf. *H.E.* II. 3.

[128] Pall. *D.V.C.* c. 17 (106. 25, 27).

[129] *V.P.* G¹ cc. 6 (4. 29), 79 (53. 18): *Praec.* 45, 54. But even here, wine appears to be allowed for the sick (Pr. 45), even if not always accepted (*V.P.* G¹ 53. 18). Apart from the Coenobium, complete abstention from wine seems to be an individual ascetic practice, even in Scetis. In *V.A.* c. 7 (853A) total abstention appears to be taken for granted. But Poemen's ὁ οἶνος ὅλως οὐκ ἔστι τῶν μοναχῶν (G Poem. 19) is in answer to praise of a certain monk for not drinking wine. The Xois who says (G Xois 1) that wine is alien to monks who live according to God, says it in answer to a question whether a third cup is too much, and is probably to be identified with the Sisoes who is twice (G Sisoes 2 and 8) recorded as facing the same problem and giving the same answer—that a third cup would not be much if there were no Satan. In Sisoes 8 the occasion is given as a προσφορά at the Mountain of St. Antony, with a 'cnidion' of wine there. Other stories show wine at feasts in Scetis (*P.J.* IV. 53 = Nau 144) and the Cells (N60: *P.J.* IV. 54 = N 148). Macarius the Egyptian (G Mac. Aeg. 10) would take wine when it was offered him, but for each cup he would go a day without water. Paphnutius (G Paph. 2) did not readily take wine, but his acceptance of a cup at the sword's point was the means of the conversion of a brigand chief. Xanthias (G Xan. 2), coming up from Scetis to Terenuthis, and offered a cup of wine, was taunted as a wine-bibber by a demon, but defiantly drained the cup, and cast out the demon in doing so. The injunction to young monks not to drink wine (MS. Berlin Phill. 1724, 216b = N (Guy) 592–45, the last anecdote in *Evergetinos* III. 42) leads on to the statement that the devil often leads old monks to offer them wine. Joseph of Panephysis would give his visitors wine, but he and his disciples secretly drank only a mixture of sea-water and fresh (G Eulogius).

[130] *Ep. Am.* c. 19 (108. 1). See also *V.P.* G¹ c. 134 (84. 30)—the women's convents employed ὠμόλινα νήθειν εἰς τοὺς λεβίτωνας.

[131] Socr. *H.E.* IV. 23.

[132] G Mac. Aeg. 2.

[133] *Ep. Am.* c. 32 (118. 14–16).

[134] Ibid. cc. 31 and 32.

[135] *H.L.* c. 7 (26. 9–12).

[136] *H.L.* c. 46 (134. 13–14): *Ep. Am.* c. 32 (118. 37–119. 4).

[137] *H.L.* cc. 10, 12, 46: *Ep. Am.* loc. cit.

[138] *P.G.* XXV, 523–34. The date of this letter (A.D. 353–4) is given by the reference (532A) to the absence abroad of Sarapion and Ammonius (cf. Soz. *H.E.* IV. 9; Festal Index, *P.G.* XXVI. 135B; and *Hist. Aceph.* 3, *P.G.* XXVI. 1443 BC).

[139] Ibid. 532A. But Athanasius, speaking of Mouis in the Upper Thebaid, Paul in Latopolis, may have confused the sees. The Festal Letters make Mouis bishop in Latopolis, Philo in Thebes. See above, note 57.

[140] Ath. *Apol. de Fuga* 7, *Hist. Ar.* 72: *Ep. Am.* c. 32: Jerome *V. Hil.* c. 30.

[141] G Am. Nitr. 1. Cf. the question to which St. John Climacus will not divulge the answer, why there were not so many luminaries among the holy Tabennesiotes as among the Scetiotes—*P.G.* 88, 1105C.

[142] *Ep. Am.* c. 35 (120. 26).

[143] *H.L.* c. 18 (47. 23).

[144] Ibid. (47. 24, 56. 15). See also c. 20 (63. 13), where Macarius tells Paul of Pherme that for sixty years he has made a regular hundred prayers a day.

[145] Ibid. c. 17 (43. 11).

[146] He was baptized sixty years before his death—*H.L.* c. 18 (58. 3–4). Sozomen, *H.E.* III. 14. 3, says he was ordained priest later than his Egyptian namesake, therefore after A.D. 340.

[147] *H.L.* c. 18 (48. 2–6).

[148] Ibid. (48. 17–24).

[149] Ibid. (48. 25–49. 8).

[150] Ibid. (52. 1–53. 13). In Syria early in the next century, St. Symeon the Stylite as a young monk provoked a similar rebellion by his extreme practices.

[151] Cf. the story edited by Draguet (*Le Muséon* 70, pp. 267–306) from MS. Vat. 2091, ff. 9r–10r, where it is inserted in *H.L.* c. 7, appearing, *pace* Draguet, to be neither more nor less genuine than the rest of the B recension of the Lausiac History. See also the story in *V.C.* S¹ pp. 3–5 (and S³ pp. 66–9).

[152] *H.L.* c. 18 (51. 10–16).

[153] Ibid. c. 17 (43. 16).

[154] G Mac. Aeg. 2.

[155] G Mac. Aeg. 4 and 20.

[156] G Chaeremon.

[157] *H.L.* c. 17 (44. 1–3).

[158] G Mac. Aeg. 7: Joh. Col. 6, 35: Esaias 5: Isaac Cell. 4, 7: Pior 1: *P.J.* XIV. 14.

[159] G Mac. Aeg. 14.

[160] G Mac. Aeg. 13.

[161] G Mac. Aeg. 39.

[162] G Olympius 1.

[163] G Mac. Aeg. 33. See Evelyn White, *History of the Monasteries of Nitria and of Scetis*, c. VII.

[164] G Mac. Aeg. 3.

[165] Cass. *Coll.* X. 2.

[166] Evelyn White, *History*, c. VII.

[167] *V.P. G¹* c. 120: Greg. Naz. *Or.* XXI, cc. 27–9: Festal Index A.D. 346.

[168] Ath. *Hist. Ar.* c. 25.

[169] Forty-eight years before Palladius' visit to him, which was probably in A.D. 394— *H.L.* c. 35 (105. 16).

[170] *Ep. Am.* c. 2.

[171] *V.P. G¹* cc. 127–31.

[172] *V.P. G¹* c. 134.

[173] *Ep. Am.* c. 7 (100. 25–30).

[174] Ibid. c. 17 (106. 5).

[175] Ibid. c. 30.

[176] Jerome, *Chronicle* (ed. Helm), p. 240 (A.D. 356)—*P.L.* 27, 687. The date is confirmed by a letter of Sarapion of Thmuis to Antony's disciples on his death, written in A.D. 356, and surviving in Syriac and Armenian, published by Draguet in *Le Muséon* 64 (1951), pp. 1–25.

[177] *V.A.* cc. 91–2 (972B–973A).

[178] On 7th Feb., A.D. 356: Ath. *Ap. de F.* 24; *Ap. ad Const.* 25; *Hist. Ar.* 48, 81: *Ep. Am.* c. 31: *Hist. Aceph.* 5: Festal Index (A.D. 356).

[179] Ath. *Ap. de F.* 7; *Hist. Ar.* 72: Jer. *V. Hil.* 30: *Ep. Am.* c. 32.

[180] *H.L.* c. 63: Festal Index for A.D. 360.

[181] *V.P. G¹* cc. 137–8: *V.C.* B⁰ c. 185, S⁵ c. 165.

[182] *Amm. Marc.* XXII. 11; *A. S. Boll.* Oct. VIII, pp. 856–88; G.C.S. 21 (Philostorgius), pp. 151–75; Theod. *H.E.* III. 18.

[183] *V.P. G¹* c. 137: *V.C.* B⁰ c. 185.

[184] Festal Index for A.D. 363. The edict for his exile had reached him on 24th Oct., A.D. 362, and he wrote his Festal Letter from Memphis.

[185] *V.P. G¹* cc. 143–4: cf. *V.C.* B⁰ cc. 200–4.

[186] *Ep. Am.* c. 34.

[187] *V.P. G¹* c. 146 (92. 12–22).

[188] Ibid. c. 145.

[189] Ibid. c. 146 (92. 22–93. 12).

[190] Ibid. c. 148.

[191] Ibid. c. 149 (95. 7–11).

[192] Ibid. c. 150.

[193] G Ammonas 3.

[194] Ibid. 8 and 10.

[195] *H.M.* c. 15.

[196] Ruf. *H.E.* II. 8.

[197] *P.O.* X. 6.

[198] *P.O.* XI. 4.

[199] G Sisoes 28.

[200] Jerome, *Chronicle* (ed. Helm.), p. 240 (A.D. 357): *P.L.* 27. 689.

[201] Jer. *V. Hil.* cc. 30–1.

[202] G Sisoes 48.

[203] Ibid. 7.

[204] Ibid. 28.

III

THE WORLD BREAKS IN

By the time of Athanasius' death, in A.D. 373, both Nitria and Scetis had come to maturity. The great majority of the monks were certainly Egyptian. But in this region we cannot assume that they were all pure Copts. Mixed blood, and bilingualism, must have been far more widespread in the regions of the Delta than in the Thebaid. Nor had any conflict yet emerged between the educated and the uneducated. Pambo, one of the first priests of Nitria, was apparently unlettered:[1] but the four Tall Brothers, of whom we shall presently hear more, were his disciples: and of these Ammonius at least was a widely-read man, not only in Holy Scripture.[2] Apart from them, no doubt there were from early times some foreigners, even as there were at Faou before Pachomius' death. Athanasius, in Rome during his exile in A.D. 340, had with him some who could serve as living examples of the monastic way;[3] and from then on, the devout in Rome had their faces turned towards Egypt.[4] One of the most moving stories of St. Macarius of Scetis is concerned with two young foreigners whose cell, after their death, Macarius would describe as 'the Martyrium of the Little Strangers'.[5] The story may have some connection with the origin of the name of Deir Bara-mûs—the Monastery of the Roman Brethren.

Basil the Cappadocian, fresh from his baptism in A.D. 357, made a monastic tour of Palestine and Egypt.[6] Whatever he may have taken over from pre-existent monasticism in Anatolia, his rule is certainly deeply indebted to this tour. Athanasius' *Life of St. Antony* was written during these years, addressed 'To the Monks in Foreign Parts', and was quickly translated into Latin. In fact, two independent translations of it had been made by the time of its author's death.[7] Exiles from the West, Hilary of Poitiers and Eusebius of Vercellae, took back with them on their return home their own experience of the monastic movement in the East, for the inspiration of St. Martin and others.[8] The names of the most famous Egyptian monks had soon become household words in the great Christian houses in Rome.[9]

Just about the time of Athanasius' death, the movement began in earnest. Jerome had already gone to Syria, and was in Antioch when

46

news reached him that his friend Rufinus was in Egypt—in Nitria—
had come to the blessed Macarius.[10] This was probably in A.D. 374,
and Jerome was still imperfectly informed—he seems to know only
of one Macarius, probably the Alexandrian. Rufinus' arrival in
Egypt more or less coincided with that of the great widow lady
Melania, coming like him from Rome. She was escorted to Nitria
by Isidore, the Bishop of Damanhur.[11] There is a famous episode
of her bringing 300 pounds of silver to the great old priest Pambo,
and being rather put out when he did not trouble to look how much
it was. When she told him, 'That you may know, sir, how much it
is, it is 300 pounds', he answered, 'My child, He to whom you
have brought it has no need of scales. He who measures the mountains in a balance, how much more does He know the sum of this
money! If you were bringing it to me, you would be saying well:
but if to God, who did not spurn the two mites, be silent.' Dying
shortly afterwards, he bequeathed her the basket he had just
finished.[12]

Melania seems to have collected quite a lot of monastic keepsakes.
Macarius the Alexandrian gave her the sheepskin that a hyena bitch
had brought him in gratitude for his healing her whelp of its
blindness.[13]

But Athanasius' death had been the signal for the forcible intrusion
of the Arian Lucius on the bishop's throne at Alexandria, under the
protection of the Emperor Valens. Athanasius' nominee, Peter, had
fled to Rome.[14] Orthodox resistance brought imperial action, and
very soon a number of bishops, with priests and monks, were on the
road to exile at Diocaesarea in Palestine. Isidore of Damanhur was
among them. Melania, having spent six months in Nitria, went to
minister to them, and dismayed the imperial officials by revealing
just who she was when they tried high-handed action against her.[15]

The two Macarii were exiled to a pagan island in the Delta. But
when the pagan priest's daughter became possessed and was healed
by them, the people of the island destroyed their temple and replaced
it with a church. The two monks were quickly allowed to return
to their desert.[16]

It was while the bishops were still in exile that a Saracen queen,
Mavia, who was harassing the borders of Arabia and Palestine,
professed her readiness to be bought off if Valens would send Moses,
an Egyptian monk, as bishop for her tribe. Moses was duly put
under arrest and sent to Lucius for consecration, but absolutely
refused to be consecrated by an Arian, and Valens found it necessary

to send him to the exiled bishops.[17] It was not long before they also were recalled.

Meanwhile—whether at the same time as the exile of the bishops, or rather later, is obscure—an armed attack by military forces had been made upon Nitria at the Emperor's command.[18] Jerome dates this in his *Chrónicle* in A.D. 375, saying that many of the monks were slain. But neither he nor Rufinus give any precise numbers. Jerome states that 'Valens lege data ut monachi militarent, nolentes fustibus jussit interfici'.[19] The reference is usually taken to be to the *Theodosian Code* XII. 18. 1 (A.D. 368) and XII. 1. 63 (A.D. 373), wherein, with particular reference to Egypt, it is enacted that men who try to escape from their public duties by going into the deserts and joining companies of monks ('specie religionis cum coetibus monazonton congregentur') should be dragged from their hiding-places and forced to return to their duties, or else have their property confiscated. The law does not, of course, speak of beating to death.[20] It is the first known reference to monks in Roman Law. Rufinus was an eye-witness, and claims to have suffered at the time, but does not state explicitly that any were killed. He stayed some six years now in Egypt, at the feet of Didymus the blind scholar in Alexandria, and then after an interval another two. He travelled up the Nile at least as far as Pispir.[21] At last he went up to join Melania and the monastic community which she had set up on the Mount of Olives soon after her service to the exiles at Diocaesarea.[22]

The Holy Places have their own special way of drawing men and women to prayer. We remember that Chariton, the protomonk of the Judaean Wilderness, came originally as a pilgrim. And we shall see later how the monastic life of that wilderness is for ever dominated by the Cities of the Incarnation along its western skyline. But it is the monasticism of the Holy Places themselves that comes first into historical prominence. Cyril of Jerusalem in the middle of the fourth century already refers to monks, apparently among his catechumens (for the monastic life did sometimes begin before baptism).[23] From the beginning probably the Church of the Resurrection had its σπουΔαῖοι—its 'devotees'. Olivet, with its two-fold view of the city and the wilderness—time and eternity—and its hallowing by the events of Holy Week and of the Ascension, already had its monks before the death of Athanasius—Innocent the Italian had been a married man and a high official at the court of Constantius. Coming to the monastic life, he raised on Olivet a shrine for relics of St. John the Baptist, rescued from their dispersal

at the hands of pagans at Samaria under Julian.[24] Not long after
A.D. 370, he was joined by a priest-monk, Palladius, apparently from
St. Basil's community at Caesarea in Cappadocia. Some friction
had arisen between Basil and his monks on his becoming bishop.
Palladius wrote about this to Athanasius, explaining also his own
reasons for joining Innocent, and Athanasius replied with high praise
of St. Basil.[25] A few years later—perhaps in A.D. 377—there was
some dissension between Innocent and Palladius, which both Basil
and Epiphanius were anxious to heal—Basil speaks of 'Innocent the
Italian and *our* Palladius'.[26] This seems most naturally to mean that
Palladius was of Cappadocian origin, but might only refer to his
having been a monk in Basil's community. In any case, the international character of the monasticism of the Holy Places stands out
from the first.

There is room enough on Olivet: and the establishment set up
by Melania and Rufinus was no doubt quite independent of Innocent
and Palladius. To it, probably in A.D. 382, came the deacon Evagrius,
in flight from a love affair in Constantinople.[27] A native of Ibora in
Pontus, he had been ordained reader by Basil at Caesarea. But after
Basil's death at the beginning of A.D. 379, he had been attracted to
the fame of Gregory of Nazianzus in the capital, and had written
back from there to the people of Caesarea excusing himself in a
letter which, surviving in the Greek under cover of St. Basil's name
(Letter 8), has long had an important but misleading place in discussion of St. Basil's Trinitarian theology. Jerome also was sitting
at the feet of Gregory about this time. Gregory ordained Evagrius
deacon; and when he abandoned the city during the Council of
A.D. 381, he left the young theologian to support his successor
Nectarius, until this personal trouble intervened. Coming to Olivet,
Evagrius fell ill for six months—something of a psychological illness
—until Melania cured him by deciding him to take the monastic
habit. He went on to Nitria, then after two years to the Cells, where
he lived for another fourteen years (Evagrius himself wrote some of
his surviving works as from Scetis: but as we have seen, this term
could be used in a wider sense). During that time he was a prolific
writer, largely in a gnomic form for ascetics to get by heart and
chew upon. Highly, sometimes rashly, speculative, in the succession
of Origen, but an original and independent thinker, he has left his
mark very deep upon Christian spirituality, providing it with
practically a new vocabulary for its Greek expression. It is he

principally who baptized the Stoic concept of ἀπάθεια—'passionlessness'—a concept which became universal in Greek ascetic theology, while it was never made at home in Latin. To him we owe the classification of the eight evil λογισμοί (thoughts, or *cogitationes*)—gluttony, fornication, avarice, grief, anger, accidie, vain-glory, pride[28]—which was taken over in a slightly different order by Cassian, and appears to be the ancestor of the 'Seven Capital Sins' of Latin moral theology. Some of Evagrius' speculations did fall wide of the Christian balance of truth. And one is suspicious at his seeming to set Knowledge above Love. But he deserves to have the credit for what he gave to the Church. Actually, such of his works as survive in Greek are mostly, though not all, under cover of some less suspect name. Others have come down to us only in Syriac, and will provide a quarry for research students for a long while to come. His very great importance is only now beginning to be appreciated.[29]

In the autumn of A.D. 385, two companies of Roman pilgrims met in Syria, the one headed by Jerome, the other by the lady Paula with her daughter Eustochium. Passing through Palestine on their pilgrimage, they came down for an extensive visit to Alexandria and Nitria before returning in A.D. 386 to settle in Bethlehem.[30]

In A.D. 388 a young Galatian, Palladius, came to Alexandria on the monastic quest[31] (*pace* Dom Cuthbert Butler, his three years' stay with Innocent on Olivet, where, as we have seen, he had a namesake, cannot well be fitted in at this point, and must be placed later[23]). He was received by the great Isidore the Hosteller, the former Nitrian monk, then seventy years old, who was said to have been one of the monks with Athanasius in Rome in A.D. 340—though he would then have been only twenty-two. Isidore entrusted the young Palladius for three years to an old man, Dorotheus,[33] at a seaside monastery five miles to the west of Alexandria. This is the old man who, when Palladius asked him why he taxed his body so excessively, answered, 'It kills me, so I kill it'. His régime proved too much for the health of Palladius, who returned to the city long before the three years were up. He does, however, seem to have continued in the region of Alexandria, where he records that there were some two thousand monks, at least into the third year. Then he went on to Nitria,[34] where a number of monks still survived from the first generation, who had known Antony and Amoun, and even Pachomius. After a year in Nitria,[35] he went on to the Cells.[36] There Macarius the Alexandrian was still priest, dying three years later at the age of a hundred. But Palladius' chief attachment was to

Evagrius, under whose tutelage he stayed until Evagrius' death after
Epiphany in A.D. 399.[37] Palladius does not seem to have remained
stationary through this time. He may possibly have been on some
mission to Palestine: for Epiphanius, writing probably in A.D. 394
to Bishop John of Jerusalem, warns him against a Galatian Palladius,
'qui quondam nobis carus fuit, et nunc misericordia Dei indiget',
preaching and teaching the heresy of Origen.[38] Certainly later in
the same year, 394, he went, on a hint from Evagrius, an eighteen-
day journey partly on foot and partly by boat up the Nile, in flood-
time, to visit the famous recluse John, who had now been forty-eight
years in his retreat of three domed cells built against the cliff face
near Lycopolis (Asiût), and died a few months later.[39] John seemed
to scent (what Palladius was a little shy of confessing) that Palladius
was of Evagrius' company, and also that he was attracted already to
ecclesiastical politics. Asking him if he wanted to become a bishop,
he was not to be put off by Palladius' playful evasion that he was
already bishop of the kitchen, consecrated by gluttony, and ex-
communicating the wine when it turned to vinegar. Long afterwards, Palladius was bitterly to remember the old man's warning.

In the autumn of the same year, John received another visit from
foreign monks.[40] A party of seven, one of them a deacon, came
from Rufinus' monastery on Olivet to make a tour of monastic
Egypt. Fear of barbarian unrest deterred them from going farther
south than Lycopolis. So the travel narrative that one of them has
left us—the *Historia Monachorum in Aegypto*—starts with an account
of their visit to John, and brings them stage by stage down the Nile
from thence, finishing with a cursory visit to Nitria, and finally an
account of the monks of Diolcus at one of the mouths of the Nile,
from whence no doubt they took ship back to Palestine. Perhaps
ten years later Rufinus, who left the East in A.D. 397, translated this
work into Latin, with embellishments and corrections.[41] No more
is known of the original author beyond a statement of Sozomen
which suggests his identity with the Timothy who was Archdeacon
of Alexandria in A.D. 412, and an unsuccessful candidate for the
Patriarchate against Cyril.[42] The work is full of wonders, and the
writer was extremely gullible. But most of his wonders are given
at second hand: and the contrast between the style and thought of
the different monks whose words he gives us suggests that he does
give these faithfully to the best of his ability. Certainly his account
of John of Lycopolis, apart from details of which I think too much
has been made at the expense of Palladius, bears out that given with

rather more detail in the *Lausiac History*. The *Historia Monachorum* describes John as ninety years old, while Palladius makes him only seventy-eight. But that is just the kind of divergence we should expect between the two writers. Palladius is more sober and more precise, and I find it hard to understand how scholars familiar with the two writers can give preference to the *Historia Monachorum* for credibility.[43]

While our other sources turn our attention at this time very much to Nitria and Scetis, it is the value of the *Historia Monachorum* to remind us how the monastic life in its various forms was pullulating up the whole length of the Nile Valley.

Some time, probably early, in the 380s—we cannot be more precise—two young men, Germanus and John Cassian, entered the monastic life in a coenobium at Bethlehem—we are not told which, and conjecture has rested on Posidonius' monastery beyond the Shepherds' Fields, where Palladius also stayed for a time, perhaps in A.D. 399:[44] but what evidence Cassian gives suggests somewhere nearer the Cave of the Nativity.[45] When shortly the two young men were inspired by an old Egyptian monk, Pinufius—who shared their cell as a novice, then proved to be a famous abbot in flight for a second time from his own fame[46]—and wanted to visit the Egyptian deserts, their community made them take an oath in the Cave of the Nativity that they would quickly return.[47] (No mention is made of Jerome, though both he and Rufinus are praised elsewhere in Cassian's writings. So it is probable, and generally assumed, that this was not Jerome's community. But the argument from silence is never conclusive.) The young men, coming to Panephysis,[48] whence they also visited Diolcus,[49] were attracted to Scetis.[50] And it was seven years—seven conscience-stricken years—before the truants came back to Bethlehem, to obtain at last forgiveness for their perjury, a ready permission to return to Scetis, and a friendly escort on their setting forth again.[51]

Cassian and Germanus certainly visited the Cells on their way from Nitria to Scetis.[52] But not once does Cassian mention Evagrius. And it has only recently been pointed out[53] in how large a measure his work is a rendering into Latin of Evagrius' teaching, without the speculations, and with certain other significant modifications. Controversial terms like 'passionlessness' (ἀπάθεια) are paraphrased or otherwise avoided: and Love is restored to its primacy above Knowledge.[54]

Probably in A.D. 394, there came to Scetis an austere personality who looms large over the next generation of its history—Arsenius,[55] who is said to have been tutor to the Emperor's sons, Arcadius and Honorius: his withdrawal to Scetis is in one account said to have been prompted by a plot of theirs against him. The gleaners of *Apophthegmata* loved to contrast this silent and somewhat forbidding figure with the simplicity and approachability of another great Scetiote, the converted brigand Moses the Ethiopian.[56]

Two other pilgrimages from the West about this time have left us literary records. That attributed to the lady Aetheria (if that was indeed her name)[57] only survives in a fragmentary condition, and in the portion which concerns Palestine, Sinai, and Syria. Its account of monastic life around Sinai is of particular interest: we may note that 'monastery' is still used here in its early sense of a solitary cell. The other account is that of Postumian, given in the *Dialogue* of Sulpicius Severus. But his pilgrimage (if it be not a literary device) was in A.D. 400–1. It contains a gentle, pained, and non-partisan view of the tragic events of that year.[58]

These two last decades of the fourth century could be looked back to as something of a golden age for Nitria and Scetis. A lurking devil of jealousy between the uneducated Egyptian monks and the intellectuals, native or foreign, would occasionally rear its head—as when one old man, scandalized at the little luxuries allowed to Arsenius in sickness, was reminded that, whereas the Roman had come from all the comforts of the palace, he himself was really better off in Scetis than he had been as a village watchman;[59] or when Evagrius, putting in his word in a debate in the Cells, was rebuked by the priest: 'We know, abba, that if you had been in your own country, you might often have become a bishop, and head over many. But now you are settled here as a foreigner.'[60]

Actually, Theophilus of Alexandria himself urged Evagrius to accept a bishopric[61]—a Coptic account says, that of Thmuis[62]—and we have surviving in Syriac a letter which may be Evagrius' reply on this occasion.[63] (The Coptic account says he fled to Palestine to avoid consecration:[64] and it would simplify our chronology considerably if we could suppose that both he and Palladius were in Palestine when he died—happy in the date of his death.) Under Theophilus' predecessor, Timothy (A.D. 381–5), Ammonius, one of the Tall Brothers, had been sought after by a city in Egypt to be their bishop. But when they came to arrest him for consecration, he cut off his left ear, and told them no mutilated man could be a bishop. When they said that was a bit of Judaism, and should not stand in the way, he threatened to cut out his tongue.[65] His brother Dioscorus was actually consecrated by Theophilus as Bishop of Damanhur in succession to Isidore some time between A.D. 391 and 394.[66]

Apart from making monks bishops, Theophilus both courted the deserts and found many other uses for their denizens, some of them rather baleful. Isidore, the monastic Hosteller of Alexandria, was frequently used as his ambassador abroad—as when, the issue being in doubt between Theodosius and the pretender Maximus, Isidore went armed with alternative letters from Theophilus of congratulation on victory, and both letters were found in his luggage.[67] In A.D. 396, he was sent by Theophilus to effect a reconciliation between Epiphanius and John of Jerusalem.[68] In A.D. 398, he was Theophilus' candidate for the episcopal throne of Constantinople,[69] and his envoy to Rome for the reconciliation between Rome and Flavian of Antioch.[70]

Meanwhile the issue with paganism at Alexandria had come to a head in A.D. 391. Some provocative action on the part of Theophilus had drawn the pagans into armed riot, in the course of which they had taken some Christians prisoner and offered them the old alternative of sacrifice or martyrdom. They then established themselves in the great Temple of Sarapis, where they stood a siege for a time. But in the end, at the imperial command, the temple and the great image of Sarapis were destroyed.[71] (A law in *Cod. Theod.* XVI. 10. 11 actually orders suppression of pagan worship, but does not speak of destruction of temples. No doubt its application would vary with local circumstances.) There is an ominous story in this connection in the *Apophthegmata*: 'Once upon a time, the fathers came to Alexandria, called by the Archbishop Theophilus that he might make prayer and destroy the temples. . . .'[72] In fact, Theophilus seems to have been discovering the use of the crowd of fanatical monks as a private army.

Pagans and Christians alike remembered the destruction of the Sarapeum as a historical landmark. The Abba Doulas would tell how his master Abba Bessarion was then on a visit to John of Lycopolis: as they were speaking together, Bessarion said: 'A decree has gone out that the temples should be destroyed'.[73] It was not only the Sarapeum that was overthrown. At Canopus also the temple became a monastery. A late Coptic account says that Theophilus first invited monks from Jerusalem to occupy the site, but that the nightly demonic apparitions were too much for them, and the Tabennesiotes were brought in in their place—native Egyptians, who knew better how to deal with Egyptian demons![74] Certain it is that the Tabennesiotes did now establish a house at Canopus.[75]

We happen to have some account of this from Eunapius, one of the less attractive of the pagan writers of the time: 'Then they introduced into the sacred places those who are called monks—men in shape, but their life is like that of pigs; and they openly underwent and performed ten thousand unspeakable ills. And yet that is what was thought pious, to despise the divine. For tyrannical power was then in the hands of every man who wore a black garment and wanted to behave himself unseemly in public. . . . And even at Canopus they established the monks, binding humanity to the service of slaves, and not good slaves at that, instead of the real gods.'[76]

The name of Metanoea—'Repentance'—given to the new monastery probably meant that it was thought of as a monument to the Conversion of the Gentiles. The prologue to the Greek *Vita Prima* of Pachomius speaks thus of 'the repentance of the Gentiles being multiplied in the Church, the bishops guiding them to God according to the teaching of the Apostles':[77] and it is not improbable that it was written, or set in order for publication, at this time. A sixth-century papyrus has a story of a visit of old Horsiesius to Theophilus in response to a letter in which Theophilus had asked him to bring with him the *Life* (not 'Lives') of Pachomius and Theodore:[78] and although the story is full of sixth-century legendary matter, this detail looks like a reference to the traditional origin of the *Vita Prima*. Certainly Theophilus would seem to have been intent on providing the new monastery with a corpus of Greek Pachomian literature as propaganda for the community now that it had come down to more cosmopolitan regions. The *Letter of Bishop Ammon* was written within a year or two—when Dioscorus was already Bishop of Damanhur, but in time for Evagrius (if we are indeed right in attributing the *De Oratione* to him and not to Nilus) to be quoting from it[79] before his death in A.D. 399. The *Rule* and the *Letters* of Pachomius and Theodore, and the *Testament* of Horsiesius, were also translated into Greek; and it was from the Greek (which does not survive except in a later selection) that Jerome in A.D. 404 translated them into Latin for the use of Latin monks at Canopus.

As we have said, Theophilus courted the monks. But there are hints of some reserve on their side. There is the story of a visit of his to Scetis, when an old man (the text says Pambo, but the great Pambo was dead, and had not lived in Scetis) would not speak to him: 'If he is not profited by my silence, neither will he be profited by my speech'.[80] Arsenius outlived Theophilus, and we cannot tell the date of the two visits to Scetis when Theophilus approached him. On the first occasion he asked to hear a word from him: there was a silence, and then, 'If I tell you, will you keep it?' On promising, he was told, 'Wherever you hear Arsenius is, don't come near'.[81] On the second visit, he sent ahead to ask if Arsenius would open to him, and received the answer, 'If you come, I open to you: and if I open to you, I open to all: and then I settle here no more'.[82]

The remaining two of the Tall Brothers, brought to Alexandria by Theophilus to help in church administration, finally sought to be relieved of their functions and return to the desert.[83]

Meanwhile in Jerusalem the young monk John had succeeded St. Cyril as bishop in A.D. 386. At Bethlehem and on the Mount of Olives, the intellectuals in concert with their bishop were using Origen as guide in their intensive study of Scripture. But Epiphanius, who could not keep his hands off his native Palestine, began to be troubled at this. For him, anything he could not understand must surely be heresy. And while he condemned the anthropomorphism of some heretics, he still felt there must be something in it.[84] Here he had, as we shall see, the unintellectual monks in his support. The *agraphon* attributed to our Lord, 'Thou hast seen thy brother, thou hast seen thy God', was basic in their spirituality:[85] and it was easy to pass from this great Christian truth to a crude humanization of the Deity.

When Epiphanius came on a visit to Jerusalem in A.D. 393,[86] he probably already knew that about the beginning of that year a certain Atarbius had come round touting for anathemas against Origen.[87] Rufinus had shown him the door. But Jerome, to everyone's surprise, had given his anathema. Atarbius had soon had to leave Palestine. Epiphanius, his suspicions aroused, tried in vain to obtain from Bishop John an anathema on Origen. He obtained only a statement of positive faith in a sermon which he could not but approve. On his next visit he drew off the gloves, and himself preached a sermon against Origen, to which Bishop John replied with a sermon against anthromoporphism.[88] There was no open breach of communion. But when Epiphanius came again the next

year, he took Jerome's brother Paulinian to his own old monastery—
in the diocese of Eleutheropolis, and so outside John's jurisdiction—
and ordained him priest, obviously for ministration to the Bethlehem
community, where Jerome, though a priest, refused to function as
such. This was not Epiphanius' only high-handed action at this
time. And yet he professed himself genuinely surprised that John
took it amiss.[89] Finally he appealed to the monks to break off communion with the Origenist John. Jerome himself seems to have
acted with some moderation, sending his brother away to Cyprus
until the trouble was over. But others of his community were more
hot-headed: and John placed under an interdict any who acknow-
ledged Paulinian's ordination—they should not enter the Church of
the Nativity, even for funerals; and they had to take their catechumens to the Bishop of Diospolis (Lydda) for baptism. It was
now that John appealed to Theophilus of Alexandria to intervene,
and Isidore came as mediator—though matters were not improved
by the discovery of a letter of his to Rufinus which seemed to show
him as by no means impartial in the matter at issue: and Theophilus
himself was at this time clearly on the Origenist side. However, in
the end he was successful in effecting a reconciliation, early in A.D.
397. When Rufinus finally left Palestine very soon after, his
old friend escorted him on the beginning of his journey.[90] A passage
in the *Lausiac History* is generally understood to mean that Melania
also played a leading part in the healing of the schism.[91] Three
years later, in A.D. 400, she too left Palestine, though she returned to
die in Jerusalem after the Sack of Rome.[92] Jerome's more violent
and lasting quarrel with her and Rufinus did not break out until
they were back in Italy, and need not concern us here.

Within a few days of Evagrius' death at Epiphany, A.D. 399,
Theophilus' Paschal Letter for the year was promulgated. It proved
to contain a strong denunciation of anthropomorphism.[93] The
intellectuals of Nitria and the Cells naturally welcomed this. But in
Scetis only one of the four Congregations, that of the Abba Paphnutius, allowed it to be read: and there also it was received with
heart-burnings. An old man, Sarapion, was convinced at last by a
Cappadocian visitor, the deacon Photinus, that anthropomorphism
was rejected by the Catholic Church. But when they all joined to
give thanks to God for his coming to see the truth, he soon broke
down in sobs: 'Ah, wretch that I am! They have taken away my
God, and I have none I can hold now, and know not whom to

adore or to whom to address myself.' Cassian represents himself, probably truly, as present on this occasion.

Elsewhere in Scetis and Nitria, Theophilus' letter was still less acceptable. Socrates tells us that a crowd of monks descended on Alexandria, where Theophilus tried to pacify them with the words, 'So have I seen you, as the face of God'. Not satisfied, they pressed him, 'If you say truthfully that the face of God is like ours, anathematize the books of Origen'. And Theophilus gave way—'for I also hold in abhorrence the books of Origen, and blame those who accept them'.[94]

This *volte-face* coincided with other happenings that were turning Theophilus against his former favourites. The Tall Brothers, Euthymius and Eusebius, had gone back to the desert from the administrative posts in which Theophilus had set them in Alexandria.[95] Isidore on his return from Rome gave evidence contrary to what Theophilus wanted in a case against the Archpriest Peter.[96] Moreover, in accordance with the terms of a will, he had spent a large legacy on the poor, without letting Theophilus know lest he should seize it for the buildings on which he was passionately set.[97] Theophilus raked up other dormant charges against him, and had him deposed in synod. Isidore withdrew to his old cell in Nitria.[98] When the Tall Brothers came to Alexandria to plead for him, Theophilus turned upon them the charge of Origenism.[99] There were riotous scenes in Alexandria and then in Nitria, where the anthropomorphist section of the monks were worked up against the intellectuals. Theophilus seems to have brought in imperial forces, and to have ousted Dioscorus from the administration of his own diocese in which Nitria lay. Origenism was condemned in synod in Alexandria early in A.D. 400.[100]

Onto this scene came the peaceful Western pilgrim Postumian. He was full of appreciation, on his return to Italy, for Theophilus' generous hospitality; and he found much that was aside from the truth in Origen's writings: but surely Origen could be read with discrimination; and here was no reason for violence between Christians.[101]

The Tall Brothers fled from Nitria, and some three hundred went with them. Many of them went up to Jerusalem,[102] and some eighty from thence to Scythopolis (Beth-Shan) in the Jordan Valley, where there were plenty of palm-trees to provide them with material for their usual trade of rope-making.[103] Fifty of them went on to Constantinople, perhaps towards the end of A.D. 401, appealing to the Archbishop, John Chrysostom, who received them hospitably, but would not give them communion; and then, against John's advice, to the Emperor.[104]

John Chrysostom was certainly no Origenist. But he knew a good man when he saw one. When, early the year before, Palladius had come on from Palestine to the capital, John quickly consecrated him Bishop of Helenopolis in Bithynia.[105] Heraclides, another monk from Nitria and disciple of Evagrius, was made Bishop of Ephesus— this appointment raised questions of jurisdiction which were soon to be used against John.[106] Germanus and Cassian, whose arrival in Constantinople must almost have coincided with that of Palladius, were ordained, Germanus to the priesthood, Cassian to the diaconate.[107]

Theophilus, blaming John for the turn of events when he was summoned to answer charges at Constantinople, worked up an agitation against him.[108] The old fanatic Epiphanius was spurred to go there inveighing against Origenism—he seems, however, to have realized when there that he was being used as a tool for other purposes, and started back for Cyprus, but died on the voyage.[109] Theophilus managed to convert the proceedings into a case against John, with himself as judge. His anger against the monks was forgotten. In fact, his Paschal Letter for A.D. 402 already suggests a desire for reconciliation.[110] Dioscorus of Damanhur died in Constantinople.[111] The other Tall Brothers and their companions, summoned to the Synod of the Oak in A.D. 403, crossed in true monastic obedience to Chalcedon, where Ammonius died.[112] Theophilus is said to have shed tears on hearing the news of his death, affirming that there was no monk of his time like Ammonius, even if he had caused him trouble. The others humbly asked forgiveness and received it.[113] Isidore also is said in the *Lausiac History* to have died in peace, apparently in this year.[114] The *Dialogue* does not, in fact, make it perfectly clear that, having withdrawn to Nitria on his condemnation, he ever left there with the Tall Brothers. But Sozomen and Socrates state that he too went to Constantinople.[115] Hierax returned to the desert.[116] So did Isaac, to continue as priest of the Cells for many years.[117] But the glory was departed from Nitria, never fully to return. Sozomen seems to think of it as little more than a region of Scetis.

The tragedy of St. John Chrysostom does not concern us further, save to note that Germanus and Cassian, coming with letters of appeal from Constantinople to Rome in A.D. 405, remained in the

West;[118] while Palladius, also fleeing to Rome,[119] but returning with the Roman envoys,[120] was separated from them,[121] imprisoned,[122] and relegated to Assuan,[123] then brought back as far as Antinoe, where he spent four years.[124] Not earlier than A.D. 408 he wrote his *Dialogue on the Life of St. John Chrysostom*[125]—a highly polemical document written in heat by one of the sufferers in the tragedy. Theophilus is, of course, the villain of the piece. Recalled from exile perhaps about the time of Theophilus' death in A.D. 412, and installed a few years later in a different Bithynian bishopric, that of Aspouna,[126] Palladius wrote his History addressed to Lausus the Chamberlain—the great record of what we have called the Golden Age of Nitria—in A.D. 419–20, in the fifty-sixth year of his life, the thirty-third of his monastic career, and the twentieth of his episcopate.[127] John Chrysostom's name had been restored to the diptychs,[128] and that ugly page of history was turned over and left behind. In the whole of this work, Palladius does not once mention Theophilus. And if he does speak of the death of Ammonius in Constantinople or Chalcedon, he gives no explanation of the need that brought him there.[129] Only Jerome comes in for a word of bitterness for his βασκανία (jealousy, 'evil eye').[130] Cassian likewise, writing in the next decade, has his word of praise, in successive chapters of his work against Nestorius, for Jerome and for Rufinus,[131] avoids the controversial name of his master Evagrius, and mitigates his teaching; mentions Theophilus only for his Paschal Letter against anthropomorphism;[132] and draws a veil over all that followed on his own departure from Egypt in A.D. 399.

.   .   .   .   .

The freshness of the first generation was fading from Scetis also. And the older monks knew it. When the barbarian Mazices devastated the valley in A.D. 407–8,[133] they accepted it as a judgement. Abba Moses the Ethiopian himself would say, 'If we keep the commandments of our fathers, I stand your surety before God that no barbarians come here. But if we do not keep them, this place must be laid desolate.'[134] The day came when the brethren were sitting with him, and he said, 'To-day barbarians are coming to Scetis: but rise up and flee'. They say, 'Then are you not fleeing, Abba?' He answered, 'For so many years have I been looking forward to this day, that the words of the Master Christ might be fulfilled which He spake, "All who take the sword shall die by the sword" '. They say to him, 'Then neither do we flee, but will die with you'. He said, 'It is no business of mine: let each one see how he is settled'. There were seven brethren, and he says to them, 'Look, the barbarians are drawing near the door'. They came in and slew them. But one of the brethren hid behind the pile of rope: and he saw seven crowns coming down and crowning them.[135]

Most of the fathers fled. Daniel, Arsenius' disciple, passed through the midst of the barbarians unseen, then said to himself, 'Lo, God has cared for me, and I am not dead: do thou also therefore the human thing, and flee like the fathers'.[136] Arsenius himself, whose cell is said to have been thirty-two miles away, perhaps remained longer—unless we are wrong in inferring from a letter of Augustine that the devastation took place in A.D. 407-8.[137] For the words attributed to him in his flight clearly refer to the events of August, A.D. 410: 'The world has lost Rome, and the monks Scetis'.[138]

NOTES TO CHAPTER III

[1] Socr. H.E. IV. 23.
[2] H.L. cc. 10–11.
[3] H.L. c. 1 (16. 6–8): Socr. H.E. IV. 23.
[4] Jerome, Ep. 127. 5.
[5] G Mac. Aeg. 33. For a full discussion of the origin of Deir Baramûs, see Evelyn White, History, c. VII. 3 (pp. 98–107).
[6] Bas. Ep. 223. 2 (337D).
[7] See Studia Anselmiana 38 (Antonius Magnus Eremita), Garitte, Le Texte grec et les version anciennes (especially pp. 5–6), and Chr. Mohrmann, Note sur la version latine la plus ancienne (pp. 35–44).
[8] Sulpicius Severus, Vita Martini c. 6, shows Martin setting up a monasterium at Milan before Hilary's return. Eusebius of Vercellae, becoming bishop in A.D. 345, set up a monastic régime in his household before his exile in 355—Ambrose, Ep. LXIV. 66.
[9] The movement was early well known enough to have its detractors—see Consultationes Zacchaei et Apollonii, P.L. 20. 1071–1166; ed. Morin, Florilegium Patristicum, fasc. 39 (1935).
[10] Jer. Ep. 3: Rufinus, Ap. ad Anast. II. 12.
[11] H.L. c. 46 (134. 13).
[12] Ibid. c. 10 (30. 4–23).
[13] Ibid. c. 18 (57. 4–13).
[14] Socr. H.E. IV. 22: Soz. H.E. VI. 19: Theod. H.E. IV. 20–22.
[15] H.L. c. 46: Paulinus, Ep. 29. 11.
[16] Ruf. H.E. II. 4.
[17] Ruf. H.E. II. 6: Socr. H.E. IV. 36: Soz. H.E. VI. 38: Theod. H.E. IV. 23.
[18] Ruf. H.E. II. 3: Socr. H.E. IV. 22 and 24: Soz. H.E. VI. 20.
[19] Jer. Chron. (ed. Helm), p. 248 (P.L. 27, 697): Oros. Hist. adv. Pag. VII. 33 (P.L. 31, 1145).
[20] S. Mazzarino, Aspetti Sociali del IV Secolo (1951), p. 429, n. 92, thinks the law referred to is one of 376, and not to be identified with either of those named above.
[21] Ruf. H.E. II. 7–8.
[22] Jer. Ep. 4. 2: H.L. c. 46.
[23] C.I. IV. 24, XII. 33: in the first passage cited, monks (μονάζοντες) are directly addressed. Scholars have taken this to mean that the audience was not restricted to catechumens—that baptized people would also attend. But the Coptic Pachomian Lives show that a monk might at this time still be a catechumen—V.C. B⁶ cc. 81, 193.
[24] H.L. c. 44: cf. Ruf. H.E. II. 28.
[25] P.G. 26, 1167.
[26] Basil, Epp. 258 and 259.
[27] HL. c. 38.

[28] *P.G.* 40, 1272–1274A (these chapters are actually cc. 6–14 of his *Practicus*). Cassian inverts grief (*tristitia*) and anger.

[29] See Guillaumont, *Les 'Kephalaia Gnostica' d'Évagre le Pontique* (1962), and his rich bibliography (pp. 339–47).

[30] Jer. *Ep.* 108 (cf. also *Ep.* 46, *Apol. c. Ruf.* III. 22).

[31] *H L.* c. 1.

[32] Butler, *Lausiac History*, II, App. V. ii

[33] *H.L.* c. 2.

[34] Ibid. c. 7.

[35] Ibid. (25. 10).

[36] Ibid. c. 18 (47. 24).

[37] Ibid. c. 38 (122. 15): see Butler, App. V. ii, etc.

[38] Jer. *Ep.* 51.

[39] *H.L.* c. 35.

[40] *H.M.* c. 1.

[41] See Butler, *L.H.* vol I, pp. 198–203, and App. I, and vol. II, n. 37, controverting Preuschen's theory put forward in his *Palladius und Rufinus*.

[42] Butler (vol. I, p. 277) puts forward this suggestion to explain Sozomen, *H.E.* VI. 29. 2. But he says that Sozomen 'stated that it was written by Timotheus, Bishop of Alexandria. In this he is certainly wrong: for Timotheus died in 385'. Was Butler only looking at the Latin translation of Sozomen? For the Greek text does *not* call Timotheus 'bishop of Alexandria,' but ὁ τὴν 'Αλεξανδρέων ἐκκλησίαν ἐπιτροπεύσας—a phrase as aptly descriptive of the work of an archdeacon as of that of a bishop.

[43] See M. Jullien, À la recherche de la grotte de l'Abbé Jean, *Études* 88 (1901), pp. 205–18: also Peeters in *A.B.* 54 (1936), pp. 368 ff., and Telfer in *J.T.S.* 38 (1937), pp. 379–83.

[44] *H.L.* c. 36 (107. 1).

[45] For dating before Jerome's arrival, see Dom Pichery's Introduction to Cassian in *Sources Chrétiennes* 42, pp. 9–13. For suggestion of the Poemenium, see Schiwietz II, 153. For position near the Cave of the Nativity, see Cass. *Inst.* IV. 31.

[46] *Inst.* IV. 30–31: *Coll.* XX. 1.

[47] *Coll.* XVII. 2, 5.

[48] *Coll.* XI. 2, 3: XX. 2. Collations XI–XVII and XIX–XXIV are sited at Panephysis.

[49] *Coll.* XVIII is sited at Diolcus.

[50] *Coll.* XX. 12. Collations I–X belong to Scetis.

[51] *Coll.* XVII. 30.

[52] *Coll.* VI. 1. Abba Theodore is described as inhabiting the Cells.

[53] S. Marsili, 'Giovanni Cassiano ed Evagrio Pontico', *Studia Anselmiana* 5, Rome, 1936.

[54] *Coll.* I. 11, etc.

[55] The two Lives, one by Theodore of Studium (*A.S. Jul.* IV. 617 ff.) and one anonymous (ed. Pereteli), are compilations based mainly on the apophthegmata found in the alphabetical collection (*P.G.* 65). But these and other stories, preserved in Varsanuphius and elsewhere, seem to be derived from an older lost Vita. Cyril of Scythopolis in the *Vita Euthymii* describes Arsenius as Euthymius' pattern, and mentions his having been tutor to Arcadius and Honorius (*V.E.* c. 21).

[56] G Arsenius 38. For Moses, see the apophthegmata in his name (but there was more than one Moses), and the account in *H.L.* c. 19.

[57] Éthérie, *Journal de Voyage*: ed. H. Pétré, *Sources Chrétiennes* 21 (Paris, 1948).

[58] Sulp. Sev., *Dial.* I. 7.

[59] G Ars. 36 and Rom. 1 (two versions of the same story?).

[60] G Evagr. 7.

[61] Socr. *H.E.* IV. 23.

[62] Coptic version of *H.L.*—Amélineau, *De Hist. Laus.*, p. 115.

[63] *Ep.* 50 (Frankenberg, p. 599)—but the evidence is tenuous, the addresses not being preserved: 'I thank the Lord and thy holiness that thou countest me with thy sheep. But it profits me, who am full of many sores, to remain outside from thy holy fold, in the wilderness.'

[64] Amélineau, op. cit. p. 118.

[65] *H.L.* c. 11: Socr. *H.E.* IV. 23: Soz. *H.E.* VI. 30: cf. Theophilus in Jer. *Ep.* 92.

[66] Dioscorus was still a priest in Nitria when (A.D. 391?) he took Palladius and Evagrius to see Benjamin—*H.L.* c. 12. He was Bishop of Damanhur by the time of the Constantinople Synod of A.D. 394, and the visit of the party from Olivet—*H.M.* (Lat.) XXIII. 2—and when

Bishop Ammon wrote his letter to Theophilus about the Tabennesiotes—*Ep. Am.* c. 32. (119. 4).

[67] Socr. *H.E.* VI. 2: Soz. *H.E.* VIII. 2
[68] Jer. *Ep.* 82; *In Joh.* c. 37 (*P.L.* 23, 390).
[69] Socr. *H.E.* VI. 2: Soz. *H.E.* VIII. 2.
[70] Pall. *D.V.C.* c. 6 (35. 11): Socr. *H.E.* V. 15, VI. 9: Soz. *H.E.* VIII. 3.
[71] Ruf. *H.E.* XI. 21, 23, 30: Socr. *H.E.* V. 16: Soz. *H.E.* VII. 15: Theod. *H.E.* V. 22. Rauschen, *Jahrbücher*, 301–3: Seeck, *Geschichte des Untergangs* . . . t. V., p. 534.
[72] G Theophilus 3.
[73] G. Bessarion 4. See also G Epiph. 2.
[74] Zoega, Catalogus 265, Nr. 160: see A. Favale, *Teofilo d'Alessandria*, p. 70, also P. Barisou in *Aegyptus* 18 (1938), p. 66.
[75] Reg. Pach., *Praefatio Hieronymi*, c. 1.
[76] Eunapius, *Vitae Sophistarum* VI. 11. 8.
[77] *V.P.* G¹ c. 2 (2. 22).⸱
[78] *Der Papyruscodex saec. VI–VII der Philippsbibliothek in Cheltenham*, ed. Crum, Strasburg, 1915, S. 41 (translation pp. 65–6).
[79] *De Oratione* c. 108, based on *Ep. Am.* c. 19.
[80] G Theoph. 2.
[81] G Arsenius 7.
[82] G Ars. 8. ⸳
[83] Socr. *H.E.* VI. 7.
[84] Epiph. c. *Haer. LXX* (Audiani), cc. 2–8.
[85] *H.M.* c. 8. 55 (68. 49–50).
[86] Jer. *Epp.* 51, 82.
[87] Jer. *c. Ruf.* III. 33.
[88] Jer. *c. Joh.* 11.
[89] Jer. *Ep.* 51 (Epiphanius).
[90] Jer. *Apol.* III. 24 (*P.L.* 23, 475).
[91] *H.L.* c. 46 (136. 7–8).
[92] *H.L.* c. 54.
[93] Socr. *H.E.* VI. 7: Soz. *H.E.* VIII. 11: Cass. *Coll.* X. 2–4.
[94] Socr. and Soz., loc. cit.
[95] Socr., loc. cit.
[96] Socr. *H.E.* VI. 9: Soz. *H.E.* VIII. 12.
[97] Pall. *D.V.C.* c. 6 (35. 14–36. 5): Soz., loc. cit.
[98] *D.V.C.* c. 6 (36. 5–37. 15): Soz., loc. cit.: Jer. *Ep.* 92 (Theophilus).
[99] Soz. loc. cit.: *D.V.C.* c. 6 (37. 15–38. 8)—a slightly different account: Jerome (Theophilus), loc. cit.
[100] *D.V.C.* c. 7 (38. 9–39. 24): Jer. (Theoph.), loc. cit. It is said that the emperors issued rescripts against Origen—Jer. *Apol. c. Ruf.* I. 12: Anastas. Pap. *Epist.* I. 5 (*P.L.* XX. 72).
[101] Sulp. Sev., *Dial.* I. 6–7.
[102] *D.V.C.* c. 7 (39. 24–8).
[103] Soz. *H.E.* VIII. 13.
[104] *D.V.C.* cc. 7–8 (40. 7–43. 18): Soz. *H.E.* VIII. 13.
[105] *H.L.* c. 35 (105. 8–11). It is not expressly stated that John consecrated him. But he certainly put him in a position of trust at the Synod he held in Constantinople in A.D. 400—*D.V.C.* c. 14 (87. 11).
[106] Socr. *H.E.* VI. 11 and 17: Soz. *H.E.* VIII. 6 and 19: Pall. *D.V.C.* c. 15 (92. 7–10).
[107] Pall. *D.V.C.* c. 3 (19. 9): Soz. *H.E.* VIII. 26. 8.
[108] *D.V.C.* c. 8 (44–5).
[109] Socr. *H.E.* VI. 10, 12, 14: Soz. *H.E.* VIII. 15.
[110] Jer. *Ep.* 98.
[111] *D.V.C.* c. 17 (105. 9–14): Soz. *H.E.* VIII. 17. 5 (Socr. *H.E.* VI. 17 is not so well informed).
[112] Soz. *H.E.* VIII. 17. 6: *D.V.C.* loc. cit. (105. 6–9): *H.L.* c. 11 (34. 13–16).
[113] Soz. loc. cit. 4–5. For the Synod of the Oak see Photius, *Bibl.* 59.
[114] *H.L.* c. 1 (15. 12–14).
[115] Soz. *H.E.* VIII. 13: Socr. *H.E.* VI. 9.
[116] *D.V.C.* c. 17 (106. 9–10).
[117] Ibid. Palladius tells here of two Isaacs. The Priest of the Cells is, it seems, the disciple of Cronius. The *Apophthegmata* (G Isaac 5) show him surviving the devastation of Scetis in A.D. 408.

[118] *D.V.C.* c. 3 (19. 9): Soz. *H.E.* VIII. 26 (Letter of Pope Innocent to the clergy and people of Constantinople). An Edict of Arcadius, of 29th Aug. 404, ordered partisans of John to return to their countries.

[119] *D.V.C.* c. 3 (19. 3): Chrys. *Ep.* 148: Innocent, *Ep.* 7 (= Soz. VIII. 26).

[120] *D.V.C.* c. 4 (22. 11–17).

[121] *D.V.C.* c. 4 (23. 8: 24. 10–19).

[122] *H.L.* c. 35 (105. 12). Chrysostom, *Ep.* 113, speaks of him in hiding.

[123] *D.V.C.* c. 20 (126. 18–20): *H.L.* Prol. (10. 5). See also Butler in *J.T.S.* XXII, no. 86, p. 141.

[124] *H.L.* cc. 58–60. The last chapter has a reference to himself as 'the exiled bishop'. We may suppose it was during this period that Palladius visited the Pachomian monastery at Panopolis (c. 32), and made friends with Aphthonius, the Second of Faou.

[125] For discussion of the date of the writing of the *Dialogue*, see Coleman-Norton's Introduction, pp. lxv–lxix. The supposed date of the *Dialogue* seems to be July 408, or a few months later—Chrysostom is already dead (14th Sept. 407), and Heraclides of Ephesus has been in prison four years.

[126] Socr. *H.E.* VII. 36.

[127] *H.L.* Prol. (9. 12–10. 2).

[128] At Antioch in A.D. 413 (Jaffe-Wattenbach 305, 306, letter of Innocent): at Constantinople soon afterwards (Cyril, *Ep.* 75—a letter of Atticus of Constantinople, answered angrily by Cyril in *Ep.* 76): perhaps even at Alexandria by A.D. 418.

[129] *H.L.* c. 11 (34. 13–16: the text is doubtful).

[130] *H.L.* cc. 36 and 41.

[131] Cass. *de Inc.* cc. 26 and 27.

[132] Cass. *Coll.* X. 2.

[133] See Evelyn White, *History*, pp. 151–61.

[134] G Moses 9: *P.J.* I*5 (Nau 361).

[135] G Moses 10. But Palladius, *H.L.* c. 19 (62. 13–15), recording his death at the age of 75, shows no knowledge of the manner of it, or of the barbarian raid.

[136] G Daniel 1.

[137] Augustine, *Ep.* 111 (Nov.? A.D. 409). Philostorgius, *H.E.* XI. 8, records that under Arcadius the Mazices 'wasted Libya and no inconsiderable part of Egypt'.

[138] G Arsenius 21. Surely Evelyn White (*History*, p. 162) is wrong in connecting this apophthegm with a second sack of Scetis c. A.D. 435, twenty-five years after the Sack of Rome.

IV

AFTER THREE GENERATIONS

JEROME buried Paula in Bethlehem in A.D. 404,[1] and Alaric's invasion
sent old Melania back in A.D. 410 to die in Jerusalem within forty
days of her arrival.[2] In A.D. 417 came her granddaughter, the younger
Melania, and her husband Pinianus, to establish themselves in a pair
of monasteries on Olivet. She was now aged thirty-four. Years
before, she had persuaded her husband to accept a brother-and-sister
relationship:[3] and she had disposed of most of her vast wealth in
time, before the Sack of Rome made it unsaleable.[4] The couple had
spent seven years in North Africa before coming by way of Alexandria to Jerusalem.[5] Now they were both intent on being enrolled
among the poor of the Church there.[6] But, in fact, Melania never
seems to have lacked for very long whatever funds she might need
for service to the Church in building or in other ways. She was
able to pay a visit to the deserts of Egypt in A.D. 418.[7] And in A.D.
437 she availed herself of the *cursus publicus* to travel to Constantinople, where her pagan uncle Volusianus was on an embassy from
the West, and to bring him to Christian faith before his death
there.[8]

When she first came to Palestine, Bishop John of Jerusalem had
just died, and so had Eustochium.[9] But Jerome was still alive in
Bethlehem. His bitterness against Origen had not diminished, nor
had his relations with the locals improved. The year before, there
had been an armed raid on his monasteries, in which a deacon had
been killed.[10] He attributed this to Pelagians seeking revenge for
Pelagius' exile from Palestine after a synod at Diospolis had condemned his heresy but found him not guilty of it.[11] But the facts
about the outrage and its perpetrators are obscure.

The young Melania was the granddaughter and namesake of the
lady whom Jerome had stigmatized as 'black by name and black by
nature':[12] and she had sheltered Rufinus in his last years.[13] One is
happy to find no hint of the old bitterness in Jerome's reception of
her and her husband:[14] he died probably two years later.[15] The
closest of relationships sprang up between Melania and her cousin,
the younger Paula, still only a girl—she had been vowed to the
convent from infancy.[16] Melania is said to have brought her to

great humility ἀπὸ πολλοῦ τύφου καὶ Ῥωμαϊκοῦ φρονήματος—'from great haughtiness and Roman presumption'.[17] When Melania died in A.D. 439, Paula was with her on her last days.[18] It is the last record I know of Jerome's Bethlehem community.

.   .   .   .   .

The Devastation of Scetis in A.D. 407–8, following so soon on the tragic happenings in Nitria, brought home to the monks that there had indeed been a falling off from the freshness of the first generation—and they were the third generation now. In the Tabennesiote community, the writer of the *Paralipomena* had recognized in his time already the beginnings of the decadence which Pachomius had foreseen.[19] In Scetis or Nitria, an old man would say, 'The prophets made their books: and our fathers came and put them into practice: and those after them learned them by heart. Then came this generation, and wrote them out, and put them away idle in the cupboards.'[20] The Abba Poemen, surviving into later years, would say that 'From the third generation of Scetis, and the Abba Moses, the brethren came no more to progress'.[21] With the Tabennesiotes, it was the growing wealth of the community:[22] the Monastery of Metanoea at Canopus, in particular, was soon to become one of the largest landowners in Egypt.[23] In Scetis, the monks felt a moral decay. They remembered a saying of Macarius the Egyptian: 'When you see a cell built near the Marsh, know that the desolation of Scetis is near: when you see trees, it is at the doors: but when you see boys, take up your mantles and withdraw'.[24] Likewise Isaac, Priest of the Cells, would in his old age say to the brethren: 'Don't bring boys here: for four Ecclesiae have become desolate in Scetis because of boys'.[25]

This temptation would appear to be refreshingly absent from the first generation—not that we do not find both Antony[26] and Athanasius[27] dealing on occasion quite objectively and healthily with questions in regard to man's sexual nature. The *Rule of St. Pachomius* does contain strict precautions against physical contact between monks:[28] but adolescents like Theodore were clearly accepted in the Community in the normal course. Dom Jean Gribomont tells me that the primary Basilian sources are also distinguished from the secondary by their freedom from the homosexual obsession,[29] which in the Pachomian sources marks one at least of the principal Coptic documents.[30] There, also, I am confident of being able to demonstrate in due course that it is one of a number of marks of the secondary character of this document as against the Greek sources.[31] In

Scetis, in the time of Macarius and Isidore, Carion was not hindered from bringing up his young son Zacharias in the desert—though murmuring did arise, as a result of which the boy immersed himself for a long hour in the natron lake, until he was disfigured almost past recognition.[32] Macarius and Moses were not ashamed to ask this boy's opinion, somewhat to his confusion:[33] and Moses and the priest Isidore were watching at his early death.[34] In the next generation, when Eudaemon came as a beardless youth to Isidore's successor, Paphnutius, he was sent away with the words, 'I allow no woman's face to stay in Scetis, because of the warfare of the enemy'.[35] (This, as we shall see, was to be taken over as the rule of the Lavras of the Judaean Wilderness in the following century.) It was in this generation that Theophilus, turning against Isidore the Hosteller, raked or faked up against him some old accusation of sodomy.[36] The same slander, half a century later, was spread abroad by the monastic opponents of Chalcedon against the Patriarch Proterius whom they murdered in A.D. 457.[37] Both the charge and the sexual obsession from which it arises belong surely to the time when the first freshness has worn off.

To the wistfulness of such an age belongs also naturally, on the positive side, the work of gathering together all that can be remembered of an earlier time. How soon stories of the desert began to be written down we cannot tell. But it is not improbable that both Palladius and Evagrius had some such written records to draw from.[38] Physical insecurity and a sense of moral decay now gave impetus to the work, with the fear lest the great Old Men and their times should be forgotten. The stage of history which we are now approaching is largely that of a progressive diaspora from Scetis: it has as its chief document that collection of *Apophthegmata Patrum* (*Gerontikon* or *Paterikon* is its older and more apposite title) which seems to have been formed about the middle of the fifth century, and from and around which all our extant collections have grown.[39] In character, it is a corpus of 'case law' of the deserts. Additions were constantly being made to it: but it is timeless in its concern with our common humanity. It is difficult to open it without quickly finding something poignant for ourselves.

While the *Lausiac History* seemed to be centred on Nitria, the *Apophthegmata* belong primarily to Scetis. But it is Scetis mainly as remembered by a later generation, probably in diaspora, with a goodly accretion already of stories and sayings of the great men of that diaspora itself. The Scetis anecdotes are in very large measure

pedigree stories: 'Abba Peter said that Abba Abraham said that
Abba Agathon said . . .' and so on. Let us now turn to the history,
so far as it can be traced, of the milieu in which it first grew.

.   .   .   .   .

For a short time Scetis was, it seems, indeed deserted. The heads
of two of the Congregations, Abba Pshoi and Abba John the Short,
are said by their later Lives[40] never to have returned, John going to
Suez and the Mountain of St. Antony,[41] Pshoi to the region of
Antinoe.[42] Abba Theodore did not go so far, moving only to the
monastic settlement of Pherme,[43] which Palladius, who clearly had
never visited it, describes as a settlement of five hundred monks in a
mountain in Egypt on the way to Scetis.[44] In view of his vagueness
it might be possible to suggest an identification with the extensive
group of monastic settlements at Khashm el Qaoud, some twenty
miles west of Scetis, which Prince Omar Toussoun discovered and
partly excavated before the war, and wanted, without justification,
to identify with the (Nitrian) Cells.[45] The finds there included an
amphora stopper stamped with a cross and the name of Paul: and
one Paul, of whom Palladius tells,[46] was the first known monk of
Pherme.

Arsenius went for a time, it seems, to Canopus, where a senatorial
lady from Rome, bearding him in his garden, was sent away broken
by his answer to her request that he should remember her in his
prayers: 'I pray God that He may wipe out the memory of thee
from my heart'.[47] He and others soon came back to Scetis, which
was destined to survive a number of devastations during the centuries that followed. The present buildings of its four extant
monasteries bear witness to the story, with the inevitable answer—
in each a square fortress-like tower—a qasr—entered over a draw-
bridge, and containing all that would be essential for the community
in case the cells should be overrun;[48] and finally—but this stage was
not reached, it seems, until the ninth century[49]—a high enclosing
wall within which the whole community, apart from a sprinkling
of anchorites in the desert outside, were huddled together as in a
coenobium.

If the chronology of the Apophthegmata is to be trusted,[50] Arsenius
finally left Scetis after a second devastation about A.D. 434, going to
the Mountain of Troe (Tura, south-east of Cairo), where, with an
interval of three years at Canopus, he stayed until his death about
A.D. 449.

But to return to the first devastation—Poemen and his seven brothers went up by the natron-gatherers' route to Terenuthis,[51] and settled for a week or so in the deserted pagan temple where Macarius, some sixty years before, had used a mummy for his pillow. They spent a week in retreat. But Poemen would see his eldest brother, Anoub, morning by morning casting stones at the idol which was still standing in the temple, and evening by evening saying to it, 'Forgive me'. Taxing Anoub with this at the end of the week, he was told that the impassiveness of the idol was to be a pattern for the brothers if they were to remain together: otherwise—'there are four gates to this temple: let each go where he will'. They accepted his rule, and set up a coenobitic life together, Anoub appointing one of their number as 'steward', and the others accepting what he provided for them without question.

In passing, we should take note of this further incentive to coenobitic development—anchorites coming together for security, and accepting a coenobitic rule as a means of retaining the anchoretic ideal in spite of being in company.

As we shall presently be turning our attention away from Egypt, it will be worth our while to dwell for a short time on Poemen and his brothers, remembering that in the alphabetical collection of *Apophthegmata* those gathered under his name occupy about a seventh of the whole work, while he figures also in a very large number of other stories in this and other collections. In fact, Bousset (whose pioneer work in analysing the collections of *Apophthegmata* provides a basis for all subsequent research) suggests that to Poemen and to his school must be attributed, in some measure at least, the compilation of the corpus. And yet outside the *Apophthegmata* he is practically unknown to history.

A distinction may be necessary. Rufinus in the 370s met a Poemen and Joseph at Pispir:[52] and this fits in very well with the recording by Poemen of anecdotes and sayings of Antony[53] and his successor Ammonas,[54] and of Pior[55] and Pambo.[56] To this group probably also belongs a question from Joseph about fasting, to which Poemen answers that as a young man he had been used to going without food every other day, or even three or four days at a time, but that the fathers had learnt by experience that it was better to eat a little every day, only very little.[57] This is the sort of thing that Cassian was being told when he was in Scetis,[58] and fits well with a Poemen who was flourishing as an elder in the last decades of the fourth century. But the Poemen who left Scetis with his brothers at its first devastation by the Mazices in A.D. 407–8 outlived Arsenius,[59] and stories were told of him by an Abba John who was exiled by Marcian after Chalcedon.[60] Can it be the same man? The differentiation is not, however, easy. If it was a later Poemen who put questions to Macarius[61] and Isidore,[62] he must have been in Scetis before A.D. 390: but attributions in these collections are not very reliable, and no Poemen is mentioned by Palladius. Poemen's chief contacts in Scetis belong to a time closer to the devastation—John the Short,[63] Agathon,[64] and, above all, Moses,[65] who wrote for him *Seven Headings of Ascetic Conduct.*[66]

At least two of his brothers, Anoub the eldest, and Paesius a younger brother, were with him in Scetis.[67] Paesius was young enough to be a nuisance, and his elder brothers decided to leave him. Paesius, finding them a long time away, looked out and saw them far off towards the horizon. He ran after them, shouting. They waited, and he came up to them and asked them where they were going. They told him they were going away because he was being a nuisance. But he did not seem to take that in: 'Yes, yes,' he says, 'wherever you will, let us go together'. When they saw his guilelessness, they turned back, knowing that it was the devil, and not Paesius of his own will, who was causing the trouble.

After they had left Scetis, Paesius came one day upon a hoard of gold.[68] He decided he would like to set up on his own, and get away from Poemen. He asked Anoub to go with him, and they started crossing the Nile. But Anoub had taken charge of the treasure, wrapping it up in his cowl, and was careful when they were in mid-stream to turn round in such a way that it fell into the river. Then Paesius consented to return to Poemen. On another occasion,[69] Paesius was quarrelling with one of his brothers, and it came to blows and shedding of blood. Anoub was shocked at Poemen's taking no notice. 'They are brothers', says Poemen, 'they will make peace again'.

This refraining from criticism, even when it might seem justified and necessary, reminds us of another trait which might seem surprising in a world where unquestioning obedience was so highly prized: it is the refraining on the part of the leader from giving commands, the insistence on showing the way by example rather than by precept. So Pachomius won the devotion of his first disciples.[70] So Isaac of the Cells used to tell of his master Cronius and of Theodore of Pherme:[71] when Isaac, wanting commands, got the older men to plead for him with Theodore, the answer came:

'Am I the head of a coenobium, to give him orders? At present I say nothing to him. But if he will, what he sees me doing he will also do himself.' So when a brother asked Poemen whether he should give orders to brethren who themselves wanted him to do so, he insisted, 'No, be to them a pattern, not a legislator'.[72]

Two other anecdotes of Poemen before we set out from Egypt. Old men asked him whether, if they saw brethren nodding in church, they should nudge them to wake them up for the vigil. Poemen answered: 'Now if I see a brother nodding, I lay his head on my knees and give him rest'.[73]

One day, Abba Isaac, seeing him washing his feet with a little water, asked him about the severity with which some ascetics treated their body, and was told: 'We were not taught to be body-killers, but passion-killers'.[74] We are tempted to suspect a direct reference to Dorotheus' answer to Palladius, 'It kills me, so I kill it'.[75]

.   .   .   .   .

The diaspora from Scetis after the first devastation spread beyond Egypt. At least one refugee from it went to Palestine, to settle for forty years in a cave above Livias, on the east side of the Jordan Valley. There he was visited, about A.D. 429, by the young Georgian prince Nabarnugi, and reeled off, unprompted, Nabarnugi's name and his ancestry.[76] But the setting of the tide towards Palestine had begun long before. The Thessalonian Porphyry, subsequently Bishop of Gaza, came, if his *Life* is to be trusted,[77] about A.D. 377, from five years in Scetis to a cave in the Jordan Valley, moving up for his health about A.D. 382 to Jerusalem,[78] where he became priest and cross-warden[79] for three years before his consecration as bishop in A.D. 395.[80] We have seen how both Hilarion and Epiphanius brought back to Palestine a monastic life they had learnt in Egypt.

Sisoes, withdrawing from Scetis after the death of Antony, did not go farther east than St. Antony's Interior Mountain, where he seems to have continued almost until the time of the Council of Ephesus,[81] though going down in his extreme old age to Suez (Clysma).[82] But he was in touch with monks of Rhaithou.[83] And Rhaithou (traditionally the little port of Tor[84]) is on one of the ways to Sinai, where Aetheria found a flourishing monastic life of anchoretic type.[85] A prominent figure here was the Palestinian Silvanus, who had been father to a community of twelve disciples in Scetis before he and they moved up to Sinai, perhaps about A.D. 380.[86] While they were still in Scetis, the others had been jealous of the favour he showed to Mark the calligrapher. But Silvanus demon-strated the reason for his favour to some visitors. He went round knocking at the door of each of his disciples in turn: 'So-and-so, come here, I need you'. None of them came quite at once except Mark. Sending him away on some service, Silvanus took his guests into the cell and they looked at his manuscript: he had broken off in the middle of the letter omega, without completing the final curve.[87]

On Sinai,[88] a guest seeing the monks hard at work said to Sil-vanus: 'Labour not for the meat that perisheth: for Mary hath chosen the good part'. Silvanus told the monk Zacharias to give the visitor a book and put him into an empty cell. When dinner-time came, nobody came to call him. In the end he came and complained to Silvanus, but was told: 'You are a spiritual man, and have no need of this food. We are carnal, and want to eat, and that is why we work. But you have chosen the good part, reading all the day, and do not want to eat fleshly food.' So he learnt that, after all, Mary needs Martha.

How long Silvanus stayed in Sinai we do not know—only that one of his monks, Netras, became Bishop of Pharan,[89] and that Mark the calligrapher died immediately before the company moved up to Syria.[90] In this case, it looks as if Syria were meant to include Palestine. At any rate, in the end Silvanus and his company settled in the Gaza region, in the sides of the Wadi Ghazzeh, near Gerara. Here at least, as one surviving story indicates, the organization was of the Lavra type—scattered cells, with a central church where the brethren could congregate on Saturdays and Sundays.[91] Another story shows Silvanus in strong opposition to Church music for monks.[92] Here he is in the Egyptian tradition which goes back to Pambo and the early days of Nitria,[93] and is found again on Sinai at the end of the sixth century.[94] Cassian similarly records how in Egypt, especially in Scetis, the office was stripped to its plainest, the day-hours being regarded as running counter to the command, 'Pray without ceasing', while in Palestine there was early a full development of the day-hours.[95] There is a story that shows Epiphanius, after he had become bishop, upholding the Egyptian tradition against the abbot of his Palestinian monastery. The latter sent to him, 'By your prayers we have not neglected our canon, but zealously perform Terce and Sext and None'. But he received the answer, 'Clearly you are neglecting the other hours of the day when you are idle from prayer. For the true monk should have prayer and psalmody in his heart without ceasing.'[96]

Sozomen tells us that Silvanus was of Palestinian birth, and that he was succeeded at Gerara by his disciple Zacharias, before A.D. 415, when the tomb of the prophet Zacharias was discovered at the village which bears his name, near Eleutheropolis.[97] But Silvanus' most famous disciple was Zeno, a little dry man, all concentrated, full of divine warmth and eagerness, and with a great gift of sympathy, so that he was much sought after for spiritual counsel.[98] He seems to have moved about considerably in Palestine and perhaps Syria.[99] But for some time towards the end of his life he was at Kefr She'arta,[100] fourteen miles north-east of Gaza. A year before Chalcedon, he shut himself up and would see no-one: he seems to have died in the course of that year.[101] We shall be hearing of him again.

But a rather later emigrant from Scetis was perhaps the most important. The Abba Esaias,[102] having had his ascetic training in a coenobium, and then gone on into the Interior Desert of Scetis,[103] found himself too popular even there (it is not suggested in our records that his flight was occasioned by a barbarian devastation) and removed himself to Palestine some time between Ephesus and Chalcedon.[104] After pilgrimage to the Holy Places, he settled for a time near Eleutheropolis, but found this easily accessible to the monks of the Judaean Wilderness, and visitors from Egypt soon found him again.[105] Presently he moved to Beit Daltha, near Gaza—about four miles from Thavatha, Hilarion's birthplace[106]—to stay there, it seems, for some forty or fifty years, until his death on 11th August, A.D. 489.[107] Farther from the Judaean Wilderness, he was more easily accessible here to Egyptian visitors, and in a fairly populous region. So he adopted another plan: he shut himself into his cell, and would see no-one except his disciple, Peter the Egyptian. If anyone wanted to consult him, question and answer must pass by way of Peter.[108] A coenobitic community seems to have been attached to him.[109] But we may suppose that he appointed another as abbot to rule over it. It is a pattern that we shall find repeated at Thavatha in the next century. In this, and in his own date and contacts, he might seem to belong to the next lecture. But in spite of his forty or fifty years in Palestine, the Syriac translation of his works still knows him as Esaias of Scetis, and it was as a living example of the old Scetiote asceticism that he must have appeared to his younger contemporaries. He is, then, something of a Janus, and it is for his backward look that I thought it good to speak of him here.

His friends were of the aristocratic and conservative party, most strongly opposed to the innovations (as they regarded them) of Chalcedon, and intent on preserving in its purity the old faith and the old life. It is not improbable that this is the milieu responsible for amassing the main primary corpus of *Apophthegmata*. Not only are Silvanus and his disciples, and Esaias himself, prominent in this collection, but its originally anti-Chalcedonian character is marked by testimonies from John who was exiled by Marcian,[110] and by a number of stories of the monks of Enaton, chief among them their abbot Longinus.[111] This monastery, at the ninth milestone west of Alexandria, and therefore in far easier contact than Nitria—let alone Scetis—with that city, seems by the time of Chalcedon to have taken over the effective leadership in Egyptian monasticism,[112] by now only too well accustomed to violent intrusions into history.[113] Longinus was, in fact, a leader of the opposition to the Council.[114] Contacts between the Gaza monks and these Egyptian circles were always close.

The works of Esaias are, unfortunately, not at present easily accessible in the original Greek. There is a Latin version in Volume XL (1105–1204) of the Greek Patrology. And an imperfect Greek text, the gaps in the MSS. used filled in by retranslation from the Latin, was published in Jerusalem by the monk Augoustinos in 1911. I bought a copy there in 1929, and now find that it is one of very few copies in Western Europe. I have also in typescript a more complete text based on a collation of the Jerusalem edition with a Bodleian MS. (Cromwell 14) containing extensive early marginal additions which seemed until recently to be the only Greek evidence for the original form of the text in some chapters, confirmed by the early Syriac and Coptic versions.[115] The Syriac, of which M. Antoine Guillaumont (who also edited the Coptic fragments[116]) has gathered material for an edition, has some matter not found at all in the Greek, including a small collection of anecdotes of the Fathers as told to Esaias by a number of his elder contemporaries. All, or almost all, these anecdotes are to be found, though sometimes summarized or curtailed, and with their pedigrees obscured, in the alphabetical and other collections of *Apophthegmata*.[117] But there is sufficient evidence that they belong originally to this Esaias collection, where they are recorded as what he himself had been told. So another set of *Apophthegmata* is added to those that can be regarded as transmitted through Esaias or his milieu. And I suspect that a close study of vocabulary would suggest the same origin for a large number of others.

Of the twenty-nine 'homilies' (λόγοι) surviving in Greek, one, a series of paragraphs beginning 'Give heed to thyself' (πρόσεχε σεαυτῷ),[118] does not seem to exhibit Esaias' vocabulary, is absent from the Syriac, and is attributed in a version in which the paragraphs begin τήρει σεαυτόν to Ammonas the successor of Antony[119]: we may suppose it to be translated from a Coptic original. A number of MSS. have for a thirtieth λόγος the first chapter ('How prayer must be put before everything') of the *Monastic Constitutions* attributed to St. Basil.[120] Some MSS. keep this attribution: some assign the chapter to Esaias. But its language and vocabulary seem to be that of Esaias, which is rather distinctive.

It is said that Esaias was unlearned, and that yet the sophist Aeneas of Gaza would bring to him problems about Plato, Aristotle, and Plotinus.[121] This is much the impression we would get from his writings. There is a great treasury of meditation on Scripture, and yet actual quotations can never be relied on for exactness. They remind us in this of the *Letters of St. Antony*, full of Scripture inaccurately remembered but wisely understood.

A large part of Esaias' work is concerned with rules for monks in all the different stages, from the novice to the solitary,[122] covering a variety of topics from practical details of conduct to the deepest things of the spiritual life: portions seem indebted to the *Rule of Pachomius*. Then we find ourselves in the midst of long and valuable applications of the allegoristic method to the interpretation of Scripture, or the same method applied in short chapters to meditation on mustard or wine.[123] There is a long letter to Esaias' disciple Peter when Peter was just entering on his ascetic career.[124] There is a chapter on the 'Branches of Vice' which gives an unusual list of seven in place of the eight 'cogitations' (λογισμοί) of Evagrius—fornication or desire, avarice, slander, wrath, jealousy, vainglory, pride.[125] Allegorism and Evagrian language are accepted without qualms. But there is little if any cosmic or theological speculation. There is a short chapter giving a classic expression to Greek Christian optimism in regard to man's true nature, wherein it is insisted that, for instance, desire, jealousy, wrath, hatred, and pride all belong to the mind by nature, as gifts of God, but sin has diverted them to wrong uses.[126] There is a long meditation on the Way of the Cross,[127] wherein a distinction has been learnt that was missed by Cassian.[128]

For experience has brought home more fully the dangers of approaching the life of the recluse or solitary without sufficient preparatory training in the common life. So the latter is seen as the *bearing* of Christ's sufferings and His Cross, while the *mounting* of the Cross is the entry into the cell of quiet. Here we have the rationale of the motif found in the decoration of some Syrian churches, where the stylite's pillar is placed in apposition to the Cross itself:[129] for as the Lord Jesus is nailed to the Cross, so stylite and enclosed hesychast are fixed irrevocably. But 'if the mind desires to mount the Cross before the senses have ceased from their sickness, the wrath of God comes upon it, because it has entered on a matter beyond its measure'.[130]

We noted earlier how in the *Lives* of Pachomius and Antony, though not in the *Letters of St. Antony*, the Name of Jesus was always accompanied by the title of Christ. In the works of Esaias the Name of Jesus is generally used without the title of Christ—'the Lord Jesus', 'the holy and great King Jesus', 'our beloved Jesus', or just simply 'Jesus'. Here we are at the heart of a spirituality which is constantly appearing again among Esaias' friends, sometimes diverted from its true balance, as when they presume upon their intimacy with the Lord Jesus to claim personal knowledge that He has but one nature.[131] Linked with it is the devotion which, when Peter the Iberian broke the Host at the fraction, could see blood spurting out upon the altar.[132] Its pitfalls need to be remembered. But simple Christians of every generation will understand it.

Esaias' friends, in their passion for the Indivisibility of the Lord Jesus, did indeed reject Chalcedon. And Esaias stood in their communion, against the Council. But there is a story which reveals a gentler and a truer mind behind his personal loyalties. Two monks from a village near Gaza had consulted him, through the medium of his disciple Peter—a strong opponent of Chalcedon—about the excessive tears of one of them, and had been told that these tears were from the demons—'Or have you not heard the Fathers saying that all that is beyond measure is of the demons?' Deciding that this was good advice, they took it into their heads to ask him whether they were doing well in remaining in communion with the Council. The old man sent to them the answer: 'There is no harm in the Council of the Catholic Church: you are well as you are: you believe well'—though he himself was not in communion with the Church. His embarrassed disciple came and told them: 'The Old Man says, "There is no harm in the Church, you are well as you are, you believe well". But I tell you that the Old Man lives in Heaven, and does not know the ills that were done in the Council.' However, the two monks preferred to follow the Old Man's advice.[133]

So we are left in hope—a hope not entirely unjustified by history in the years that followed—that Chalcedonian Orthodoxy would in the end be able to reconcile to itself a proportion at least of those whose very devotion to the Person of the Lord Jesus at first turned them against it. And may not that same direct devotion have preserved in true faith, in spite of inadequacies of expression, those Christian peoples who never have been so reconciled?

NOTES TO CHAPTER IV

[1] Jer. *Ep.* 108. 34; *Praef. in Reg. Pach.* c. 1.

[2] Pall. *H.L.* c. 54 (148. 1): cf. Augustine, *Epp.* 124–6. Melania and her party had left Rome for Sicily (where Rufinus died) before Alaric's invasion. From thence she went straight to Jerusalem, while the rest of the party went to Africa.

[3] *Vita Melaniae Junioris (Anal. Boll.* 22: *Sources Chrétiennes* 90), c. 1: *H.L.* c. 61 (155. 16–156. 3).

[4] *V.M.J.* cc. 10–11, 15, 19–20: *H.L.* loc. cit. (p. 156).

[5] *V.M.J.* c. 34.

[6] c. 35.

[7] cc. 37–9.

[8] cc. 50–6. The occasion was the marriage of Valentinian and Eudoxia. *V. Petr. Ib.* p. 29) is mistaken in dating the visit to their betrothal some twelve years earlier, *c.* A.D. 425. The writer of the *Vita Melaniae* was himself concerned in these events, and his evidence must be accepted.

[9] Jer. *Epp.* 143, 151, 153, 154. For John's death, see Zosimus, *Ep.* 2 *ad Africanos* (Coll. Avellana 46), dated 21st Sept., 417, which speaks of John's decease and a letter received from his successor Praylius.

[10] Augustine, *de Gestis Pelagii* 66 (*P.L.* 44, 358). Jerome, *Epp.* 135–7 (Innocent I), 138–9.

[11] Aug. *de G. Pel.* 62–5; *c. Julianum* I. 19 (*P.L.* 44, 652–4): Jer. *Epp.* 138, 143: Marius Mercator, *Comm s. nom. Caelestii* III. 4–5 (*P.L.* 48, 100–1).

[12] Jer. *Ep.* 133. 3—'eam cujus nomen nigredinis testatur perfidiae tenebras'.

[13] Ruf. *Prol. ad Urs. in Hom. Orig. in Num.* (*P.G.* 12, 586).

[14] See Jerome's *Ep.* 143 to Augustine—'Sancti filii communes, Albina Pinianus et Melania, plurimum vos salutant'.

[15] See Cavallera, *S. Jérome*, II. 56–63.

[16] Jer. *Ep.* 107. 3.

[17] *V.M.J.* c. 40.

[18] cc. 62, 68.

[19] *Paral.* IX. c. 17 (141. 13)—ὧν τὰς ἀρχὰς ἡμεῖς οἱ γράψαντες Διήλθομεν.

[20] *P.J.* X. 114 (Nau 228): G Mac. Aeg. 25 shows Macarius already telling Poemen of a decadence.

[21] G Poemen 166. Cf. G Joh. Col. 14: G Ischyrion: *P.J.* I*5 (Nau 361): *V.P. Paral.* IX. c. 18 (143. 1–10).

[22] *Paral.* IX. c. 17 (140. 21)—τὸν μέλλοντα πλατυσμὸν γενέσθαι τῶν μοναστηρίων. This had already begun in Theodore's time—*V.P.* G¹ cc. 127 and 140.

[23] For a later period, see E. R. Hardy, Jr., *The Large Estates of Byzantine Egypt*, pp. 46–7; and P Cairo 67286, 67347; P Lond. 995, 996, 1152.

[24] G Mac. Aeg. 5.

[25] G Isaac Cell. 5.

[26] *Ep. Ant.* I. 35–41 = G Ant. 22.

[27] Ath. *Ep. ad Amunem Monachum* (*P.G.* 26, 1169–76).

[28] *Praec.* 93–6, 109.

[29] See also his article 'L'Exhortation au Renoncement attribuée à Saint Basile', in *Or. Chr. Per.* XXI, 3–4, especially pp. 387–9.

[30] That represented by the fragmentary S[10] (*Vies Coptes*, pp. 21–39), which can be in large measure completed from Amélineau's Arabic text.

[31] Lefort took, of course, the opposite view, and on this point I have not yet convinced Dom Gribomont. See *Vies Coptes*, Introduction, pp. lxxiii–lxxv, and my article, 'Pachomian Sources Reconsidered', in *J.E.H.*, Vol. V, no. 1, especially pp. 68–70.

[32] G Carion 2.

[33] G Zacharias 1 and 3.

[34] G Zach. 5.

[35] G Eudaemon.

[36] *D.V.C.* c. 6 (36. 6–37. 9).

[37] *Plerophories* XXXIV (*P.O.* VIII. 1).

[38] See Butler, 'Palladiana III', in *J.T.S.* 22 (1921), pp. 222–38, especially p. 233. Draguet, (*Le Muséon* 57, p. 56) appears to have overlooked this article.

[39] See Bousset, *Apophthegmata* (Tübingen, 1923): J.-C. Guy, 'Recherches sur la tradition grecque des *Apophthegmata Patrum*' (*Subsidia Hagiographica* 36, Brussels, 1962).

[40] Coptic *Life of John the Short* by the seventh-century Bishop Zacharias of Sakha, *A.M.G.* XXV, pp. 316 ff.; *Life of Pshoi*, attributed to John the Short himself, extant in Greek (as *Life of Paesius*, ed. Pomialovsky), in Syriac (*A. M.S.* III. 572–620—*Life of Mar Bishoi*), and in Arabic (unpublished) in Bibliothèque Nationale, Fonds arabe, No. 4796, ff. 119 sqq. Evelyn White (*History*, pp. 111–15) notifies but does not use the Syriac version.

[41] *A.M.G.* XXV, p. 390 ff. *Life of Bishoi* (Arabic), f. 153; (Syriac) p. 604.

[42] So apparently the Arabic Life (loc. cit.). The Syriac (p. 605) simply has 'Maris' (= the Upper Thebaid): but a story of this period of his life shows him sending a disciple to an old man near Antinoe (p. 611, l. 2), which cannot therefore have been far away.

[43] G Theod. Pherm. 26.

[44] *H.L.* c. 20.

[45] Prince Omar Toussoun, 'Cellia et ses Couvents', *Mémoires de la Société Royale d'Archéologie d'Alexandrie*, Tom. VII, 1 (1935).

[46] *H.L.* loc. cit.

[47] G Arsen. 28.

[48] Evelyn White (*History*, pp. 165–7, 227, 231, etc.) claims it as *certain* that towers had already appeared by the middle of the fifth century. But his actual evidence is slight and late—a Coptic Synaxarion (for Tobh 29) on the forty-nine Martyrs of Scetis, whose story falls before Chalcedon; a reference to the building of towers by order of Zeno in the Syriac version of the legend of Hilaria. The building of towers in the time of Justinian is witnessed by Severus of Ashmunein, *Hist. Patr.* (ed. Evetts, p. 193).

[49] Evelyn White, *History*, pp. 327–9.

[50] G Arsen. 42.

[51] G Anoub 1.

[52] Ruf. *H.E.* II. 8.

[53] G Poemen 75, 87, 125; Antony 3.

[54] G Poemen 2, 52, 96.

[55] G Poemen 85.

[56] G Poemen 47, 75, 150.

[57] G Poemen 61.

[58] Cass. *Coll.* II. 17–26.

[59] G Arsen. 41.

[60] G Poemen 183: perhaps Anoub 1.

[61] G Mac. Aeg. 25 (the answer implies a late date in Macarius' life).

[62] G Poemen 44; Isid. 5—and another anecdote following Isid. 6 in some MSS., and found in Syriac (Bedjan 425): G Zacharias 4 and 5 also take Poemen back to the days of Isidore.

[63] G Poemen 46, 74, 101: Joh. Col. 13.

[64] G Poemen 61 shows Joseph surprised at Poemen's calling the young Agathon 'Abba Agathon'. This fits well with the Poemen and Joseph whom Rufinus met. And Poemen 41 and 55 give two stories of Alonius, who is questioned by Agathon in Alonius 4. But Poemen 67, and N (Guy) 495 (=MS. Wake 67, f. 113r; MS. Berol. Phill. 124, 189a) show Agathon's

disciple Abraham coming to Poemen. The same Abraham is found in the Syriac collection of Abba Esaias' works as recounting a number of anecdotes of Agathon to Esaias. One of these (a greatly deformed version of it is found in G Agathon 1) shows Agathon as a young monk in the Thebaid—which would fit with Poemen 61. The rest belong to Scetis. But G Agathon 28 and 29 show Agathon back by the Nile, apparently near Troe in the time before Arsenius came there (c. 434 A.D.?)—which suggest that Agathon also left Scetis at the first Devastation.

[65] G Poemen 166, Zacharias 5, Moses 12.

[66] G Moses 14–18 (in better MSS.): *P.J.* IV. 1–7: Syriac (Bedjan) 121*–7*.

[67] G Poemen 180 does not actually name the two brothers, but their identification is justified by reference to other stories. G Poemen 2 shows Poemen questioning Ammon as about Paesius. This suggests that, indeed, Poemen may be a single person. If he was born c. 345 A.D., he might already have been notable by 375, and still lived to the late 440s.

[68] Berol. 1624, 176a (also in Evergetinos, II. 6): N (Guy) 448.

[69] G Poemen 173.

[70] *V.P.* G¹ cc. 24–5.

[71] G Isaac Cell. 2.

[72] G Poemen 174.

[73] G Poemen 92.

[74] G Poemen 184.

[75] *H.L.* c. 2 (17. 6).

[76] *V. Petr. Ib.* (ed. Raabe), pp. 85–7 (Syr.).

[77] Marc le Diacre, *Vie de Porphyre évêque de Gaza*, ed. H. Grégoire and M.-A. Kugener, Paris, 1938. The editors seem to me to have established a stronger case against the authenticity of this Life than they themselves would allow. See also P. Peeters, *La Vie Géorgienne de S. Porphyre de Gaza*, in A.B. 59 (1941), pp. 65–100 (text, pp. 101–216).

[78] *V. Porph.* c. 4.

[79] c. 10.

[80] cc. 11–16.

[81] G Sisoes 28—Sisoes said he had been there seventy-two years, which would bring us to A.D. 429 as a *terminus a quo*. See also G Sisoes 7–9, 15, 18, 25. Sisoes 48 shows him coming down at least on one occasion to the 'Outer Mountain' of Pispir.

[82] G Sisoes 21, 26, 50; Tithoes 5; Pistus. See also Sisoes 3.

[83] G Sisoes 17 and 26—Amoun of Rhaithou. The second of these at least shows this Amoun visiting Sisoes at Clysma—therefore, we may suppose, not earlier than A.D. 429. This may be the Amoun who is found questioning Poemen in G Amm. Nitr. 2—it is certainly not Amoun of Nitria.

[84] See Devreesse, 'Le Christianisme dans la Péninsule sinaitique' in *Revue Biblique* XLIX. 2 (April 1940), pp. 205–23—especially pp. 210 and 217—arguing against the identification of Rhaithou with Tor. But 'Ammonius's' account of Rhaithou seems on the map to fit Tor better in one respect—a plain stretching far to the south, but twelve miles wide between the sea and the mountain wall.

[85] *Itin. Aeth.* cc. 1–5. The Church which she found on the mountain-top was, we suppose, that said to have been built by the Syrian ascetic Julian Saba when he spent some time on the mountain, perhaps c. A.D. 360 (Ephraim, *Hymn. XX de Jul. Saba*, in Lamy III, 910–16: Theod. *Hist. Rel.* II, 1316BC). Another Syrian hermit of not more than a generation later, Symeon the Ancient of Mount Amanus, visited Sinai and spent a week in prayer on the summit (*H.R.* VI. 1361A–1364C). Theodoret's mother had known him.

[86] Soz. *H.E.* VI. 32.

[87] G Marc. 1: see also Marc. 2 and 3: Marc. 4 tells of the departure to Sinai. G Silvanus 11 shows Moses questioning Silvanus—which fits with an earlyish date in Scetis.

[88] G Silvanus 5: see also Silv. 4 and 8.

[89] G Netras (312A).

[90] G Marc. 5.

[91] Ed. Nau in *P.O.* VIII, pp. 178–9, from MS. Coislin. 127, f. 136. The story is also found in MS. Wake 67, f. 95 (94)ᵛ; N (Guy) 403.

[92] Ed. Nau in *P.O.* VIII, p. 180, from MS. Par. 1596, f. 649; Evergetinos II. 11 (374c–375b): MS. Cromwell 18, περὶ κατανύξεως (cf. *P.J.* III), c. 25: B.M. Add. 28825 (Ascetic Anthology of Nicodemus Rhacendytus) c. 103 (ff. 44–5); Sin. 448, 726.

[93] MS. Par. 1596, ff. 647–9: Everg. II. 11 (371: overlooked by Bousset as under heading Παλλαδίου): Nic. Rhac. c. 104 (ff. 45–6): Christ and Paranikas XXIX*; Sin. 448, 758.

⁹⁴ Nic. Rhac. c. 105 (ff. 46 sqq.); Pitra, *Jur. Eccl. Gr. Hist. et Mon.* II, p. 220: Chr. and P. XXX*: Sophronius and John (Moschus) telling of Nilus.

⁹⁵ Cass. *Inst.* III. 1–3.

⁹⁶ G Epiph. 3.

⁹⁷ Soz. *H.E.* VI. 32, IX. 17. The latter passage shows us Zacharias as a man of varied learning, able to cite a non-canonical Hebrew book for the explanation of a child's body with accoutrements of royalty found at the feet of that of the prophet Zacharias.

⁹⁸ N (Guy) 509–11 (cf. Berol. 1624, 191c–193a; Wake 67, f. 118; Armenian 10*171); three anecdotes referred to Zeno, told in the first person as what the narrator had been told by Zeno's disciple. They are followed in the Armenian by an Esaias extract, and the Abba Esaias might well be the narrator.

⁹⁹ G Zeno 1, 3, 6, 8. G Zeno 5 shows him in Scetis—which would take his monastic career back probably before A.D. 380. *Plerophories* VIII call him methkarkânâ ('gyrovagus'). See also *Pleroph.* LII, *V. Petr. Ib.*, p. 47.

¹⁰⁰ *V. Petr. Ib.* p. 50: *Pleroph.* VIII.

¹⁰¹ *Pleroph.* loc. cit.

¹⁰² *Vita Esaiae* by Zacharias Rhetor, ed. Brooks, C.S.C.O. Ser. Syri. III. 25, 1/16 (1/10).

¹⁰³ Op. cit. p. 4—Scetis is not mentioned here by name, but is implied in his Syriac description as Esaias of Scetis, and in the stories he recounted therefrom.

¹⁰⁴ *Pleroph.* XII shows him still in Egypt in A.D. 431.

¹⁰⁵ *V.Es.* pp. 6–9.

¹⁰⁶ p. 9: *V. Petr. Ib.* p. 102.

¹⁰⁷ *V. Petr. Ib.* p. 124.

¹⁰⁸ *V. Es.* pp. 9–10: *V. Petr. Ib.* p. 102.

¹⁰⁹ *V. Es.* p. 9, l. 24: *Pleroph.* XLVIII (101. 13).

¹¹⁰ G Poemen 183: perhaps also G Anoub 1: the John in question came down from Syria, and did not know Coptic.

¹¹¹ G Theodore of Enaton (196B–197A), Lucius (253BC), Longinus (256C–257B): many other stories of Longinus in unpublished MSS. of the 'Systematic Collection'—Guy VII. 13; XV. 113, 114; XVI. 7; XVIII. 11, 12; XIX. 7, 9; in the 'Anonymous', N (Guy) 558–61. See also N (Guy) 541 (Eulogius) and 585. The Arabic (Jacobite) Synaxarion (P.O. XI, pp. 764 ff.), commemorating Longinus on 27th Jan., tells how he and Lucian (Lucius?)—an older man— were Cilician monks who left their home country when Lucian was elected abbot and wanted to escape. After a time in Syria, Longinus came on to Enaton, where he became abbot and Lucian joined him.

¹¹² For a fuller account of Enaton, see P. van Cauwenbergh, *Étude sur les moines d'Egypte*, pp. 64–72. The Arabic Synaxarion (P.O. XI, 766 ff.) describes the reception there of the news of Chalcedon. It was here that Severus came in exile in A.D. 518, and started his controversy with his fellow exile Julian of Halicarnassus. Justinian's letter *contra Monophysitas* (A.D. 540–46: P.G. 86. i, 1103–46) is addressed to the monks of Enaton. Later in the sixth century the monophysite-Patriarchs, refused entry to Alexandria, took up their residence at Enaton— see Severus of Ashmunein, *History of the Patriarchs* (ed. Evetts), pp. 206, 210. Its monasteries were sacked by the Persians in A.D. 617—ibid. p. 221.

¹¹³ I have not repeated here the oft-told story of the monastic riots in support of St. Cyril against the prefect Orestes, and the murder of Hypatia—Socr. *H.E.* VII. 14–15.

¹¹⁴ *Chronicle* of Zacharias of Mitylene, IV. 1: *V.P. Ib.* pp. 64–5.

¹¹⁵ See note 125 below.

¹¹⁶ *L'Asceticon copte de l'abbé Isaïe*, fragments sahidiques édités et traduits par Antoine Guillaumont—publications de l'Institut francais d'Archéologie orientale, Bibliothèque d'études coptes—tome V, Cairo, 1956.

¹¹⁷ This small collection begins, 'My brethren, what I saw and heard with the Old Men, these things I relate to you, taking away nothing and adding nothing'. There follow, as related to him, stories identical with or closely related to G Anoub 1; Paphnutius 3; Cronius 1 (Cronius not named); Amoun 'Nitr.' 2; Peter Pionita 2; Agathon 1, 2, (11–12), 23, 24, 29b, 3, 8, 9, 10, 16 (very much fuller), and some more material about Agathon not so clearly represented in the alphabetical collection; Pistus. The Agathon material is all given as told to Esaias by Agathon's disciple Abraham. The compiler of the alphabetical collection, finding the first of those Agathon stories immediately following the words of Peter disciple of Lot to Esaias (who, in the Syriac, speaks in the first person of himself as the questioner), supposed that it also was what Peter had said to the brother. Hence the beginning in G Agathon 1: 'Abba Peter of Abba Lot said . . .'.

[118] Oratio 27 (*P.G.* 40, 1193–7). MS. Cromwell 14 has here much extra material in the margin.

[119] *P.O.* XI. 4, pp. 458–71. All the extra material in Cromwell 14 is included here also—but in a different order and in a slightly different version. It may be noted that the material common to all Greek MSS. is in the same order in Esaias and Ammonas: it is the material added in the margin of Cromwell 14 that is inserted in different places and in a different order here and in Ammonas.

[120] Ed. Garnier, vol. II, 767–75 (535A–540D).

[121] *V. Es.* p. 12.

[122] Orr. 1, 3, 4, 5, 6, 9.

[123] Orr. 11, 12.

[124] Or. 25. A number of passages in this letter have parallels in the Macarian corpus. But the resemblances do not amount to actual quotation, and are insufficient for us to judge whether either work is indebted to the other. See Villecourt, *Note sur une Lettre de l'abbé Isaie a l'abbé Pierre*, *R.O.C.* 22 (1920–1), pp. 54–6.

[125] Or. 28. The Greek MSS. generally give us a short recension of this work. But a longer one survives in Syriac, and in part in Coptic fragments—and in marginal additions in Cromwell 14, and extracts in the *Alphabetical Apophthegmata*. Recently Mr. Timothy Ware has identified a complete copy of the Greek—many times as long as the usual Greek text—attributed to Mark the Monk in an eleventh-century MS. at Athens, Atheniensis 549, pp. 433–63.

[126] Or. 2.

[127] Or. 13.

[128] Cassian, *Inst.* IV. 34–5.

[129] E.g. at Qalb Lozé. See Lassus, *Sanctuaires chrétiennes de Syrie*, p. 279, pl. xlvi.

[130] Or. 8. 6 (*P.G.* 40, 1133c).

[131] *Pleroph.* LXI, p. 119: cf. XXI, p. 45; XXVI, p. 65; LVI, p. 111; LXXXVI, p. 140.

[132] *V.P. Ib.* p. 56: cf. *Pleroph.* LXXVIII, p. 135. A similar story to prove the reality of the Chalcedonian Eucharist is found in a Greek collection (Paris gr. 1596) and published in *P.O.* VIII, pp. 174–5.

[133] *P.O.* VIII, p. 164 (also from Paris gr. 1596).

V

NEW BEGINNINGS

LATE in the year A.D. 405 there came to Jerusalem a young priest, in his twenty-ninth year, from Melitene on the Euphrates in Lesser Armenia. Euthymius, born as an answer to prayer, had been vowed before birth to the service of God.[1] Baptized after his father's death in his third year by Otreius, Bishop of Melitene, and ordained reader as soon as he could read if not before, he was given an enlightened education, under the bishop's supervision, by two young readers, Acacius and Synodius, both of them future bishops of Melitene.[2] Scrupulous and devout in all the liturgical order of the Church, but ever of an austere character seeking retirement and solitude, he was at last ordained priest, and given the charge, young as he was, of all the monks of the diocese. This was more than he was prepared long to stomach. He soon fled to Jerusalem,[3] and thence to St. Chariton's first Lavra at Fara, establishing himself, we are told, in an anchoretic cell outside the Lavra, and settling down to learn the lowly monastic occupation of rope-making.[4]

Euthymius brought with him from Melitene a practice which was to have considerable influence on the future of Judaean monasticism. On the octave of the Epiphany—the Feast of Our Lord's Baptism—he would go off after the Lord's example into the Utter Desert, remaining there until it was time to come up to Jerusalem for Palm Sunday.[5] In A.D. 411 he set out with his friend Theoctistus for the πανέρημος—'utter desert'—of Coutila towards the Dead Sea; the region of Qumrân. Their way would take them, after two or three miles of hills and valleys, over a more level stretch (the trough of a syncline) beyond which the strata rise to a limestone scarp running south-west from above Jericho, climbing up over the wilderness to the neighbourhood of Tekoa, its south-eastern face falling away sharply to the Utter Desert which stretches, line beyond line, to the south, between the Dead Sea and the Judaean horizon. Through this mountainous ridge the wadis break in fantastic gorges—jagged torrent-beds where water, apart from rare thirsty pools, is only seen for a few hours after rain; their sides riddled with caves, large and small. It is to these remote gorges that the monastic centre of gravity will presently be moving from the neighbourhood of the villages.

While passing down one of the most beautiful of them, the Wadi Mukellik, the two monks came upon a great cave in its northern cliff, entered it after a dangerous bit of rock-climbing, and were overjoyed to find a retreat prepared by God for them. They managed to survive on the herbs growing around, until two shepherds from Bethany (the Lazarium) found them there, and the village took to supplying their scanty needs. Report reached Fara, and other monks began to join them.[6] The danger of passage for the night office from other caves in that precipitous valley to the main cave, which was marked for the church, persuaded them not to make the place a lavra, but to gather the brethren together in a coenobium built along the edge of the last drop into the torrent-bed, at the foot of the cliff in which the cave was, with a tower (since fallen away) built up against the cliff-face to give access to the church-cave, in which Euthymius would stay through the week, making himself approachable only on Saturdays and Sundays.[7]

One day, which was neither Saturday nor Sunday, an Arab tribe appeared in the valley clamouring for Euthymius. When Theoctistus tried to put them off to the week-end, the sheikh took him by the hand, showed him his boy with his whole right side paralysed, and told him their story. He himself had been in command (his name, Aspebet, is a Persian title—'master of horse') over the Arabs under Persian suzerainty. Reported for protecting Christians in their flight from persecution renewed in the last year of Yazdigerd (A.D. 420), he had taken refuge with the Romans, and had been appointed to a similar command ('phylarchy') by Anatolius, *magister militum per Orientem*. He was still a pagan. But the sick boy, whom physicians and magi in Persia could not help, had at last betaken himself to the God of the Christians (should we say, 'of the Romans'?), and had been directed in a dream by a monk with greying hair and a great beard, to come to the gorge which lies south of the Jerusalem-Jericho road. To cut a long story short, Euthymius (whom the boy could recognize from his dream) came down and healed him. The tribe was converted, and baptized in a little baptistery constructed in the cave. The sheikh took the name of Peter. His brother-in-law Maris remained in the valley as a monk: when Theoctistus died forty years later, Maris succeeded him as head of the coenobium.[8]

Once more Euthymius was irked by popularity, and very soon fled away southwards with a young Melitenian, Domitian, along by the Dead Sea, to establish himself for a time, it appears, on the top of the old Jewish stronghold of Masada, where a ruined church still remaining is probably that set up by him. Even he seems to have found a prolonged stay here impracticable, and he moved up to establish a monastery and convert some Manichees in the region of Ziph to the east of Hebron—where Saul had hunted David.[9] Once more he was soon fleeing from popularity, and came back to settle with his disciple in a cave on that level stretch in the midst of the wilderness over or near which he must have passed on his way down with Theoctistus in A.D. 411 from Fara to the Wadi Mukellik. News spreads fast in that wilderness, and Theoctistus was soon up begging him to return to his monastery three miles away. This he would not do, only going down there for the Liturgy on Saturdays and Sundays.[10] Peter Aspebet was also quickly on the spot with his tribe and a crowd of new catechumens, whom Euthymius took down to the Wadi Mukellik for baptism. Peter built the saint a great two-mouthed cistern, a bakery, and three cells, with an 'oratory or church' in the midst of the three. Not unnaturally, Euthymius did not concede Peter's request for his tribe to stay there, but installed them, with a church in the midst of their tents, in a suitable place between the two monasteries, visiting them frequently until they were provided with their own clergy. Finally Peter was consecrated bishop for his tribe, now distributed in a number of camps.[11] He was to play a not inconspicuous part in the Council of Ephesus.[12]

Euthymius had no desire to convert his new solitude either into a coenobium or a lavra. Any postulants who came to him he would send on to Theoctistus. But at last he was directed in a dream to accept three Cappadocian brothers, and no longer to refuse all who came. Soon there were a dozen brethren with him. Peter Aspebet built small cells for them, and adorned the church παντὶ κόσμῳ ('with all adornment'). The place became a lavra 'after the pattern of Fara', and Juvenal of Jerusalem came down to consecrate the church on 7th May, A.D. 428.[13]

Cyril of Scythopolis, writing the *Life of Euthymius* more than a century later, knew that in his day the monastery was a thoroughfare on the way to the other desert monasteries, and tried to think how lonely, by comparison, it must have been when Euthymius first came there. Really, its position is by nature rather central in the wilderness, and one is surprised at Euthymius' choice of it, unless somewhere in his commanding mind there was recognition of its strategical importance. During his lifetime it had to be a lavra to suit his

own character. But he knew also that the site was better fitted for
a coenobium, and left instructions for its conversion into one after
his death.[14] Meanwhile, he set the pattern for the Judaean organization in treating the 'Lower Monastery' of St. Theoctistus, the
coenobium, as a novice-house from which young monks should
graduate to the near-anchoretic life of the lavra.[15] In the Antonian-
Pachomian stage, the anchoretic and coenobitic vocations were
separate. St. Basil regarded the coenobitic as definitely superior.
In Nitria and Scetis there are approaches to the Judaean order, but
the situation is not crystallized. In the Euthymian system, canonized
by Sabas in the next generation, the coenobium is ancillary to the
lavra, to which it normally forms an indispensable preliminary
stage.

The list of Euthymius' first twelve disciples in the lavra is revealing. Four of them (as well as Euthymius himself) were from
Melitene, three from Cappadocia, three from Rhaithou in the Sinai
Peninsula, one from Antioch, and one—just one—a Palestinian, a
native of Tiberias and priest of Scythopolis. This last and one of
the Rhaithou brethren who was also a priest continued to serve in
this office in the lavra, apparently for the rest of their lives. Domitian of Melitene and Domnus of Antioch were ordained as deacons
for the lavra, Domitian continuing to serve there as such until his
death. Domnus, a nephew of the Patriarch John of Antioch, went
after Ephesus, in spite of Euthymius' prophetic warnings, to help
his uncle, whose successor he became. At the 'Robber Council' of
Ephesus in A.D. 449, he was ousted from his throne although he had
given his signature, and returned penitent to Euthymius.[16] Three
others of the brethren became bishops—the Cappadocian Cosmas
of Scythopolis,[17] the Melitenian Stephen of Jamnia,[18] his brother
Gaianus of Madaba.[19] Cosmas was cross-warden in Jerusalem
before he was made bishop: he was succeeded in this office by his
brother Chrysippus,[20] who has left us a number of rather rhetorical
sermons.[21] The third Cappadocian brother, the eunuch Gabriel,
became hegumen of Eudocia's Church of St. Stephen: he could
speak and write in Greek, Latin, and Syriac.[22] Andrew, the third
of the Melitenian brothers, was installed by the lady Bassa as
hegumen of her martyrium of St. Menas in Jerusalem.[23] Only the
remaining two brethren from Rhaithou are left in obscurity.

Euthymius was prepared to look for his models to the Egyptian
deserts which he had never visited. But we are not surprised to read
that his favourite pattern was the austere and highly-cultured

Arsenius, who was still alive, and of whom travellers from Egypt would bring him reports.[24]

Antony was an illiterate layman, and the majority of the Egyptian monks were much the same. Euthymius was an ecclesiastic almost from birth, and his disciples such as we have described.

. . . . .

When Juvenal came down to consecrate the Church of St. Euthymius' Lavra, he brought with him the theologian Hesychius and the Chorepiscop Passarion.[25] Hesychius lived on until after Chalcedon, but we know little of his life. His extensive writings, mainly commentaries on Scripture, survive only in a scattered and fragmentary condition, but would repay fuller research:[26] the writings of Euthymius' disciple Chrysippus seem to show some dependence on him. Passarion, of whom we have neither writings nor life, is the first of whom we are told (in this passage of the *Life of Euthymius*) that he was 'Archimandrite of the monks'—that is to say, Archimandrite in the special sense given that word in Jerusalem, of those who had oversight of all the monks in the diocese. Hence his coming down for the consecration of St. Euthymius' Church. He died less than seven months later, towards the end of November.[27] He was looked back to as a primary figure in the monastic life of Jerusalem, where he founded a famous almshouse (πτωχοτροφεῖον) outside the east gate of the city,[28] and a great and beautiful coenobium within the walls of Holy Sion for the 'devotees' of that shrine, 'for the service and psalmody of those who without ceasing glorify the Lord'.[29] The stress on liturgical order once more marks a contrast between Palestinian and Egyptian monasticism. In this, in his coenobitic order, and in his attention to the poor, Passarion seems to be in the tradition of St. Basil.

On Olivet, as we have already seen, the younger Melania had settled with her husband in A.D. 417. Her monasteries also were of the coenobitic type, and there are echoes of the *Vita Pachomii* in the account of how she would take the menial work upon herself. She would not even be abbess, but appointed another to that office—a severe figure whose austerities Melania herself would try surreptitiously to mitigate for the sisters.[30] Here also the liturgical order is stressed,[31] and we note the multiplication of shrines over relics of saints,[32] and Melania's care in her last years to ensure, by building a great monastery, the regular performance of the Liturgy at the place of Our Lord's Ascension, and at the Cave of His instruction to His Apostles [33]

Pinianus and Melania took under their care a Jerusalem boy, Gerontius, whom in due course they made a monk—laying the habit on the stone of the Holy Sepulchre, and praying that he might be vouchsafed the threefold grace of right faith, holiness, and tears. Soon he was ordained to be their priest, celebrating, it seems, three times a Sunday—once at the Ascension, once in the men's monastery, and once in the women's; while he celebrated every day privately for Melania according to the custom of the Church of Rome.[34] He wrote her *Life*, which survives in Greek and Latin. After her death, he remained at the head of the double monastery, sharing with Passarion's successor, Elpidius, the office of Archimandrite, which, as we have said, meant in Jerusalem the supervision of all the monks of the diocese.[35]

It must have been within a few months of the consecration of St. Euthymius' Church that Pinianus and Melania received as guests the young Iberian (Georgian) prince Nabarnugi and his friend Mithridates the eunuch, who had come in pious flight to Jerusalem from the palace of Theodosius, where Nabarnugi was being religiously and lovingly brought up, a hostage for the friendship of his country with the Roman Empire.[36] In the last lecture we heard of their visit to the Scetiote hermit beyond Jordan. It was not long before the two had received the monastic habit at the hands of Gerontius, taking the names of Peter and John by which they are generally known.[37] They seem to have had little idea at first of submission to monastic discipline—constantly going off into the solitude of the wilderness, and then, inspired by the example of Passarion,[38] building a house on the left of the way from the Tower of David to Sion, and there receiving pilgrims and the poor indiscriminately, up to twenty tables a day, spending thereon the remains of the money they had brought with them.[39] It was here that the old Abba Zeno intervened, warning them that young men needed the discipline of a coenobium: and into a coenobium they went, staying there (for a year?) until Zeno said they could come out.[40] Zeno from this time appears as Peter's spiritual director, though he certainly was not normally in Jerusalem. Peter and John returned to their monastery, which continued after their time to be known as the Monastery of the Iberians. But funds no longer allowed their former hospitality. While they were here, Juvenal, passing by on the way to a festival on Sion, sent to arrest Peter for ordination. But Peter, getting wind of it, jumped down from a roof at the back and escaped.[41]

Juvenal himself had been a monk and was a lover of monks.[42]
But the monks on their side appear already to have viewed him with
reserve. Stories told against him in anti-Chalcedonian works, which
may be coloured by later events, tell of corruption and negligence
in the Church of Jerusalem at this time, and put it all down to him.[43]
Euthymius also seems to have had his doubts. Before Ephesus, he
told Peter Aspebet to conform his actions to Cyril of Alexandria
and Acacius of Melitene, with no mention of Juvenal who had
consecrated Peter.[44] We get the impression of a somewhat aristocratic monastic society regarding Juvenal as a parvenu.

Aristocratic it certainly was. Melania was very much at the centre
of the picture when the Empress Eudocia came on pilgrimage to
Palestine in A.D. 438, and Cyril of Alexandria came up on the same
occasion for the consecration of the first shrine of St. Stephen in
May of that year, followed next day by that of other shrines on
Olivet.[45] Five years later, when Eudocia came again, estranged from
her husband but still with imperial pomp, to settle in Jerusalem, one
of her first cares was to seek to renew contact with the young
Iberian prince whom she had helped to bring up as a boy in Constantinople. Dutifully, he saw her once. More than that he had no
wish for. Seeking out old Zeno, he was told, 'Save, save thyself!'
Leaving their Jerusalem monastery to the care of others, he and John
withdrew (not later than A.D. 444) to a community between Gaza
and the port of Maiuma.[46] They did not long avoid ordination to
the priesthood, though Peter after ordination still refused to celebrate
the Liturgy.[47]

One of our sources[48] speaks of Peter's monastery at this time as
a lavra.

We hear little echo of upheaval in Palestine in connection with
the Latrocinium of Ephesus in A.D. 449. Domnus, the deposed
Patriarch of Antioch, returned penitent to St. Euthymius' lavra.[49]
Thither also came Auxolaus, who had succeeded Peter Aspebet as
Bishop of the Arab Camps. He, too, had signed at the Robber
Council: he died ἐν ἀγανακτήσει—in (or should we say 'of'?) the
saint's displeasure.[50] Elsewhere, peace seems to have reigned. But
there were dire forebodings. Pelagius, a refugee from Edessa and
its Bishop Ibas, was heard one day on Calvary crying out, 'Juvenal!
Juvenal! Juvenal!' Asked to explain, he told how Juvenal, whom
they now saw carried along by the monks and clergy, would one
day be so carried along by the Romans and the demons.[51]

Summoned with his bishops to Chalcedon, Juvenal bade those who stayed behind to anathematize him himself if he ever accepted the Tome of Leo.[52] And then, of course, he signed once more on the winning side: and his bishops did the same. Hastening back ahead of the bishops, the monk Theodosius raised an outcry against Juvenal's treason. Eudocia and the great majority of the monks, and some bishops, were won to his support.[53] An army of monks came down to Caesarea, so great that the governor did not dare let them inside the city, to meet Juvenal on his return, and expostulate with him in vain.[54] He prudently withdrew to Constantinople.[55] Theodosius was consecrated in Jerusalem to occupy his throne, and began filling with opponents of the Council all the vacant sees in Palestine, whether their lawful bishops were alive or no.[56] It was so that Peter the Iberian himself was carried up to Jerusalem—unwillingly, but obedient in the end to what he believed to be the voice of God—to be consecrated as Bishop of Maiuma, returning thither to be enthroned on 7th August, A.D. 452.[57]

Almost all the monks of Palestine had joined with Theodosius—the Archimandrites Elpidius and Gerontius: Romanus, another disciple of Passarion, who from his coenobium by Tekoa had gone out three times to long prayer in the wilderness before he succeeded in wresting from Heaven a clear anathema on Chalcedon.[58] Only Gelasius at Nicopolis, and Euthymius, are recorded to have remained firm. Theodosius brought Gelasius up to Jerusalem hoping to consecrate him bishop, but entirely failed to obtain from him recognition of any Bishop of Jerusalem but Juvenal.[59] As for Euthymius[60]—Stephen Bishop of Jamnia and John Bishop of the Arab Camps had come back from the Council 'at a run' and gone straight to him, fearing lest they should have done the wrong thing, and should suffer the fate of John's predecessor Auxolaus. For the language of Chalcedon was, in fact, unwonted in the East, and Juvenal was no safe example to follow. But Euthymius found no fault with the Definition, either now or when the two Archimandrites came down from Theodosius to seek his support. Elpidius was, in fact, convinced by Euthymius' reasoning, though he did not yet break with Theodosius. Gerontius remained as before. As the intruder continued to importune him, Euthymius betook himself to his Lenten retreat in the Utter Desert of Rouba near the Dead Sea. Other true seekers of quiet joined him there, including a number who had been led away by Theodosius, but whom Euthymius now persuaded to accept Chalcedon. Among these was a recent arrival from Lycia, who after monastic prowess in his home country had come to establish himself in the Plain of Jordan.

Gerasimus (to whom originally belongs the story of the lion, the donkey, and the camels, which Jerome—Hieronymus—was to filch from him through the ignorance of Latin pilgrims many centuries after they both were dead)[61] established a system different from the normal Judaean type, of which we are fortunate in possessing a somewhat detailed account, though its attribution to Cyril of Scythopolis may be questioned.[62] Here a coenobium itself formed the centre of a lavra of about seventy anchorites in cells scattered over the Plain, to which the novices in the coenobium would expect to graduate in due course. The anchorites would spend the five days from Monday to Friday in their cells, living on bread and water and dates, without lamps, heat, or cooked food. On Saturday they would bring their handiwork of rope and baskets to the coenobium, where they would receive Communion on Saturday and Sunday, partake of cooked food and a little wine, and return to their cells on Sunday evening with their week's supply of bread, water, dates, and palm-blades for their handiwork. The total furniture for each would be his clothing of one colobium, pallium and cowl, one rush-mat for his bed, and one pottery vessel for water to serve both for his drinking and for moistening the palm-blades. The rule was that the cells should be always left open, and any brother in need should be at liberty to take what was found in a cell if its occupier was absent. When the people of Jericho began to bring them all sorts of comforts on Saturdays and Sundays, some of the anchorites would take to flight as soon as they saw them. Of Gerasimus himself it was said that he would subsist the whole of Lent on his weekly Communions.

In A.D. 453, Juvenal returned with the support of imperial arms to Palestine. Theodosius seems to have offered armed resistance, being defeated in something like a pitched battle at Neapolis—unless the anti-Chalcedonian writers are right in representing this as a slaughter by Roman soldiers and Samaritans of unresisting monks.[63] Juvenal was restored, Theodosius fled to Egypt with a price on his head,[64] Romanus was arrested and sent a prisoner to Antioch.[65] The other intruder bishops were extruded.[66] It seems an exception would have been made for Peter the Iberian: but he would not accept it, and went in voluntary flight to Egypt.[67] The Chalcedonian bishops were restored, and Euthymius returned to his lavra from two years of retreat in Rouba.[68]

But the Empress and the great majority of the monks remained unreconciled. However, the events of A.D. 455 in Rome and Africa, and the appeals of her relatives, raised doubts in Eudocia's mind.[69] Even so she would not forget that she was an empress: if she was to be converted, she must be converted in style. She sent the Chorepiscop Anastasius—another disciple of Passarion,[70] and, it would seem, somewhat of a neutral in the present conflict—to consult Simeon the Stylite on his column to the west of Aleppo.

Perhaps Theodosius got wind of this. At any rate, it cannot have been long before this that he went up to Syria from Egypt—some said, to win over Symeon the Stylite from Theodoret: but others said it was to heal a dispute between anti-Chalcedonians in Antioch. Disguised as a soldier, he was recognized at the gate of that city, and taken off to imprisonment in the monastery of Dius at Constantinople.[71]

Symeon wrote back to Eudocia in no uncertain terms what he thought of Theodosius, and expressed his joy at Eudocia's seeing the light, but his surprise that, when she had the fountain near at hand, she sought to draw the same water from a distance: 'Thou hast there the God-bearing Euthymius. Follow his teachings and admonitions, and be saved.'

Three miles south of St. Euthymius' Lavra is the great massif now known as Jebel Muntar, the highest point in the wilderness below Jerusalem, from which a magnificent view is to be had of Jerusalem itself and Bethlehem on the western sky-line, of the whole length of the Dead Sea, of the wilderness between it and the Judaean heights, of its eastern wall of the Mountains of Moab, of the Jordan Valley stretching far away northwards, and of St. Euthymius' Lavra itself spread out over its plain. Here, empress-like, Eudocia had a tower built for herself, and sent Anastasius with Cosmas the Cross-Warden to seek Euthymius. But the bird had flown. Hearing what was afoot, he had gone down once more to Rouba. Taking Theoctistus to support them, they went down thither to find him, and hardly persuaded him to come up to the Tower, and bid Eudocia leave the communion of Dioscorus and join Juvenal. Thereupon she returned to Jerusalem and entered into communion with the Patriarch, bringing over with her a crowd of laymen and of monks, Elpidius at their head. Gerontius would still have none of it.[72] Invited at least to meet Juvenal, if not to communicate with him, he replied, 'God forbid that I should see the face of Judas the traitor'.[73] Elpidius' disciple Marcian was also recalcitrant, and withdrew to be head of a coenobium at Bethlehem.[74] Romanus, still in Antioch, wrote to Eudocia telling her of the divine anathema on Chalcedon.[75]

Juvenal and Eudocia combined to appeal to the Emperor Marcian for an amnesty for him and the other exiles.[76] It seems they were successful—but the emperor may have been dead before it could be put into effect. At any rate, Romanus had returned well before the death of Juvenal. He preferred, however, not to go back to Tekoa, which was in the Jerusalem diocese, and so directly subject to Juvenal. He transferred himself to a hill-top to the west of Eleutheropolis, on a property belonging to Eudocia, who, in spite of her acceptance of Chalcedon, persuaded him to build there a great and beautiful monastery.[77]

No-one quite knew which way the new Emperor Leo would turn.[78] In Egypt the opponents of the Council, who formed the great majority, were emboldened to consecrate a successor, Timothy called 'the Cat', to Dioscorus who had died in exile. Peter the Iberian was called out of hiding to partake in his somewhat irregular consecration, apparently with only one other bishop. Twenty days later, on Good Friday, A.D. 457, the Chalcedonian Pope Proterius was lynched.[79] But it was three years before the government despaired of compromise and sent Timothy into exile, in A.D. 460,[80] replacing him with a very mild Chalcedonian of the same name,[81] apparently a Tabennesiote monk of the Canopus monastery, to which he retired when Timothy the Cat was restored fourteen years later.[82] It seems that this Tabennesiote monastery to the east of the city did take the Chalcedonian side,[83] while monastic opposition to the Council was led by the monastery of the Ninth Mile-Stone on the other side of Alexandria, under its abbot Longinus.[84]

While in Egypt uncertainties as to the future encouraged murder, in Palestine there was an atmosphere making for peace and reconciliation. So when two monks from Nitria came to the Judaean Wilderness at this time, it may have been for peace and quiet rather than as Chalcedonian refugees. We may note that neither of them was of Egyptian origin, Martyrius being from Cappadocia, and Elias from Arabia. Both of them were later to become patriarchs of Jerusalem. The standard of comfort at St. Euthymius' Lavra does not seem to have come up to that of Nitria: and each of them soon went his own way, Elias to the Plain south of Jericho, and Martyrius to a hill-top cave about a mile and a half up from St. Euthymius' Lavra towards Jerusalem.[85]

These two, like Gerasimus, were established in their monastic careers before coming to Palestine. But the years following Chalcedon brought to Jerusalem also a number of younger aspirants to the monastic life who were to leave their mark upon history. It will be well to give a quick survey of the places ready to receive them. On Olivet, Gerontius at the head of Melania's monasteries led the opposition to Chalcedon.[86] Down the slope, in the region of Gethsemane, another Roman lady, Flavia, had established a church and monastery of the martyr Julian, to which came a young Cappadocian monk, Theognius, in A.D. 454–5.[87] Somewhere between that and the east gate of the city was Passarion's great almshouse.[88] But it was on the western ridge—a region that had been left ruinous and sparsely inhabited, and where now the authorities were encouraging squatters[89]—that the main hostelries were growing. We have already heard of Peter the Iberian's settlement there, apparently not far from the present Anglican Christ Church.[90] But in and around the Tower of David itself, the 'devotees' of the Church of the Resurrection were installing themselves with no special organization.[91] Farther south, in the present Armenian Patriarchate, a chapel of St. Menas may be assumed to mark the site of the shrine and convent founded by another Roman lady, Bassa, a friend of the Empress, where Euthymius' disciple, Andrew the Melitenian, was installed as hegumen.[92] In the precinct of Holy Sion itself, Elpidius was at the head of Passarion's coenobium.[93] In the same region yet another monastery had been founded before A.D. 466 by Eustorgius.[94]

To Longinus, an old Cappadocian in the Tower of David, came before the death of the Emperor Marcian[95] a young compatriot from Mogarissos, a village in one of those valleys now famous for their cave-churches of later centuries.[96] This Theodosius had been a cantor (ψάλτης) from boyhood, deeply versed in Scripture and in the liturgical order of the Church.[97] Now he had heard the old call of the Holy Land: 'Get thee out from thy country ... unto a land that I will show thee'. On his way to Jerusalem he had visited Symeon the Stylite.[98] Wanting after a time to pass on from Jerusalem to the wilderness, he was diverted by Longinus to be enrolled among the 'spudaei' attached to the establishment of another Roman lady, Icelia, at Cathisma on the road to Bethlehem—somewhere near the Well of the Magi and the present monastery of Mar Elias.[99] This was the lady who had introduced from Rome into Palestine the custom of celebrating the Feast of the Presentation with candles.[100]

On her death, Theodosius was appointed steward of the monastery. But when the hegumen died and he was put forward to succeed him, he fled into the wilderness,[101] to learn its ways from two of the earliest disciples of Euthymius in the regions north-east of Bethlehem,[102] before settling, about A.D. 479, on the hill-top where his monastery now stands.[103]

In A.D. 456-7 another Cappadocian, Sabas, came as a boy in his eighteenth year from a coenobium two miles from his home at the foot of Mt. Argaeus, whither he had fled at the age of seven from the quarrels of two uncles who were acting as his guardians during his father's absence as an officer on military service.[104] He came to the monastery of Elpidius, who had recently been reconciled to Juvenal. Another old Cappadocian sponsored him there.[105] Very soon, with Elpidius' approval, he went down to Euthymius, who, true to his rule of not accepting the beardless in a lavra, sent him on to Theoctistus for further training in the coenobium.[106] There for a long time he was the monastery donkey-boy.[107] Once, when a brother begged leave to go to Alexandria to put his family affairs in order, he was allowed to take Sabas with him. While there, Sabas made himself known to his own father and mother. His father, John Conon, who was now in command of the *numerus Isaurorum* there, tried in vain to persuade Sabas to stay and become *presbyterus* ('priest'? or 'ancient'—*senator*—a known army rank?) of the *numerus*.[108]

It was in the autumn of A.D. 466 that yet another seventeen-year-old came to Sion, this time to the monastery of Eustorgius.[109] Cyriac was a nephew of the Bishop of Corinth, and Reader in the church there. Hearing one Sunday the Gospel in church, 'If any will come after me, let him deny himself and take up his Cross and follow me,' he slipped out of church without a word to anyone, down to Cenchreae, and away by ship to Palestine.[110] After wintering in Jerusalem, he also was sent on, by Eustorgius, to the Lavra of Euthymius, where he had two Corinthian acquaintances, brothers, one of them a priest. He received the habit at the hands of Euthymius himself, but, of course, was too young to be allowed to remain there. Theoctistus having died the previous September, Euthymius sent him down to Gerasimus, who kept him in his coenobium in the Jordan Plain, and turned him onto wood-cutting, water-carrying, and cooking.[111]

Meanwhile Juvenal had died, probably on 1st July, A.D. 459, and had been succeeded by the Chorepiscop Anastasius,[112] who, as we

have said, appears to have been somewhat of a neutral on the issue
of Chalcedon—in fact, very much Eudocia's man: for her conversion
does not appear to have put a stop to her patronage of opponents
of the Council. She gave Romanus the site for his new monastery:[113]
and her tower on Jebel Muntar, the place chosen for her conversion,
was taken over by strongly anti-Chalcedonian monks.[114] Euthymius,
who had foretold Anastasius' patriarchate years before,[115] treated
him much as Arsenius had treated Theophilus at the turn of the
century; excusing himself from receiving him,[116] and only meeting
him when he came down for the funeral of Theoctistus.[117] Anastasius, on his side, showed marked attention to Euthymius, coming
down twice to his obsequies in A.D. 473.[118] The important office of
cross-warden was held throughout his patriarchate by disciples of
Euthymius.[119]

Eudocia remained true to type to the end. Among her innumerable foundations, she set in hand a Church of St. Peter and a great
cistern at a point where the Roman road from Jerusalem to Jericho
debouches from the side of a valley onto a spur commanding a full
view of St. Euthymius' monastery about two miles away.[120] Coming down to visit the work in the days after Easter, A.D. 460, she sent
Gabriel to beg his old master to come and see her there. The reply
was also typical: she must not expect to see him in the flesh again:
she herself would be dead before winter; let her spend the summer
in recollection and in preparation for her exodus, and not remember
him any more while in the flesh—and not leave him anything in her
will either—'But when you depart to the Master of All, there
remember me'. Greatly vexed—for she had wanted to leave him a
large income—she hurried back to the Holy City, sent for the
Patriarch and had him consecrate the Church of St. Stephen, still
unfinished, on the 15th June, then rushed him around Palestine
consecrating all her unfinished churches until her death on the 20th
October.[121]

．　　．　　．　　．　　．

Theoctistus, dying on 3rd September, A.D. 466, was succeeded by
the Arab Maris, and he on his death two years later by one Longinus.[122] Sabas, in A.D. 469, having reached the age of thirty,
obtained permission from Longinus (who sought Euthymius'
approval) to go out and occupy a cave on the southern cliff opposite
the coenobium. There for the next five years he would stay without
food from Monday to Friday, going out from the coenobium on
Sunday evening with palm-blades for his week's work, and returning

at dawn on Saturday with fifty baskets completed.[123] Euthymius now thought Sabas ready to join him on his annual Lenten retreat into the Utter Desert.

What a party that must have been in Euthymius' last years, from A.D. 470! Euthymius himself, aged over ninety, and his faithful deacon Domitian; the future patriarchs, Martyrius and Elias; Sabas; Gerasimus from the Jordan Plain; and with Gerasimus, the lad Cyriac still in his early twenties.[124] They would set out for Rouba on 14th January, each armed with a trowel for digging up for food those roots of melagrion, or 'meliagrion', which St. Sophronius at least identifies in his *Anacreontics* with St. John the Baptist's food of 'wild honey'—ἀκρίδες πελὲν τὸ βρῶμα μελιαγρίου τε ῥίζαι.[125] Scattered in solitude through the week, they would assemble on Sundays to receive Communion at the hands of Euthymius. They would return in time for Palm Sunday to their monasteries, or, armed with those lovely little flowers of many colours that show themselves in the spring in the most barren places of the wilderness (for the thirsty soil is fertile when water can reach it), to Olivet and Jerusalem for the annual rehearsal of the events of that day and the week that follows.

Once at least, when Euthymius took Domitian and Sabas on from Rouba to the remoter wilderness along the Dead Sea, Sabas fainted for thirst, and Euthymius after prayer dug with his trowel and came to water.[126]

In A.D. 473, the company was assembled at Euthymius' Lavra on the 14th January, some to send him forth on his journey, some to go with him. But no! Euthymius told them, 'I stay this week, and on Saturday night I go forth'. At the vigil of St. Antony on the Tuesday night, he took the priests into the sacristy and told them his death was at hand. In the morning he summoned the whole community and bade them elect his successor. When they unanimously asked for Domitian, he told them that could not be. Then they asked for Elias, a native of Jericho, who was steward of the Lower Monastery. Euthymius commissioned him, with instructions for the conversion of the lavra into a coenobium, and for the building work therein involved, and with rules for hospitality and the canon of the psalm-singing. He stayed in the sacristy, and on the Saturday night he fell asleep.[127] That night in the Coenobium of St. Gerasimus, young Cyriac, who was then serving as cook, was staying up to clean the vegetables for the fathers, when about eleven o'clock Gerasimus summoned him to put on his cloak and sandals

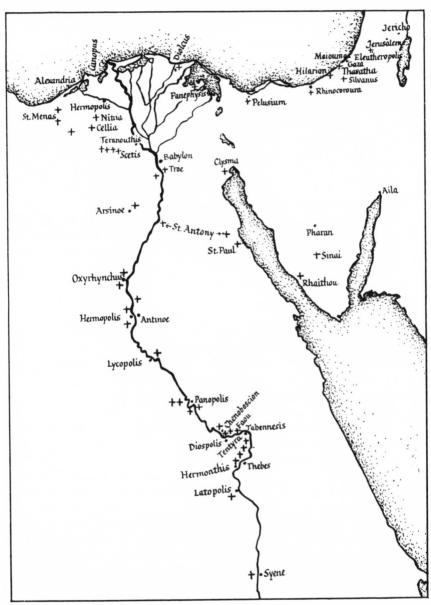

I. Monastic Egypt, Sinai and Southern Palestine.

II.

THE JUDAEAN MONASTERIES.

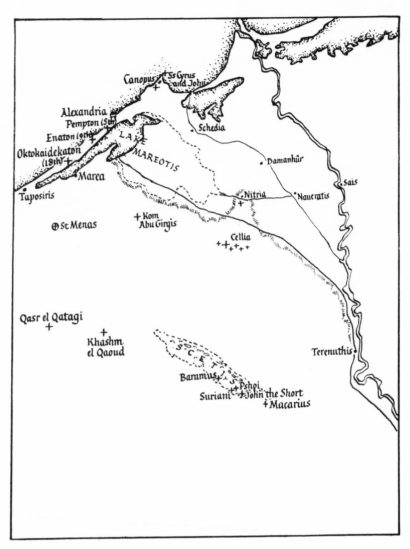

III. Alexandria, Nitria and Scetis.

1. Choziba (pp. xv, 150, etc.).

2. MONASTERY OF ST. THEOCTISTUS in the Wadi Mukellik (pp. 83, 106, etc.). The aperture in the cliff-face high up to the right is a secondary entrance to the Church cave.

3. Eudocia's Church of St. Peter (Qasr 'Ali: her latest foundation) looking south-east (Moab in the background). St. Euthymius' monastery lies in the plain in the middle distance, 2 miles away (pp. 84, 95, 157).

4. Monastery of St. Euthymius (Khan el Ahmar) from the north-east, during excavation in 1928 (pp. 84-6, 97, 102-3, etc.).

5. The view Westward from JEBEL MUNTAR. Jerusalem and Mt. of Olives on the sky-line (p. 91).

6. The view south from JEBEL MUNTAR (pp. 91, 106). Monastic ruins in fore-ground. Mar Saba two miles away towards the right end of the picture.

7. MAR SABA from the North-East. The dome of the Theotokos Church is seen at the centre. The Women's Tower appears behind (outside the walls of the monastery).

8. MAR SABA from the West (the track from Deir Dosi)—the two towers are in front of the Cedron gorge. The Dead Sea and the Mountains of Moab in the distance.

9. CASTELLIUM (pp. 108–11).

10. LAVRA OF ST. FIRMINUS (p. 129), in the Wadi Suweinit near Michmash: the central group of cells, El 'Aleiliyât. The left-hand group of seven interconnected cells can only be reached along a narrow ledge on the cliff face, on which Mr. Markoff can be seen. The separate long cave to the right, the ascent to which was even more difficult, contains a Baptistery with Syriac inscriptions.

11. SOUKA (pp. 14–15, 126–8, etc.). Cave in foreground. Tower of Lavra of St. Chariton below the sky-line at the centre. Herodium (Jebel Fureidis) in background.

12. CELL OF ST. CYRIAC at Sousakim (pp. 127–31).

13. SOUSAKIM (pp. 127–8, 130–1). The Wadi Mukta' el Juss, in the foreground, comes down to join the Wadi 'l Mu'allak. St. Cyriac's cell is seen on the spur between the two wadis.

14. MAR SABA. St. Sabas' Tower is at the top of the picture. The cupola of his Tomb appears to the right of the Guest-House near the centre, with the cliff containing the God-built Church behind it (p. 106).

15. THE BODY OF ST. SABAS RETURNS TO JERUSALEM, 26th October, 1965 (p. 118).
—*Photo by Elia Photo Services, Jerusalem.*

16. The Relic is restored to its first resting-place, 19th November, 1965. (The Cupola in front covers the Saint's Tomb: the doorway behind is that of the Theotokos Church: the God-built Church is in the cliff to the left.)—*Photo by Rittas, Jerusalem.*

17. The monk Panteleimon feeding St. Sabas' birds.

and follow him. When they came near Jericho, Cyriac asked what it was all about, and Gerasimus told him that about the third hour of the night he had seen a lightning-flash from heaven to earth, which remained as a pillar of light from earth to heaven, and had been told that it was the soul of Euthymius being taken up.[128]

Such a crowd was assembled with the Patriarch for the funeral that soldiers had to be used to disperse it before the body could be set in the coffin and buried at three o'clock in the afternoon.[129]

Seven days after his master, Domitian also fell asleep.[130]

The Patriarch left the deacon Fidus to supervise the building of the 'cemetery' in the place of the cave that had been Euthymius' first retreat on the plain. This was completed in three months, the rock roof of the cave being destroyed and replaced with a fine barrel-vault running north and south, the tomb of the saint being in the centre of the chamber, with plenty of room for bodies of later abbots and other holy men to be buried around him.[131] We excavated this chamber in 1928 and 1929. Its flagged floor had often been relaid. One slab proved to be part of a marble chancel-screen laid face downwards. In the centre of the chamber the flags had gone, and there was a rough empty tomb of slabs laid on edge, with space for the coffin or body of a small man. Between its foot and a little altar built against the east wall on a firmly cemented foundation, we uncovered below the floor level many earthenware lamps, one with the word Ἀνάστασις—'Resurrection'—stamped on it in reverse. On the north side of this space, under flags still in position, seven skeletons were piled on top of each other.[132] I know no record of where the saint's body was taken when the monastery was finally abandoned by the monks in the twelfth or thirteenth century.

On the 7th May—the anniversary of the church's consecration— the Patriarch came down with the great stone lid to be set over the tomb, the silver funnel to be fixed in it, and the marble screen to be set around it. The coffin was laid in place, and fixed, it was supposed, against all possibility of being moved.[133] The rest of Cyril of Scythopolis' *Life* of the saint makes it abundantly clear how Euthymius continued to reign from his tomb over the wilderness. He is the real effective founder of that Judaean monasticism which for the next four crucial centuries was to be the primary formative influence in East Christian monastic order, and to play a leading part also in the development of liturgy, hymnody, and dogma. Generally unknown in the West,[134] he is placed in the Byzantine hymns of the Ascetics second only to St. Antony.[135]

NOTES TO CHAPTER V

[1] Cyril of Scythopolis, *Vita Euthymii*, c. 2.
[2] cc. 3–4.
[3] c. 5.
[4] c. 6.
[5] c. 7.
[6] c. 8.
[7] c. 9.
[8] cc. 10 and 36.
[9] cc. 11–12.
[10] c. 14.
[11] c. 15.
[12] He was appointed to a delegation to call on Nestorius (Schwartz, *Act. Conc. Eph.* III. 17, 21) and reported on the result (II. 9. 17; III. 18. 5). See also II. 4. 38, 20. 1, 34. 29, 59; VII. 85. 38.
[13] *V.E.* c. 16.
[14] c. 39.
[15] cc. 16 and 31.
[16] c. 20.
[17] cc. 16 and 37.
[18] c. 20.
[19] c. 34.
[20] cc. 20 and 37.
[21] cc. 30 (49. 18) and 37 (56. 5). For an account of his writings, see Sigalas, *Des Chrysippos von Jerusalem Enkomion auf den hl. Johannes den Taufer*—Texte und Forschungen zur byzantinisch-neugriechischen Philologie, Nr. 20 (1937). Along with a text of the Encomium on St. John the Baptist, Sigalas gives here an account of his other encomia (on St. Theodore, the Mother of God, the Archangel Michael) and a very full bibliography. For his indebtedness to Hesychius of Jerusalem, see Martin in *R.H.E.* 1939, pp. 54–60.
[22] *V.E.* cc. 30 and 37.
[23] c. 30.
[24] c. 21.
[25] c. 16 (26. 17–20).
[26] See K. Jüssen, *Die dogmatischen Anschauungen des Hesychius von Jerusalem* (1931 and 1934): articles by C. Martin in *R.H.E.* 1935, pp. 356–9, and 1939, pp. 54–60. For his surviving Chalcedon, see *Pleroph.* X.
[27] *V.E.* c. 16 (17. 3)—μήπω τοῦ ἑπταμηνιαίου πληρωθέντος χρόνου. The *Narratio de obitu Theodosii Hierosolymorum et Romani monachi* (ed. Brooks, C.S.C.O., scr. Syr., ser. tertia, XXV), p. 27, gives the commemoration of Passarion and of Romanus on 25th Nov. (Teshrin II), six days before that of Peter of Alexandria. But the Palestino-Georgian Calendar (ed. Garitte, Brussels, 1958) gives the commemoration of Peter on 25th Nov., that of Passarion on 21st.
[28] The aforementioned Calendar places the commemoration of Passarion in the πτωχεῖον. See also *Narr. de ob. Theod.*, loc. cit., and *V. Petr. Ib.*, p. 35.
[29] *V. Petr. Ib.*, ibid.: cf. Pal. Georg. Calendar, 3rd Nov. Here Sabas was first received in Jerusalem (*V. Sabae*, c. 6).
[30] *V. M. J.*, c. 31.
[31] cc. 46, 47, etc.
[32] c. 48.
[33] cc. 49, 56. See also *V. Petr. Ib.*, pp. 27–30.
[34] *V.M.J.* c. 49 (34. 24–6): *V. Petr. Ib.*, p. 31.
[35] *V.E.* cc. 27 (42. 12–14), 43 (62. 20), 45 (67. 15).
[36] *V. Petr. Ib.*, pp. 27–30.
[37] p. 32. Peter was just twenty (see p. 33).
[38] *V. Petr. Ib.*, p. 35.
[39] pp. 45–6.
[40] p. 47.
[41] *Pleroph.* XLII: *V. Petr. Ib.* p. 50.
[42] *Pleroph.* XVI, XVII, XL.
[43] *Pleroph.* XVIII.
[44] *V.E.* c. 20.
[45] *V.M.J.* cc. 57–8: *V. Petr. Ib.* p. 33.

⁴⁶ *V. Petr. Ib.* pp. 48–9.
⁴⁷ p. 51.
⁴⁸ *Pleroph.* II (13. 8).
⁴⁹ *V.E.* c. 20 (33. 28)—but see *Act. Conc.* t. II. 3, p. 444, 17 ff.
⁵⁰ *V.E.* c. 27 (41. 12, 16)—cf. *Act. Conc.* t. II. 6, p. 14.
⁵¹ *Pleroph.* IV.
⁵² Zach. Mit. *Chr.* III. 3. Cf. *Pleroph.* XX (42. 1–5) and XXV (58. 12–59. 3): *V. Petr. Ib.* p. 52. 1–9.
⁵³ Zach. Mit. loc. cit.: *V.E.* c. 27 (41. 22–42. 1): G Gelasius 4.
⁵⁴ Zach. Mit. loc. cit.: *Pleroph.* X (24. 4–17), XXV (61. 9–14), LVI (111. 13–113. 4): *V. Petr. Ib.* p. 52. 9–13.
⁵⁵ Evagr. *H.E.* II. 5: Zach. Mit. loc. cit.
⁵⁶ *V.E.* c. 27 (42. 1–5): G Gelasius 4 (149CD): *V. Petr. Ib.* p. 52. 13–53. 4: *Pleroph.* XXV (61. 14–62. 9): Evagr, *H.E.* II. 5 (52. 15–7).
⁵⁷ *V. Petr. Ib.* pp. 53–6: Zach. Mit. *Chr.* III. 4: Evagr. loc. cit. (52. 17–19).
⁵⁸ *Pleroph.* XXV. Romanus's leading part in the raising of Theodosius was no doubt the ground on which he was exiled to Antioch.
⁵⁹ G Gelasius 4.
⁶⁰ *V.E.* c. 27.
⁶¹ J. Mosch. c. 107: *Vita Divi Hieronymi.* Mediaeval Latin pilgrims would never have heard of Gerasimus: and with the softening of the sound of the initial Γ, there remained the effective difference of only two letters between the two names.
⁶² The account of his system appears as c. 35 of the *Vita Euthymii* in Avgoustinos' edition (Jerusalem, 1913), which is based on Sinai MS. 524. It is also to be found incorporated in the composite Life of Gerasimus attributed to Cyril of Scythopolis, published by Kleopas Koikylides (Αἱ παρὰ τὸν ʼΙορδάνην Λαύρα Καλαμῶνος καὶ ἁγίου Γερασίμου—Jerusalem, 1902), of which a Syriac version is found in the British Museum MS. Add. 12174 (ff. 244 ff.). See also A. Grégoire, 'La Vie anonyme de S. Gérasime', in *B.Z.* 23 (1914), pp. 119–35.
⁶³ Evagr. *H.E.* II. 5 (52. 21–7): Zach. Mit. *Chr.* III. 5–6: *Pleroph.* X (222–4): *V.E.* c. 30 (47. 10).
⁶⁴ *De ob. Theod.* 21. 4–6: *V. Petr. Ib.* 57. 17–20.
⁶⁵ *De ob. Th.* 21. 7–9: *Pleroph.* XXVI (62. 11–12).
⁶⁶ *De ob. Th.* 21. 10–13: *V. Petr. Ib.* 57. 12–17.
⁶⁷ Zach. Mit. *Chr.* III. 7: *V. Petr. Ib.* 58. 1.
⁶⁸ *V.E.* c. 28.
⁶⁹ *V.E.* c. 30.
⁷⁰ *V.E.* c. 22 (35. 3–5).
⁷¹ *De ob. Th.* pp. 21–3: Zach. Mit. *Chr.* III. 9 gives a variant account of his capture.
⁷² *V.E.* c. 30.
⁷³ *V. Petr. Ib.* 32. 8–16.
⁷⁴ *V.E.* loc. cit. (49. 12).
⁷⁵ *Pleroph.* XXV (62. 10–63. 5).
⁷⁶ *De ob. Th.* 26. 1–10.
⁷⁷ *De ob. Th.* 26. 10–23: *V.E.* (49. 12) is mistaken in dating the foundation of the Tekoa monastery to this time.
⁷⁸ Cf. Evagr. *H.E.* II. 9.
⁷⁹ *V. Petr. Ib.* 64–8: Zach. Mit. *Chr.* IV. 1–2: Evagr. *H.E.* II. 8.
⁸⁰ *V. Petr. Ib.* 69–70: Zach. Mit. *Chr.* IV. 3–9: Evagr. *H.E.* II. 9–11.
⁸¹ *V. Petr. Ib.* 70. 19–22: Zach. Mit. *Chr.* IV. 10: Evagr. *H.E.* II. 11.
⁸² Liberatus (*P.L.* 68), c. 16: Evagr. *H.E.* III. 11: cf. Zach. Mit. *Chr.* V. 4.
⁸³ Salophaciolus' abortive successor as Chalcedonian Patriarch, John Talaia, was also a Tabennesiote of Canopus (Zach. Mit. *Chr.* V. 6: Liberatus, c. 16: Severus, *Hist. Patr.* 183). So in the next century was Paul, installed as Chalcedonian Patriarch in A.D. 537, and deposed three years later (Liberatus, c. 23: *Hist. Patr.* 202). The chronicler Victor of Tonnuna, refusing to condemn the Three Chapters, was interned here with some others by Justinian, c. A.D. 560 (*P.L.* 68, 961 ff.). See van Cauwenbergh, op. cit. pp. 153–9.
⁸⁴ *V. Petr. Ib.* 64: Zach. Mit. *Chr.* IV. 1.
⁸⁵ *V.E.* c. 32.
⁸⁶ *V.E.* cc. 27 (42. 13, 44. 7) and 30 (49. 8).
⁸⁷ Cyr. Scyth., *V. Theogn.* 241. 18–242. 3: Paul El., *V. Th.* (Anal. Boll. 10).
⁸⁸ *V. Petr. Ib.* 35: *De ob. Theod.* 27.

[89] *V. Petr. Ib.* 44–5: see Chabot, 'Pierre l'Ibère', in *R.O.L.* III, p. 309.

[90] *V. Petr. Ib.* 45: see Vincent and Abel, *Jerusalem Nouvelle*, fasc. III, pp. 516–17.

[91] *V. Sabae,* c. 31 (116. 6–7): *V. Theod.* p. 236. 11–13.

[92] *V.E.* c. 30 (49. 20–2): V. and A. fasc. III, pp. 544 and 547.

[93] *V. Petr. Ib.* 35: *V.S.* c. 6 (90. 20–1).

[94] *V. Cyriaci,* p. 224. 13–15.

[95] *V. Theod.* (Cyr. Sc.) p. 236; (Theod. Petr.) c. 7.

[96] *V. Th.* (C.S.) p. 236. 3–5; (Th. P.) c. 3.

[97] *V. Th.* (C.S.) p. 236. 5–8.

[98] *V. Th.* (Th.P.) cc. 4–5.

[99] *V. Th.* (C.S.) p. 236. 14–17; (Th. P.) c. 7.

[100] *V. Th.* (C.S.) p. 236. 23–5.

[101] p. 236. 7–237. 2.

[102] p. 237. 2–6: *V.E.* c. 8 (16. 10–16): *V.S.* c. 29 (114. 3–6).

[103] *V. Th.* (C.S.) p. 237. 7–10; (Th. P.) c. 7: *V.S.* c. 29 (114. 6–8). *V.S.* c. 14 (97. 19–21) shows that Theodosius had not yet founded his monastery when Sabas was guided to the site of his own lavra in A.D. 478. For an account of the remains of St. Theodosius' monastery, see E. Weigand, 'Das Theodosioskloster', in *B.Z.* 23 (1914), pp. 167–216.

[104] Sabas' birthplace, Moutalaska, is identified with the modern Talas. *V.S.* cc. 1–2.

[105] *V.S.* c. 6.

[106] c. 7.

[107] c. 8.

[108] c. 9. Must we resist the temptation to find here reference to a regimental chaplaincy? Each numerus had its priest and deacon—Soz. *H.E.* I. 8. *Senator* in Greek papyri is transliterated σινάτωρ. See Jones, *Later Roman Empire,* c. xvii, pp. 632–3 and n. 55.

[109] *V. Cyr.* 224. 9–15.

[110] 223. 1–224. 9.

[111] 224. 16–225. 2.

[112] *V.E.* c. 33: see also *V.S.* cc. 11 (95. 4–5) and 15 (98. 12–14); and *V. Cyr.* 224. 10.

[113] *De ob. Theod.* 26. 16–23.

[114] *V.S.* c. 38 (127. 15–20).

[115] *V.E.* c. 22.

[116] *V.E.* c. 33.

[117] c. 36.

[118] cc. 40 and 42.

[119] c. 37. Cosmas on becoming Metropolitan of Scythopolis in A.D. 467 was succeeded as cross-warden by his brother Chrysippus, who held the office for twelve years, therefore up to the death of Anastasius.

[120] c. 35 (53. 7–9). See Beauvery, 'La route romaine de Jérusalem à Jéricho', *Revue Biblique* LXIV. 1 (1957), pp. 72–101.

[121] *V.E.* c. 35.

[122] c. 36: *V.S.* c. 10.

[123] *V.S.* c. 10.

[124] *V.E.* c. 38: *V.S.* c. 11: *V. Cyr.* 225. 10–12.

[125] Sophr. *Anacr.* V. 24–5 (*P.G.* 87. 3, 3756c).

[126] *V.E.* c. 38 (56. 29–57. 11): *V.S.* c. 11 (94. 20–95. 2).

[127] *V.E.* c. 39.

[128] *V. Cyr.* 225. 13–17: *V. Ger.* (ed. Koikylides) c. 5 (p. 5).

[129] *V.E.* c. 40.

[130] c. 41.

[131] c. 42.

[132] *P.E.F. Quarterly Statement,* Oct. 1932, pp. 200–2: also Barrois in *R.B.* XXXIX. 2 (April 1930), pp. 272–5.

[133] *V.E.* c. 42.

[134] He is not mentioned in Dr. Cross's *Dictionary of the Christian Church.*

[135] See the Triodion, for Vespers of Friday in the Cheese-week, Sticheron to the 'Κύριε ἐκέκραξα'—'Ἀντώνιον τὸν κορυφαῖον, τὸν φαεινὸν Εὐθύμιον, καὶ ἕκαστον καὶ πάντας ὁμοῦ—': Saturday Mattins, Cathisma after Second Stichology—''Αντώνιον ὁμοῦ καὶ Εὐθύμιον πάντες, σὺν πᾶσι τοῖς λοιποῖς θεοφόροις πατράσιν—': after Third Canticle of the Canon—''Αντωνίου τὸ πρᾶον καὶ καθαρόν, Εὐθυμίου τὸ μέγα καὶ θαυμαστόν—'.

VI

BATTLE FOR THE FAITH

ANASTASIUS took Martyrius and Elias back with him from the reburial of Euthymius, and ordained them Priests of the Anastasis.[1] Within the next year Sabas, feeling that times had changed, withdrew from the Wadi Mukellik to four years in the deserts of Coutila and Rouba towards the Dead Sea.[2] In that same year, A.D. 474, the Emperor Leo died and was succeeded almost immediately by his son-in-law Zeno. Then in January, A.D. 475, power was seized for twenty months by Leo's brother-in-law, Basiliscus, who promulgated an *Encyclical* anathematizing Chalcedon.[3] It seemed a moment of triumph for the opponents of the Council. Timothy the Cat returned to Alexandria to occupy the patriarchal throne until his death in July, A.D. 477.[4] At Antioch, Peter the Fuller, the propagator of the addition to the Trisagion—'Who wast crucified for us'— which was to become a slogan of the monophysite party, established himself for a third time.[5] It was he who ordained to the priesthood one John Rufus of Samosata, an ardent opponent of the Council, who had been a law student at Beirut.[6] Peter the Iberian had come back before this to Palestine, not to his see of Maiuma, but to the region of Ascalon: he seems, however, to have journeyed about considerably, making propaganda against Chalcedon, and building up a strong monastic movement along the coast:[7] among others he converted to the monastic life a young lawyer, Theodore of Ascalon, who had been a fellow-student at Beirut with John Rufus.[8] Gerontius was still in possession on Olivet, Marcian at Bethlehem, Romanus by Eleutheropolis. Even on Jebel Muntar there were two anti-Chalcedonian monks. When Gerasimus died in A.D. 475, and young Cyriac moved up from his monastery to that of St. Euthymius,[9] nothing had been done towards carrying out Euthymius' instructions for converting the lavra into a coenobium.[10] Anastasius, the Patriarch of Jerusalem, accepted the *Encyclical*,[11] and did not dare to accept its cancellation in the *Antiencyclical*. But he appears to have remained in communion with both sides.[12] He died on the 1st July, A.D. 478, just nineteen years after his predecessor:[13] his name appears on that day in the Chalcedonian calendars surviving in Georgian.[14] Martyrius, who succeeded him as patriarch, at once found himself in trouble, with Gerontius ready to take a line suggestive of that of Theodosius after Chalcedon. Martyrius, we are told, sent the deacon Fidus to Constantinople with letters that were too outspoken (παρρησιαστικώτερον)—but Fidus was shipwrecked and miraculously returned to Jerusalem with a story of a vision of Euthymius, and a message from him to Martyrius not to worry about the 'aposchists', but to get on with the neglected work of turning Euthymius' lavra into a coenobium.[15] Martyrius acted on this: and sure enough, 'within a few days' Marcian called together his monks at Bethlehem and proposed that it was time the matter was settled—let them cast lots as between the Church of the Monks and the Church of the Bishops. The lot fell for the bishops, and there was great festivity in Jerusalem, with all the lights of the Anastasis blazing, to celebrate this *Second Union* (the first would have been that of Eudocia and Elpidius). Only Gerontius remained— to be turned out from Olivet where he had governed for forty-five years.[16] Down in the wilderness, the two opponents of the Council were ejected from Eudocia's Tower on Jebel Muntar.[17] At Eleutheropolis and in the Coastal Plain, there was no question of expulsions.

What Cyril of Scythopolis does not tell us is that there were any conditions attached to this *Second Union*. But Zacharias of Mitylene gives us Martyrius' pronouncement on the occasion,[18] and it proves to be a precursor of the *Henotikon* of Zeno—no explicit anathema on Chalcedon, but an anathema on those who accept any other doctrine than that of Nicaea, wherever it arose, at Ariminum, Sardica, Chalcedon or any other place.

Fidus meanwhile was commissioned to proceed with the conversion of St. Euthymius' lavra into a coenobium, which he completed in three years.[19] Cyriac was active in the work: he was sent down with a monk Thomas to buy ἁπλώματα—curtains or veils— for the coenobium from the Pope of Alexandria[20]—probably at this time the restored Chalcedonian Timothy, though he seems to have died before the work was completed: the anti-Chalcedonian Peter Mongus was in hiding.[21]

The cells of the lavra were destroyed to their foundations. The coenobium was surrounded with an enclosing wall, and a strong tower was built in the middle—which we did not place, unless, indeed, it surmounted the cemetery. The line of the walls of the old church can in part be traced in the refectory which now occupied the central vault under the new church. The orientation was slightly altered.[22]

All was ready for the date of consecration to be fixed once more for 7th May—in A.D. 482. But there had been a drought that year, and the donkeys of all the neighbouring monasteries were assembled on the eve of the event to go and bring water from the perennial spring of Fara, when the hegumen Elias sent them all back to their places, having been told by Euthymius in a dream to do so. In the three hours after dawn there came, in fact, one of those freak downpours which are well known, if rare, occurrences in the wilderness, just around the monastery itself, filling its two great cisterns and then stopping.[23]

One is tempted to relate this occasion with that of a similar downpour in the days before Whitsun after three years of drought in the region of Madaba, where Peter the Iberian was travelling to visit the hot springs for his health.[24] Certainly it was within a year or two.

John Rufus was with him on this journey. When Peter the Fuller was once more ousted from Antioch, and after a time of some anarchy the Chalcedonian Calandion was installed, in A.D. 479,[25] John, rather than accept him, had fled, at the invitation of his friend Theodore of Ascalon, to Peter the Iberian in Palestine.[26] Henceforward he was constantly with Peter until Peter's death ten years later, and wrote his life, which for these ten years is a first-hand personal record.[27] He was also the author of a series of *Plerophories* ('Assurances') against Chalcedon which survives, like the *Life of Peter*, in Syriac translation. Later he seems to have become Bishop of Maiuma.[28]

On returning from Transjordan, Peter stayed some months on an old property of Eudocia's a few miles north of Jerusalem, but would not enter the Holy City, whose Patriarch was compromised with the Council.[29] Then he passed down to the Coastal Plain, spending some time near Ascalon, but finally settling for nearly three years at Migdal Thavatha—the birthplace of Hilarion.[30] Meanwhile the Henotikon of Zeno had brought all four Eastern patriarchs into communion with each other. But Peter absolutely rejected the compromise, and would not allow his biographer to accept a pressing invitation from Peter the Fuller (now restored on acceptance of the Henotikon) to return to Antioch.[31] At Thavatha, he was only four miles from the old Scetiote Abba Esaias. The two kept in close contact.[32] In A.D. 487, Zeno in his efforts to bring about a complete reconciliation sent to summon both of them to conversations in Constantinople. But Esaias prayed successfully that he might be prevented from going by illness, while Peter the Iberian fled with his biographer to Phoenicia, staying there for over a year until he had definite news that he was excused attendance.[33] Then the party returned to Palestine, taking its time, and settling finally not at Thavatha but near Jamnia.[34] There news reached them of the death of Abba Esaias, which took place on 11th August, A.D. 489.[35] And there Peter himself died four months later, in the night leading to Friday, 1st December.[36] In his last instructions to his disciples, he bade them give heed to the *Ascetica of St. Basil*.[37]

In the morning the Mass was celebrated in the presence of his body, and postulants received the habit at his dead hands.[38] Then the four who were named his heirs[39] carried the coffin speedily away, halted at evening for a short while in a church outside the walls of Ascalon, and went on through the night to reach his old monastery outside Maiuma before dawn, and lay the body in the sarcophagus there prepared for it, next to his old companion John the Eunuch, before the townsfolk of Gaza or Maiuma could hear the news and come and carry it off to one of their churches.[40] Theodore of Ascalon, the fourth of his heirs, was appointed abbot there,[41] and quickly set to work to replace the few neglected cells of Peter's little lavra with the buildings of a fine coenobium in an enclosing wall.[42] John Rufus and the other brethren had already joined him there from Jamnia in time for the fortieth-day memorial.[43]

On his journey back through Phoenicia, Peter had been in contact with a remarkable society of young law students at Beirut,[44] conspicuous among them John Rufus' younger brother Evagrius, Severus from Sozopolis in Pisidia, and Zacharias of Gaza: Severus and Zacharias had known each other earlier as students in Alexandria.[45] A number of the society had joined Peter before his death.[46] Now Evagrius and a further company came to Maiuma. Among them was Zacharias, somewhat hesitant, especially when he thought of the proximity of his family at Gaza. Sure enough, he soon returned to Beirut, carrying with him letters from Evagrius to Severus, and from the sophist Aeneas of Gaza to his compatriot Zenodorus.[47]

Severus had discouraged Zacharias from going in the first place. He himself, while already leading an extremely ascetic life, proposed to return to his home and practise there as a lawyer—he bought the

gown that would be necessary. But first he must make a pilgrimage
to the Holy Places. Leaving his luggage at Beirut in charge of
Zacharias, he went with one old slave up to Jerusalem, then down
to pay a last visit to his monastic friends at Maiuma—and all was
changed. He sent his old slave back to Beirut, with a message to
Zacharias to despatch his slaves and his goods home to Sozopolis,
and himself remained at Maiuma as a monk.[48] It was not long
before he was seeking the eremitic life, and went with one other to
the wilderness near Eleutheropolis, but soon fell ill, and was taken
in and cared for at the monastery of Romanus,[49] thence returning
to the Gaza sea-board to settle as a solitary near Maiuma, close to
Peter's monastery,[50] but very soon having himself to build and
equip a monastery for those who came seeking to live under his
obedience.[51]

Meanwhile Zacharias, having completed his training, came home
to Gaza, but had to go on his father's business to Constantinople,
where he stayed to practise as a lawyer.[52] To him we owe a short
Life of the Abba Esaias,[53] a *Life of Severus* written while the latter was
still in power as Patriarch of Antioch,[54] and four out of twelve books
of a *Church History* published under his name[55]—all these surviving
in Syriac translation. His contact with Aeneas the sophist of Gaza
suggests a close relationship between our highly-educated monastic
circles and the more secular literary school of Gaza flourishing just
at this time.[56] The subject deserves close attention, which I have not
given it. In connection with it, we should remember that Severus'
supporters were the first to quote from the corpus of mystical works
attributed to Dionysius the Areopagite.[57] Some scholars have even
suggested that Severus was their author.[58] More recently arguments
have been brought forward for attributing them to Peter the Iberian.[59] I cannot myself feel that they belong to Peter's character. But
this milieu does at least suggest itself as their most probable source.

An account of the deaths of the intruder Theodosius of Jerusalem
and of the Abba Romanus is probably the work of John Rufus.[60]
John Rufus and Zacharias of Mitylene (he seems to have finished
up as bishop of that city, possibly on the Chalcedonian side![61]) are
writing often as first-hand witnesses of identical or overlapping
events, giving us something of a stereoscopic view of a lively piece
of history.

. . . . .

After his four years wandering in the Utter Desert, Sabas came
to spend the night in prayer on the mountain of Eudocia's Tower

(we are tempted to ask what he was doing there, when two opponents of Chalcedon were in possession of the tower).[62] An angel
pointed out to him the gorge of the Cedron below him, two miles
away to the south-south-west, and told him, if he would make a
city of the wilderness, to go and stand on its eastern brink: he would
see opposite him an untouched cave, where he should dwell.
Thither, then, he came, early in A.D. 478, fixing a rope at the mouth
of his cave because of difficulty of access, and fetching his water
from a cistern a mile and a half away. Arabs who presently found
him there without possessions began to bring him at intervals portions of their own fare of dry bread, cheese, and dates. Five years
he spent there alone in quiet converse with God,[63] cleansing his
intellectual eye to reflect as in a mirror the glory of the Lord, the
evil spirits being now defeated by his ceaseless prayer and nearness
to God. At last he was called to turn his swords into ploughshares—
to turn from fighting the demons to the peaceful cultivation of other
souls. Many scattered anchorites and grazers (βόσκοι) came to join
him, including a number who were later to found their own lavras
(or in one case a coenobium) up and down Palestine. To each he
allotted a cave with a small cell at its mouth: remains of such are
still to be seen in the valley and elsewhere in the wilderness where
the same pattern was followed. The company grew to seventy, 'a
new choir of seventy apostles'. Sabas built a tower on an impreg-
nable hill in the bend of the wadi to the north of his cave to mark
the limit of the lavra, and a small oratory in a central position where
any visiting priest could celebrate the Liturgy for the brethren—
since Sabas would not himself be ordained, and none of his company
were priests. Water was still a problem.[64] But as he prayed in the
little oratory one night of full moon, he heard the beating of a wild
ass's hoof in the valley below, and leant out to see the animal
digging deep into the gravel, then bending down and drinking.
He went down and found, indeed, living water at the foot of the
cliff—an even supply that never fails.

Another night[65] he saw a pillar of fire from earth to heaven at the
point where his tomb now stands. Climbing up in the dawn, he
found a great cave with a wide opening to the south, a natural apse
in its eastern side, and on its inner, northern side, a chamber for a
sacristy (Διακονικόν). Here was a God-built church—θεόκτιστος:
it must at once have reminded Sabas of the cave-church of St.
Theoctistus where he had served his novitiate, which is in plan

remarkably similar, though on a smaller scale. Here from henceforth the company, which had soon grown to a hundred and fifty,
came for the office on Saturdays and Sundays—though fear of being
ordained made Sabas put off the thought of its consecration. On
the top of the high cliff above the cave-church he built himself a
tower from which a secret tunnel (blocked after his death by the
construction of cisterns) led down to the sacristy. Gifts began to
come in, which he spent mostly on building. The Patriarch
Martyrius knew him of old, and no-one dared oppose him.

But when Martyrius died and was succeeded by Sallust in A.D.
486,[66] grumblers arose who after a year or two went up to ask the
patriarch for a hegumen. Being pressed, they had to confess that
they came from the valley already known by the name of Abba
Sabas—but complained that he was a boorish fellow, who refused to
be ordained or allow anyone else to be, although there were a
hundred and fifty brethren. Sallust sent for Sabas on some other
pretext, and ordained him in their presence, then came down and
consecrated the God-built church on 12th December, A.D. 490.
During the year that followed,[67] three Armenians, an older man
and two disciples, came to the lavra, and Sabas gave them a cell and
cave to the north of his original cave, and the use of the first little
oratory for the office in Armenian on Saturdays and Sundays. In
the same year[68] there came incognito to the lavra as a postulant an
ascetic bishop, John of Colonia in Roman Armenia, in flight from
the worldly cares of his bishopric. We shall be returning to him
later. In the same year also Sabas' father, John Conon, died in
Alexandria,[69] and his wife Sophia sold her property and came up
to Jerusalem. She also died shortly, and her son used her money to
buy a hostelry and gardens in Jericho, and arrange their water-
supply, and to build the guest-house in the lavra itself.

Sabas inherited from Euthymius the practice of going out into
solitude after Epiphany.[70] But now he would keep the Feast of St.
Antony, on 17th January, in his own lavra, then go to his old
master's monastery for his memorial on the 20th, after which he
would go off into the wilderness, to return to his lavra on the eve
of Palm Sunday. He seems to have gone in his wanderings even
farther afield than Euthymius. Once he went up to the sources of
the Jordan at Panias.[71] Another time he went to the south end of
the Dead Sea, towards the traditional Zoar,[72] and saw a small island
which looked suitable for a Lenten fast. But when he tried to reach
it (other records show that the sea used to be fordable)[73] he fell into

a patch of bituminous eruption, and narrowly escaped with his face
so burnt that on his return to his lavra he could only be recognized
by his voice. His beard never grew properly again. Another year
he took a disciple, Agapetus, with him.[74] As Agapetus lay asleep,
and Sabas was praying, a great lion (I think all Cyril's lions are
παμμεγεθέστατοι—'all greatest') came and sniffed Agapetus all over
from foot to head. Sabas prayed for him, and the lion went off,
driven away as by a whip, lightly brushing Agapetus' face with his
tail and waking him up.

In A.D. 492 Sabas did not go farther for his retreat than the spur
two miles to the east known as Castellium[75] from the ruins on it of
the old Herodian fortress-prison of Hyrcania.[76] The shepherds
regarded it as haunted with demons—understandably enough, for it
is riddled with unexpected holes and caves into which it is only too
easy to find one's self slipping down loose gravel slopes. Sabas
sprinkled the place with oil of the Holy Cross, and stayed there in
the face of all demonic terrors until, after a last supreme but in-
effectual effort against his prayers, they left at midnight with a
tremendous din like a multitude of crows. The shepherds saw and
heard it, and came and found Sabas alone. After Easter he returned
with others to tidy the place up and make a coenobium of it. Under
the rubbish they found a great double-vaulted building[77] which he
converted into a church. It was the first of several Sabaite monasteries which, like St. Euthymius' first monastery in the Wadi
Mukellik, owed their origin to a Lenten retreat.

Perhaps because of its practical dangers, Castellium was to be a
coenobium, but for tried monks, not for novices.[78] For the latter,
provided they were of age, Sabas built in the following year a small
coenobium just north of the lavra itself, saying that the coenobium
is to the lavra as the flower to the fruit. The beardless he would
not accept even there, but would send them to Theodosius in his
great hill-top coenobium three miles up to the west. To him let us
now turn.

If the Magi came from Persia or Mesopotamia to Bethlehem, and
wanted to return another way without passing through Jerusalem,
they would almost inevitably take an ancient road across the wilderness from Bethlehem to Jericho. Close to this route, on a conspicuous hill-top five miles east of Bethlehem, is a cave where
tradition says that they spent the first night of their return journey.[79]
To this cave, within a year or so of Sabas' settlement in the gorge of
the Cedron, came Theodosius, already initiate into the ways of the

desert. After he had spent some time alone there feeding upon herbs, he began to be a centre of attraction. There is a story of his going out, when others had begun to join him and he did not know whether this was indeed the right place for him, swinging all over the wilderness a censer laden with charcoal and incense, but unlit. Only when he came back to his hill-top did it begin to smoke.[80] When one day he found that an illustrious visitor had secretly left him a store of money, he used it to build a hostelry over the cave.[81] By gradual growth there arose the largest and most highly organized of Judaean coenobia, with over four hundred brethren at the time of the founder's death in A.D. 529,[82] and so hospitable that legend began to place there the Feeding of the Five Thousand.[83] Here were hostels and hospitals for monks, for worldly visitors, and for the poor; a home for the aged;[84] and a 'monastery within a monastery' for monks mentally afflicted after excessive or ill-judged asceticism.[85] Apart from a special church for these last, there were three churches in the ordinary monastery, where Greeks, Armenians, and Bessi respectively would perform the office and the Liturgy of the Cate-chumens in their own language, coming together in the main church of the Greeks for the Liturgy of the Faithful.[86]

Theodosius, we are told, was famous for three things especially—exact asceticism with true faith throughout life; glad hospitality without distinction of persons; and concentration almost without ceasing in the divine office.[87] He appears alone in the Judaean Wilderness in holding to the Basilian ideal, which we have noted before in Passarion and in Peter the Iberian. And it is significant that Theodore of Petra in his panegyric on Theodosius shows him delivering to his disciples a long extract from St. Basil's *Regulae Fusius Tractatae*.[88] Elsewhere quotations from Basil are rare in our Palestinian monastic literature.

A couple of stories show Marcian of Bethlehem in friendly relations with Theodosius:[89] and another shows Marcian sending supplies to Sabas when there was a shortage at Castellium during building operations in A.D. 492.[90] The *Second Union* seems, indeed, to have been effective here. But this brings us to the subject of diocesan monastic administration. We have seen how in the middle of the century it was in the hands of the two Jerusalem Archiman-drites, Elpidius and Gerontius.[91] Their successors in the 480s, after Gerontius' expulsion, had fallen away from the high pitch of monastic strictness—ἀκρίβεια, and were occupied with earthly cares and worldly incomes.[92] Anarchy was increased by the freedom given to the 'Aposchists' on the accession of the new emperor Anastasius in A.D. 491. The Patriarch Sallust stepped in to appoint Marcian as Archimandrite. But Marcian died in November, A.D. 492.[93] Thereupon the monks of the wilderness went up to the Patriarch, himself already a sick man, and asked for and obtained Sabas and Theodosius as Archimandrites of the anchorites and cell-dwellers and of the coenobia respectively.[94] Each of them was given a Second—for Theodosius, the head of the coenobium of Martyrius; for Sabas, the hegumen of the lavra of St. Gerasimus. So the diocesan administration of the monks passed down from the cities to the wilderness itself. Sallust the Patriarch died on 23rd July, A.D. 494.[95] He was succeeded by Elias, whose harmony with the two monastic leaders over the next twenty years helped to build up a sober Chalcedonianism against which a monophysite emperor had little power.

One of Elias' first steps in the city was to assemble the 'spudaei' of the Church of the Resurrection from their scattered cells in and around the Tower of David into a comfortable monastery near the episcopal house[96]—the beginning, we may suppose, of the present Orthodox Patriarchal Monastery. Sabas seized on the opportunity to buy the cells and make of them three hostelries, one for his own lavra, one for Castellium, and one for visiting monks.[97] This is not the first we hear of such hostelries. Back in A.D. 485, we read of the hegumen of St. Theoctistus' paying two hundred *nomismata* to the monks of St. Euthymius' so that his monastery could have to itself the hostelry which the two monasteries had hitherto shared.[98] The monks of St. Euthymius' spent the money on a hostelry near the Tower of David which they bought from the monks of Souka.[99] In Jericho also, Sabas built in one of his gardens a hostelry for Castellium.[100]

When two Isaurian architects, Theodulus and Gelasius, came to the lavra, Sabas quickly set them on to building a bakery and a hospital, and above these (so it seems they were in its undercrofts) the great Church of the Theotokos which remains the principal church of the lavra, separated from the God-built church by a court-yard beneath which lies the cemetery of the monks and the saint's own tomb. Elias came down and consecrated the new church on 1st July, A.D. 501.[101] The Armenians, now too numerous for the small oratory, were transferred to the God-built church. But Sabas, perceiving that in singing the Trisagion in Armenian they were introducing the Antiochene addition, 'Who wast crucified for us', insisted that that hymn should be sung in Greek.[102]

Meanwhile, Bishop John of Colonia, on his arrival in A.D. 491, had been entrusted as a novice to the 'steward' of the lavra,[103] and had obediently carried out all the menial jobs, carrying water up from the valley, and cooking for the builders.[104] At the time for the change of functionaries in the First Indiction (A.D. 492–3), the new 'steward' appointed him guestmaster and cook.[105] After a year of this, Sabas allowed him a cell for quiet, and he stayed there for another three years, only coming out on Saturdays and Sundays.[106] Then (A.D. 496–7) he was himself made steward of the lavra for a year.[107] Towards the end of A.D. 497, Sabas, thinking him suitable for the priesthood, took him up to Jerusalem for ordination.[108] Elias came to Calvary for the purpose, and John was duly put under arrest. But he asked the Patriarch, 'Father, since I have some sins, I beg I may lay them privately before your beatitude: and then, if you think me worthy, I will accept ordination'. Taking Elias to the approach to Golgotha, and obtaining his promise of secrecy, he told him that he was already a bishop, and of what city. The Patriarch, keeping the secret, called Sabas and told him: 'He has confided certain things to me, and it is impossible to ordain him: but from to-day let him be in quiet, and let no-one trouble him'. Sabas, deeply grieved at the thought that he should have so misjudged his man, withdrew to a cave near Castellium and prayed for an explanation, which in due course he received. Then he went and told John, but promised to keep the secret to himself.[109] For four years John remained in his cell, seeing no-one but his attendant, and only coming out for the consecration of the Great Church.[110]

Not long after that, Sabas, finding the grumblers increased to forty, withdrew from his own lavra.[111] Thereupon John also withdrew to a cave in the Utter Desert of Rouba, from which he would come out every two or three days to gather melagria.[112]

Sabas spent some time in the neighbourhood of Scythopolis and Gadara, sowing there the seeds of a coenobium.[113] Then he returned to his lavra, but found the grumblers increased to sixty, and went away to Nicopolis, where yet another new coenobium sprang up.[114] Meanwhile the grumblers went up to the Patriarch to ask for a hegumen, reporting that their abba had become food for lions (λεοντόβρωτος γέγονεν) near the Dead Sea. Elias was not going to believe that, and bided his time, seeking for Sabas. Presently he recognized him when he came up from Nicopolis for the Encaenia

(Holy Cross Day), and insisted on his returning to his lavra with a letter from himself commanding obedience.[115] The grumblers in anger destroyed Sabas' tower, casting wood and stones down into the valley, and went away, first seeking in vain a refuge at Souka, and finally settling in the ruins of Romanus' old monastery by Tekoa. In the end Sabas found them there, and stayed five months, building them a bakery and a church, which was consecrated in A.D. 507. So began the New Lavra—a source of trouble for the next forty years.[116]

Meanwhile, John was continuing in his solitude. It was just at this time that the Lakhmid prince Al Moundhir was terrorizing the provinces of Arabia and Palestine with his raids.[117] The fathers of the lavra sent to call John back for safety. But he would not leave the sweetness of his quiet, entrusting himself to God's protection with the words of Arsenius' disciple Daniel at the Desolation of Scetis: 'If God does not take care of me, why should I live?'[118] God sent him a great lion for his protection. The first night, John was a little frightened at finding the lion lying down beside him. But when he saw the beast following him day and night, inseparable from him, and warding off the barbarians, he gave thanks to God who 'letteth not the rod of the ungodly come into the lot of the righteous'.[119]

At last Sabas himself came down to him, again with the words of old Daniel at the Desolation of Scetis: 'Lo, God has protected thee: do now thou also the human thing, and flee like the fathers'.[120] He returned then to the lavra, and Sabas enclosed him, in A.D. 509,[121] in the cell where he still was, aged nearly 104, when Cyril of Scythopolis wrote his *Life* forty-seven years later.[122]

Four other dependent monasteries sprang up within two or three miles of the lavra in the next few years.[123] Their story must not delay us here, save for that of the Tower of Eudocia on Jebel Muntar.[124] Here two Nestorianizing monks had replaced the two monophysites driven out at the time of the introduction of the *Henotikon*. Muntar dominates all Sabas' monasteries, and it was natural that he should be anxious for their conversion, which in the end by prayer and persuasion he achieved. Then he took and entrusted them to Theodosius, installing one of his own disciples, John Scholarius, on the great hill with a few companions. One day in the autumn of A.D. 511, John Scholarius met in the Anastasis in Jerusalem a servant of God on pilgrimage, whom (as his own monastery had as yet no hostelry in Jerusalem) he took to the

Hostelry of the Great Lavra, and introduced to Sabas. Then with Sabas' permission he took him down to his tower, where he entered with a will into the life of the community.[125] Actually, he was Abramius, who for ten years had been priest and hegumen of a monastery of his founding at Cratea in the province of Honorias (between Paphlagonia and Bithynia), and was fleeing from popularity.[126] His bishop Plato, having sought him high and low, at last heard of his Palestinian retreat, and wrote begging him to come back.[127] Finally in despair he excommunicated him, when he had been four years with John Scholarius.[128] Scholarius brought him then to Sabas, and Sabas to the Patriarch, seeking a way out. But Elias was firm that an excommunication could only be lifted by the bishop who had imposed it, and Abramius had to return to Cratea, where he was quickly restored to his former position.[129] But on Bishop Plato's death not long afterwards, Abramius was made bishop in his place.[130] Fifteen years later he took advantage of a visit on diocesan business to Constantinople to escape from his bishopric and return to John Scholarius.[131]

One more story illustrating Sabas' ways at this time.[132] Passing, one Lent, from Rouba to the Reed-bed ('Calamon') of Jordan, he met a great lion limping, with a splinter in its foot, and sat down and pulled out the splinter, after which the lion would follow and serve him through Lent. Sabas had at that time down in Rouba a Syrian disciple, Flavius, with a donkey for service. When he sent Flavius on any errand, he would bid the lion look after the donkey. All went well until one day Flavius was sent up to Jerusalem, and fell into grievous sin there. That same day the lion ate the donkey. Flavius hearing of it, understood the cause, but did not dare face the old man, and returned to his village in despair. Sabas sought him out diligently, and with gentle persuasion brought back the lost sheep, who shut himself into his cell in penitence from the heart, and became greatly well-pleasing to God.

. . . . .

Meanwhile on the Coastal Plain and around Eleutheropolis, the opponents of the Council had seemed to be having it their own way. But about A.D. 508 a fire-brand monk, Nephalius, who twenty years before had been a violent opponent of the *Henotikon* in Alexandria,[133] appeared in circumstances which are somewhat obscure as a strong Chalcedonian in Palestine, ousting or threatening to oust the 'Aposchists' from their monasteries. This took Severus to Constantinople as apocrisiarius for Theodore of Ascalon and the other monks of the Maiuma region.[134] He stayed there for three years organizing opposition to the Council, obtaining, it seems, a complete ascendancy over the Emperor Anastasius, and achieving the deposition of the Patriarch Macedonius, though not his own election in his place.[135] Then he returned to his own monastery by Maiuma—but not for long.[136]

Of the subsequent history of the Judaean monks' fight for Chalcedon I have written elsewhere[137] and hope some day to write again more fully—of Sabas' winter spent in the capital in A.D. 511–12, and his championing of Elias before the emperor;[138] of his bringing round Mamas, hegumen of Romanus' monastery by Eleutheropolis, to acceptance of Chalcedon;[139] of the ousting of Flavian of Antioch and his replacement by Severus;[140] of the refusal of Elias and the monks to accept Severus' synodicals or to anathematize Chalcedon;[141] of the letter of the monks to Alcison of Epirus, seeking to bring into concert all Chalcedonian resistance;[142] of the expulsion of Elias in A.D. 516, and his replacement by his deacon John;[143] of John's vacillation, and his final submission to his monks in the vast concourse in the Church of St. Stephen outside the walls of Jerusalem (the only church large enough to hold them), when Theodosius and Sabas mounted the ambon on either side of John, and the three with one voice anathematized all who did not accept Chalcedon— Theodosius adding his anathema on 'any who does not accept the Four Councils even as the Four Gospels';[144] of their subsequent great letter of protestation proclaiming the Faith of the Holy Places against the Emperor himself;[145] of Anastasius' death and that of the exiles Elias and Flavian within ten days in July, A.D. 518;[146] and of the great festival on 6th August in that year, when by command of the new Emperor Justin the Four Councils were inserted in the diptychs.[147] Here I will only make certain points in summary. Especially, we note how an international Orthodoxy centred on Jerusalem, and achieved not by force but by patience, is seen standing up against imperial monophysitism. We see, too, how as a temporary measure (in the end, of course, it had to go) the *Henotikon* had a positive historical value in giving people time and freedom to think—so that the successors of those who, like Marcian of Bethlehem, had been hesitant to accept anything but a downright anathema on Chalcedon, were now ready to die in defence of that Council. We have seen the power of the Holy Places in keeping their devotees to a sober historical Faith.

Our story has shown us also the full integration of the monks into the diocesan system. And it has shown them to us coming out as agents in history in a manner fraught with moral and spiritual dangers, but not without its nobility or rightness on occasion. We can note also in Sabas and others a frank acceptance of the use of wealth which may seem rather far removed from St. Antony and the monks of the first generation. But along with this is found a sense of responsibility towards society as a whole, of which we shall soon be hearing more.

Sabas was the chief of the embassy which the Patriarch John sent round Palestine, and to the two civil capitals of Caesarea and Scythopolis, to report the good news.[148] On his return John, in spite of the five years' drought which had begun with the exile of Elias in A.D. 516, invited him and the other hegumens to dinner, and set him between himself and his brother, the Bishop of Ascalon.[149] Sabas, who could go for weeks without food, was prepared to eat twice a day and above satiety when the laws of hospitality required it of him, and did not suffer from doing so. Now the two bishops were plying him with food until he said: 'Let be, fathers, I am taking as much as I need'. Theodosius seeing it, said cheerfully: 'Master Sabas is so hungry that the two of you, who after God keep Palestine fed, especially in this time of drought, are competing to serve him with food'. The Patriarch answered: 'Pardon, fathers, for all of us bear neither fasting nor satiety: but the Man of God partakes of the Apostolic gift, and knows both how to be abased and how to abound: he has learned the secret in everything and in all things both to be filled and to be hungry, both to abound and to be in want, and to be strong for all things in Christ who strengtheneth him'.

Sabas would say playfully to Theodosius, 'Sir Abba, you are a hegumen of children, but I a hegumen of hegumens: for each of those under me is independent, and is hegumen of his own cell'.[150]

Theodosius died on 11th January, A.D. 529.[151] Four months later in the same year (which is that of Justinian's great Edict against Paganism) the Samaritans rose up in revolt, sacking and burning churches and villages of the Christians, murdering the Bishop of Neapolis and many priests and others, and proclaiming an emperor of their own race.[152] The revolt was suppressed, and the Patriarch Peter of Jerusalem (John had died in A.D. 524) begged Sabas to go up to Constantinople and plead for a grant of public funds to make good the damage. This he did in April, A.D. 531,[153] returning in September with his five requests granted:[154]

1. Two bishops were to inspect damage to buildings in the two provinces of Palestine, and three *centenaria* of gold from the taxes for A.D. 530–32 (the 9th and 10th Indictions) should pay for repairs.

2. The same bishops should inspect damage to churches, to be repaired out of public funds or Samaritan property.

3. A hospital of 100 beds should be built in the midst of the Holy City with a yearly income of 1,850 *nomismata*—this was afterwards increased to 200 beds, with income increased in proportion.

4. The great New Church of the Theotokos in Jerusalem, started by Elias, was to be completed.

5. A *castrum* was to be built in the wilderness below Sabas' monasteries, with a garrison of soldiers against Arab raids (Sabas came back with funds for this: but on his death his successor handed the money over to the Patriarch, who never used it for the purpose for which it was intended).[155]

In return, Sabas had promised Justinian the reconquest of Africa and Rome and the rest of Honorius' empire, and the suppression of Arianism, Nestorianism, and Origenism.[156] What he had pointedly not promised, in spite of solicitation, was a son to Theodora.[157]

We are reminded that when Sabas had visited the Emperor Anastasius in A.D. 511–12, he had thanked him for the remission of the *chrysargyrum* years before, and had pleaded (though here he had been thwarted) for the remission of the *perissopractia*.[158] The desert monk was in both cases a cogent ambassador for the practical needs of the people.

In A.D. 511 when Sabas had arrived at the Palace, the *silentiarii* had let the other monks in, but seeing Sabas' rags had turned him away, thinking him a beggar.[159] When he was missed and they were sent to look for him, they found him standing in a corner of the *consistorium* reciting psalms. In A.D. 531, when he had submitted his requests to Justinian, and the emperor was discussing the details of them with the Quaestor in the Magnaura, Sabas went a little apart and began quietly saying Terce.[160] The deacon Jeremias, his disciple, rebuked him: 'Honoured father, when the emperor is showing such eagerness to fulfil your requests, why are you yourself standing apart?' He answered: 'My child, they are doing their proper work. Let us also do ours!'

Returning to Jerusalem with the imperial orders, he distributed among his monasteries the gold given him. The deacon Jeremias was displeased at the distribution, and moved off from the Lavra to settle in a valley east of Jebel Muntar, which Sabas then helped him to turn into a lavra. It was Sabas' last foundation.[161]

At the Patriarch's request, he was once more the emissary to carry the imperial orders to Caesarea and Scythopolis.[162] Returning to Jerusalem, he made the round of the Holy Places as if saying good-bye to them, then went down to his lavra, and soon fell sick.[163] The Patriarch came down to visit him, and found him with no comfort in his cell but a few carobs and old dates. He put him in a litter and took him up to the patriarchate and cared for him with his own hands. But after a few days Sabas knew the end was near, and asked to be taken back to his own cell. There in his tower on 1st December he assembled the fathers of the Lavra, and gave them for hegumen Melitas of Beirut, handing to him in writing the Traditions delivered to the monasteries under him, and bidding him keep them unaltered. Four days he remained without food, then as the night drew on to Sunday the 5th December, A.D. 532, he asked for and received Communion, and with a last 'Lord, into thy hands I commend my spirit', he gave up his soul. He was in his ninety-fourth year.

The Patriarch and other bishops and leading men of the city, and an immense crowd of monks and laity, came down to lay his body in the vault under the courtyard between the churches, at the point above which his cenotaph now stands. Fifteen years later, at the burial of one of his successors, his biographer went down into the vault and saw the saint's body still uncorrupt.[164] In spite of many vicissitudes, and not a few Bedouin devastations, his monastery has continued with an unbroken history to the present day.

His younger contemporary Benedict, who was settled at Monte Cassino by the time of Sabas' death, has bequeathed his Rule to us. Sabas' *Life* would seem to imply that he also left behind him a written Rule.[165] It has not come down to us, though a collection of Rules for his monastery of several centuries later does survive in two MSS. on Sinai, and is of very great interest, perhaps retaining reminiscences at least of the original Rule.[166] Maybe it is more in keeping with the spirit of East Christian monasticism that the written Rule should not survive, while there remains the pattern of his living monastery, whose Typikon has continued through the centuries to take perhaps first place among the Typika which regulate the liturgical order of the Eastern Orthodox Church. When Egypt had slipped off into heresy or schism, and the

Athonite monasteries were far in the future, the Lavra of St. Sabas, with the other surviving Judaean monasteries only less tenacious under the lordship of Islam, was moulding the shape of Orthodox monasticism for the centuries to come, developing its hymnody and liturgical order, and gathering up its dogma, with a continued intellectual life of which St. John of Damascus is only one, though the supreme, example.

> By the channels of thy tears
>   Thou didst cultivate the barrenness of the Wilderness:
> And by thy groanings from the depth
>   Thou didst bear fruit of thy toils an hundredfold;
> And becamest a light unto the world,
>   Shining with miracle,
>   Sabas our father holy.
>   Intercede unto Christ our God
>   For our souls' salvation.[167]

.   .   .   .   .

The little cupola which marks St. Sabas' tomb in the court between his two churches has for centuries been a cenotaph, his bones having been carried off to Venice at the time of the Crusades, This book was already in proof when news came that they were to be restored to their first resting-place—a fitting and generous gesture of reparation from the Western Church, to mark and to strengthen our brotherhood in the One Inheritance of the Saints; by whose prayers, made effectual in our lives, may the Lord Jesus bring healing to the divisions of His Church!

NOTES TO CHAPTER VI

[1] *V.E.* c. 42 (61. 31–62. 2).
[2] *V.S.* cc. 12–14.
[3] Zach. Mit. *Chr.* V. 1–2: Evagr. *H.E.* III. 3–4: Theod. Lect. I. 28–32: *V. Petr. Ib.* 78. 23–79. 10.
[4] Zach. Mit. *Chr.* V. 4–5: Evagr. *H.E.* III. 6 and 11: Theod. Lect. I. 30–1.
[5] Theod. Lect. I. 20–2, 30–1: *Gesta de Nomine Acacii* 12 (Thiel, *Epp. R.P.*, p. 518).
[6] *V. Petr. Ib.* 79, 10–15—Raabe fails to understand this in the text of his translation, but gets nearer to it at the end of his footnote. *Pleroph.* XXII (47. 6–7): *V. Severi, P.O.* II, 86–7, 224–5.
[7] *V. Petr. Ib.* 77–8.
[8] *V. Petr. Ib.* 78. 2–3.
[9] *V. Cyr.* 225. 17–25.
[10] *V.E.* c. 43.
[11] Zach. Mit. *Chr.* III. 2: Evagr. *H.E.* III. 5.
[12] Zach. Mit. *Chr.* III. 5.
[13] *V.E.* c. 43 (62. 11–13): *V.S.* c. 15 (98. 11–14).
[14] Kekelidze, *Ierusalimskii Kanonar VII vieka*, p. 118: Garitte, *Le Calendrier Palestino-Géorgien*, p. 266.

[15] *V.E.* c. 43.
[16] Zach. Mit. *Chr.* V. 6: *V.E.* c. 45—Cyril's statement that it was now that Romanus left Tekoa is refuted by *De ob. Theod.*
[17] *V.S.* c. 38 (127. 15–19).
[18] Zach. Mit. *Chr.* V. 6: Schwartz (*Kyrillos von Skythopolis*, p. 368) retranslates this into Greek.
[19] *V.E.* cc. 43–4.
[20] *V. Cyr.* 225. 25–226. 3.
[21] Zach. Mit. *Chr.* V. 5: Evagr. *H.E.* III. 11: for full references see Stein, *Histoire du Bas-Empire*, II. 22, n. 1.
[22] *P.E.F.Q.S.*, Oct. 1928, pp. 175–8; Jan. 1930, pp. 43–7; Oct. 1932, pp. 188–203.
[23] *V.E.* c. 44.
[24] *V. Petr. Ib.* 89–90.
[25] See Stein, pp. 20–1.
[26] *V. Petr. Ib.* 81–2: *Pleroph.* XXII (48. 4–7): *V. Sev.* 86–7.
[27] *V. Petr. Ib.* 83. 9–13.
[28] *P.O.* VIII, Introd. pp. 6–7: *Pleroph. Tit.* (1. 5): *V. Sev.*, 86.
[29] *V. Petr. Ib.* 96–100.
[30] 100–1.
[31] *Pleroph.* XXII.
[32] *V. Petr. Ib.* 101–2.
[33] Zach. Mit. *Chr.* VI. 3: *V. Es.* 14–15: *V. Petr. Ib.* 103–11.
[34] *V. Petr. Ib.* 111–23.
[35] *V. Petr. Ib.* 124. 4. The date is often given as A.D. 488. This is impossible on the following grounds: The spatharius Cosmas was sent to Alexandria in A.D. 487, returning by Palestine to summon Peter and Esaias to Constantinople. Peter to avoid receiving the summons moved off to Phoenicia, wintering at Orthosias and staying there over Epiphany, Easter and Pentecost (A.D. 488: *V. Petr. Ib.* 106. 10). Then he moved to Gishra near Tripolis, where he received news that he was excused the visit to the capital, and started on his journey back to Palestine. He took his time over it, and when he did reach Caesarea, he went to stay in a monastery at Aphthoria, twelve miles away, for four months, including again Easter and Pentecost (A.D. 489: *V. Petr. Ib.* 121. 3). He then moved to Azotus: but his friend the Tribune Elias installed him after Holy Cross Day, in the autumn (123. 3; *Teshriatha* here means 'autumn', not more specifically the months of October and November), outside Jamnia, where he received news of Esaias' death.
[36] 137. 11. 145. 14–15 speaks of his dying before the dawning of Sunday, 1st Dec.: but, 1st Dec. in A.D. 489 did actually fall on a Friday.
[37] *V. Petr. Ib.* 135. 9–12.
[38] 138. 1–7.
[39] 134. 1–6.
[40] 138–42.
[41] 134. 4–6: *V. Sev.* p. 86.
[42] *V. Petr. Ib.* 143. 18–144. 23.
[43] 143. 12–18. John Rufus does not mention that he himself became Bishop of Maiuma: *V. Sev.* 86 only says that he was 'set apart for the altar', while Theodore was appointed abbot. But he is called Bishop of Maiuma in the Title of the *Plerophories.*
[44] *V. Sev.* 46–85.
[45] *V. Sev.* 11 ff.
[46] 83–6, 95.
[47] 87–9.
[48] 91–3.
[49] 96–7.
[50] 97.
[51] Ibid.
[52] 95.
[53] C.S.C.O., Scr. Syr. ser. tertia, XXV. 3–16: also a fragment of a Life of Peter the Iberian, 28.
[54] *Patrologia Orientalis*, II. 7–115.
[55] *Chronicle of Zachariah of Mitylene*, text in Land, *Anecdota Syriaca*, III. 2–340; translation by F. J. Hamilton and E. W. Brooks, London (Methuen) 1899 (only books 3–6 are really by Zacharias).

[56] *V. Sev.* 90.

[57] At the Constantinople conversations of A.D. 533—Mansi VIII, 820c–823D: Schwartz, *Act. Conc.* IV. 2, 169–84.

[58] J. Stiglmayr in *Scholastik*, 1928, pp. 1–27, 161–89; 1932, pp. 52–67. See Lebon in *R.H.E.* 1930, pp. 880–915; 1932, pp. 296–313.

[59] Honigmann, *Pierre l'Ibérien et les écrits du Pseudo-Denys l'Aréopagite*, in Mémoires de l'Académie Royale de Belgique, Classe des Lettres et des Sciences morales et politiques, XLVII. 3, Brussels, 1952, pp. 6–7. See bibliography in *Sources Chrétiennes* 58, Denys l'Aréopagite I, *La Hierarchie céleste*, introduction, p. xvii, nn. 1 and 2. For the whole subject and its bibliography, see also the article on 'Denys l'Aréopagite (le Pseudo-)' by R. Roques in *Dictionnaire de Spiritualité*, III.

[60] C.S.C.O., Scr. Syr., ser. tertia, XXV. 21–7.

[61] He was present at the Constantinople synod of A.D. 536, being a member of the first commission sent to look for the defaulting Patriarch Anthimus: but his name does not appear among the signatures to the decrees, nor anywhere after the fourth session—Mansi VIII, 878c, 926c, 927A, 934BC.

[62] *V.S.* c. 15.

[63] c. 16.

[64] c. 17.

[65] c. 18.

[66] c. 19.

[67] c. 20.

[68] c. 21.

[69] c. 25.

[70] cc. 22–4.

[71] c. 24.

[72] c. 22.

[73] References in G. Adam Smith, *Historical Geography of the Holy Land* (ed. 1935), p. 507, n. 5.

[74] *V.S.* c. 23.

[75] c. 27.

[76] See Abel, *Géographie de la Palestine*, II. 350.

[77] *V.S.* c. 27, p. 111. 21–2. οἶκον βιωτικὸν μέγαν in Schwartz's edition. I prefer the obscurer but equally well-attested reading βητικόν (at least two MSS. not collated by Schwartz support it, in addition to the two quoted for it by him), interpreting it as a 'beta-shaped house', and understanding it of two barrel vaults seen in section ∞.

[78] *V.S.* c. 28.

[79] *V. Theod.* (Th. P.) c. 8.

[80] c. 15.

[81] *V. Th.* (C.S.) 238. 1–18.

[82] *V. Th.* (Th. P.) c. 25: 693 brethren had predeceased him—ibid.

[83] c. 21.

[84] c. 18, where it is said that round about a hundred tables were set a day.

[85] c. 23.

[86] c. 24.

[87] c. 61 (ed. Usener, 99. 22–100. 5): *V. Th.* (C.S.) 238. 24–8.

[88] c. 28–9.

[89] c. 40: *V. Th.* (C.S.) 237. 10–23.

[90] *V.S.* c. 27 (111. 26–112. 13).

[91] *V.E.* c. 27 (42. 12–14).

[92] *V.S.* c. 30.

[93] *V.S.* c. 27 (112. 13–16).

[94] cc. 30 (115. 14–26) and 65: *V. Th.* (C.S.) 239. 1–12.

[95] *V.S.* c. 31 (115. 28–116. 3). The Palestinian Georgian Calendar (ed. Garitte, pp. 80 and 286) nearly confirms Cyril's dating, giving the commemoration of Sallust on 24th July.

[96] *V.S.* c. 31 (116. 4–8).

[97] Ibid. (116. 9–24).

[98] *V. Cyr.* 226. 15–17.

[99] Ibid. 17–19.

[100] *V.S.* c. 31 (116. 24–5).

[101] c. 32 (117. 1–19): *V. Johannis Hesychastae* 208. 26–7.

[102] *V.S.* c. 32 (117. 19–118. 5).

[103] *V.J.H.* 205. 5–7.

[104] 205. 15–19.

[105] 205. 26–206. 35. As the new coenobium was at this time being built a mile to the north, his office involved carrying their food to the workmen that distance away.

[106] *V.J.H.* 206. 15–207. 2.

[107] 207. 2–5.

[108] 207. 5–28.

[109] 208. 1–23.

[110] 208. 23–209. 5.

[111] *V.S.* c. 33.

[112] *V.J.H.* 209. 6–20.

[113] *V.S.* cc. 33 and 34.

[114] c. 35 (120. 13–121. 2: 122. 12–18).

[115] Ibid. (121. 2–122. 11).

[116] c. 36: *V.J.H.* 212. 15–16.

[117] *V.J.H.* 211. 15–19. Cyril dates Al Moundhir's raid after the Fall of Amida, which was on 10th Jan., A.D. 503.

[118] *V.J.H.* 211. 19–212. 3: G Daniel 1.

[119] *V.J.H.* 212. 4–14.

[120] 212. 15–22.

[121] 212. 23–6.

[122] 222. 8–12.

[123] *a.* The Coenobium of the Cave to which he had retired when Elias did not ordain John—*V.S.* c. 37: *V.J.H.* 208. 2–4. A.D. 508?

b. The Lavra of the Heptastomos—*V.S.* c. 39.

c. The Coenobium of Zannos—*V.S.* c. 42.

[124] *V.S.* c. 38 (A.D. 511—see *V. Abramii* 245. 6).

[125] *V. Abr.* 245. 2–19. Dates have to be fitted in with Sabas' absence in Constantinople during the winter of A.D. 511–12.

[126] *V. Abr.* 244. 21–34.

[127] 245. 20–8. The first result was only the conversion of Bishop Plato's emissary Olympius to the monastic life on Muntar, where in due course he became a priest, and Second of the monastery.

[128] 246. 9–14.

[129] Ibid. 14–27.

[130] 247. 1–5.

[131] 247. 12–22, and the Arabic version (*Anal. Boll.* XXIV), p. 354 ff.

[132] *V.S.* c. 49.

[133] Zach. Mit. *Chr.* VI. 2 and 4: Evagr. *H.E.* III. 22: see Stein II. 35.

[134] Evagr. *H.E.* III. 33 (132. 4–15): *V. Sev.* p. 104.

[135] *V. Sev.* p. 109 ff.: see Stein II. 170–1 and note.

[136] *V. Sev.* p. 110.

[137] 'Jerusalem after Chalcedon, A.D. 451–518', in *The Christian East*, Vol. II, New Series, no. 1, pp. 22–32.

[138] *V.S.* cc. 50–54.

[139] c. 55: Evagr. III. 33 (*Letter to Alcison*, p. 133. 7–9).

[140] *V.S.* c. 56 (148. 16–22): Zach. Mit. *Chr.* VII. 10: *V. Sev.* 110–14: Evagr. *H.E.* III. 32. See Stein II. 173 and note 1 (for references).

[141] *V.S.* c. 56 (148. 23–149. 6).

[142] Evagr. *H.E.* III. 31 and 33.

[143] *V.S.* c. 56 (149. 27–150. 11).

[144] Ibid. (150. 11–152. 5): *V. Theod.* (Th. P.) c. 36.

[145] *V.S.* c. 57: *V. Th.* (Th. P.) cc. 32–3.

[146] *V.S.* c. 60 (161. 3–162. 10).

[147] Ibid. (161. 10–18).

[148] c. 61.

[149] c. 64.

[150] c. 65.

[151] c. 70 (171. 26–9): *V. Th.* (C.S.) 239. 26–30—cf. *V. Th.* (Th. P.) c. 56.

[152] *V.S.* c. 70 (172. 1–173. 4).

[153] cc. 70–2. The date has been the subject of controversy, as from this point on Cyril's indictional dating seems to indicate one year earlier than that given by all his other synchronisms. Diekamp (*Die origenistischen Streitigkeiten im sechsten Jahrhundert*, pp. 11–15) accepted the later dating. Schwartz (*K. von Sk.*, pp. 340–55) argued for the accuracy of the indictions. But Stein, reviewing Schwartz's edition in *A.B.* 62 (1944), pp. 171–80, seems effectually to vindicate Diekamp: and I accept his dating.

[154] cc. 73–4.

[155] c. 83 (187. 28–188. 3).

[156] cc. 72 (175. 20–176. 2) and 74 (178. 22–179. 7).

[157] c. 71 (173. 28–174. 11).

[158] c. 54.

[159] c. 51.

[160] c. 73 (178. 9–18).

[161] c. 74 (179. 12–25).

[162] c. 75.

[163] c. 76.

[164] c. 77.

[165] c. 76 (182. 21–3), etc.

[166] MSS. Sin. 531 and 1906, published by Dimitrievsky, *Works of the Kiev Spiritual Academy* I (Kiev, 1890), pp. 170–92; and by Kurtz, *B.Z.* 3 (1894), pp. 169–70.

[167] Dismissal Hymn of the Feast of St. Sabas (5th Dec.).

VII

THE MONASTERIES UNDER JUSTINIAN

WHEN Sabas came to Scythopolis in the autumn of A.D. 531, the bishop's chancellor, John, was in constant attendance on him.[1] Twelve years before, he and his wife and house had received the saint's blessing when he came to announce the triumph of Chalcedon on the accession of Justin to the empire.[2] Now John had a boy, Cyril, with him. When the boy bowed down to receive the saint's blessing, Sabas raised him up and embraced him, and turned to his father with the words: 'This boy is from henceforth my disciple, and a son of the Fathers of the Wilderness'. Then he addressed the Metropolitan: 'Great Sir, I entrust this boy to you: give heed to him, for I need him'. Cyril's mother being eager to see the saint, John arranged for this to take place during a visit to the hesychast Abba Procopius. When Sabas saw the boy with his mother, he exclaimed: 'Why! Here is my disciple Cyril.' Again he told John: 'Teach him the Psalter, for I need him: for indeed henceforth he is my disciple'. He kept the boy with the male party while they had a meal with the hesychast, and when they returned to the bishop's house. Next day, being about to leave for Jerusalem, he went to John's house and blessed it and the family.[3] From that time the Metropolitan would often ask John, 'How is Abba Sabas' disciple?' and would press him to teach the boy the *Psalter* and the *Apostle*. It was not long before he blessed and tonsured him, and set him on the first step of the ecclesiastical ladder.[4] Nearly twelve years after Sabas' visit, Cyril received the monastic habit in the monastery, and at the hands of Abba George, to whom he was later to address his writings; then went with George's blessing to Jerusalem for the consecration of the great New Church of the Mother of God in November of that year (A.D. 543)—but really intending to go and settle in the Judaean Wilderness.[5] He could expect a welcome there. For ever since Sabas' visit his home had been open to visitors from the wilderness, and had in fact become a kind of hostelry for them in Scythopolis.[6] Knowing or suspecting his intention, his mother instructed him to do nothing without the approval of John the Bishop and Hesychast. She was afraid of his being led astray by the Origenists who were then gaining power in Jerusalem.[7]

That is a long and complex and distressing story. Back in A.D. 514, Sabas' disciple Agapetus, taking over the headship of the New Lavra from a very simple monk, Paul, who had fled from the responsibility after six months, quickly expelled from it four monks, headed by one Nonnus, whom Paul had accepted unsuspecting. They were infected with Origenist teaching about *Pre-existence* and *Apocatastasis*:[8] and it is natural to conjecture a connection between them and the Stephen Bar-Sudaili against whose teaching Philoxenus of Mabbug wrote.[9] This Stephen had certainly moved from Edessa to the region of Jerusalem—Philoxenus says he would have written to warn the Patriarch of Jerusalem against him had they not been out of communion with each other. He is supposed to have been the author of the secret *Book of the Holy Hierotheus*, a book (surviving and probably originally written in Syriac) which would certainly justify an outcry of the Orthodox against it.[10] On Agapetus' death five years later, the four monks managed to get back to the New Lavra, hiding their teaching so long as Sabas was alive.[11] One of them, by name Leontius of Byzantium, was with Sabas on his visit to Constantinople in A.D. 531, and was left behind by him there. Cyril of Scythopolis says that Sabas detected his Origenism hidden under his defence of Chalcedon, and separated from his company both him and some supporters of Theodore of Mopsuestia. But one may suspect that he left them behind quite normally as his representatives, and that Cyril's account is coloured by later events.[12]

Certainly 'Origenist' teaching spread quickly after Sabas' death, especially among the more intellectual monks, not only in the New Lavra. Two of these, Theodore Ascidas of the New Lavra and Domitian of the Monastery of Martyrius, coming with others to Constantinople for the doctrinal debates in the summer of A.D. 536, were by the influence of Leontius (which had become considerable) rapidly raised to the metropolitical sees of Caesarea in Cappadocia and of Ancyra.[13] In the following winter, Melitas, the hegumen of the Great Lavra, died, and was succeeded by Gelasius, one of the two Isaurian architect brothers who had been active in the buildings of the Lavra at the turn of the century.[14] The new hegumen's strong attack on Origenism roused opposition led by the deacon and canonarch John, an Antiochene, who, being expelled from the sanctuary for his heresy, formed a band with John called the Thunder-demon and about forty others. Driven out of the Great Lavra, they sought refuge at the New Lavra, whither Leontius had recently returned from Constantinople. Leontius gathered the

Origenists together into something of an army. Having failed to obtain support from Sophronius, the successor of St. Theodosius, they set out armed with picks and shovels and crowbars, intent on destroying the Great Lavra. But about the second hour of the day there fell upon them a mist and a darkness, and after stumbling about the rough and pathless places of the wilderness, they found themselves next day in the region of Marcian's monastery by Bethlehem, and gave up the attempt.[15] But subsequently by representing Gelasius as a trouble-maker they managed, about A.D. 540, to force him to a choice between accepting them back and expelling their chief opponents in the Great Lavra. Gelasius chose the second alternative, and six brethren left the Lavra. But going to Antioch they appealed to the Patriarch Ephraim, who summoned a local synod in which Origenism was condemned. Thereupon the Origenists at court (Leontius had by now returned there) set to work to force the Patriarch Peter of Jerusalem to omit the name of Ephraim from the diptychs. But Peter incited Gelasius and Sophronius to produce a *libellus* against the Origenists, urging him not to break with Ephraim. This he sent to Constantinople, where the Roman legate Pelagius was already working in the same direction. In consequence, early in A.D. 543 Justinian issued an edict against Origenism, which the bishops, including Theodore Ascidas and Domitian, were compelled to sign. But when Domitian (now Metropolitan of Ancyra) found that some had managed to avoid signing, and that Theodore Ascidas, although he had signed, was carrying on exactly as before, he shaved his beard and cut himself off from the Church and died of dropsy in Constantinople without communion.[16] In Jerusalem, the Origenists on hearing of the edict left the New Lavra and withdrew to the Plain. But very soon Ascidas' threats had forced Peter rather lamely to allow them back. Meanwhile Ascidas (Leontius died about this time) was seeking to regain ground against Pelagius and Peter by agitation against the *Three Chapters* (Theodore of Mopsuestia, etc.). Peter earned imperial disfavour by taking to Constantinople another *libellus* from the Archimandrites, pleading against the condemnation of the *Three Chapters*, and was compelled by Ascidas to accept two Origenist assessors (*syncelli*), and to appoint John the Eunuch, Domitian's successor at the Monastery of Martyrius, as hegumen of the New Church of the Mother of God.[17]

It was in the midst of these events that the young Cyril came to Jerusalem in November, A.D. 543.[18] After visiting the Holy Places, he went down to the Great Lavra to see John the Bishop and Hesy-chast, who told him, if he wanted to be saved, to go and settle in the Coenobium of St. Euthymius. But Cyril in his youthfulness went instead to the Jordan Plain, and fell ill for six months in the Lavra of Calamon. At last, in July, A.D. 544, John appeared to him in a dream and told him he had been punished enough for his dis-obedience, and should now go to Jericho, to St. Euthymius' hostelry there, where he would find a monk who would take him up to the monastery. So at last he came to settle there, going frequently to seek counsel of John the Hesychast, now about ninety years old, who from his enclosed cell was the inspiration of the Great Lavra's opposition to the Origenists.

On one of the first of these visits,[19] Cyril was sent on by John to the Old Lavra, Souka, with letters for the other great old anchorite, Cyriac, now well over ninety, describing the riotous conditions prevalent in Jerusalem (where the Sabaite hostelry underwent something like a siege, and it was unsafe for a Sabaite monk to show himself)[20] and asking for all the strength of his prayer.

A generation earlier, the spiritual life of the wilderness seemed to be focused round the two great abbots, Sabas and Theodosius. But now that the monasteries themselves were becoming deeply en-meshed in the intrigues and ugliness of ecclesiastical politics, the centre of gravity seems to have moved on—or back—once more to the great solitaries. And it will be fitting here to glance at the life-story of Cyriac, whom we remember as a boy of seventeen, back in A.D. 466, running away from his home in Corinth to the Judaean Wilderness,[21] and whom we last heard of assisting in the work of transforming St. Euthymius' lavra into a coenobium.[22] When in A.D. 485 St. Euthymius' two monasteries had fallen apart, and the Upper Coenobium had bought its hostelry in Jerusalem from the fathers of Souka, Cyriac, grieved at the division, had himself moved on to Souka,[23] serving there in four successive years as baker, hospitaller, guest-master, and steward.[24] After this, having been already ordained deacon at the monastery of St. Euthymius, he served four years in the sanctuary (ἱερατεῖον) before being ap-pointed treasurer (κειμηλιάρχης) and canonarch. After thirteen years in this office he was ordained priest, but continued in the same functions for another eighteen years—thirty-one years in all, during which he could claim that the sun never saw him eating or angry, and he would not finish beating the lavra's wooden gong for the nightly psalmody until he had recited the whole of the 119th Psalm (the 118th in LXX numbering: known from the first verse as *The Undefiled*).²⁵ Then at last, in A.D. 525, at the age of seventy-six, he went on with a disciple to the Utter Desert of Natoupha. As there were no *melagria* in these parts—only squills—he prayed to God who created all things and is able to change the bitter into sweet, to let the squills serve as food for them; and he bade his disciple go and gather and boil them. The disciple did so—boiled them thoroughly and served them with salt—and the two continued feeding on them for four years.²⁶ After that, a leading villager of Tekoa, hearing about them from the shepherds, went down to them with his donkey laden with warm loaves, which he left with them. After they had eaten of the bread, the disciple without consulting the old man boiled some squills and ate them as usual, and was struck down voiceless from their bitterness. The old man learning the cause, prayed over him, raised him up, gave him Communion, and restored him to health. Next time they had nothing but squills, the disciple did not dare to touch them: so the old man blessed them and began eating them first, and the disciple took courage and ate them without harm.²⁷

After another year, the healing of a lunatic boy made Cyriac too famous in those parts, and he fled down to Rouba, where he stayed five years feeding on 'roots of melagria and hearts of reeds'.²⁸ Once more fleeing from popularity, he came at last to a place utterly desert and secret called Sousakim, where the wadis from Souka and from the New Lavra meet in the depth of the wilderness—the 'Rivers of Etham', some said, of which David wrote: 'Thou driedst up rivers of Etham' (or 'mighty rivers').²⁹ Here he spent seven years until at last in the time of the Great Plague (A.D. 542-3) the Fathers of Souka came and persuaded him to come up to the 'hanging cave' of St. Chariton outside the lavra.³⁰ It was in that cave that Cyril first found him when he came with Bishop John's letter, probably in A.D. 544, and obtained from him his account of the Origenists' intrigues, and of the reasons for rejecting their doctrine.³¹ When Cyriac heard that Cyril was from the coenobium of St. Euthymius, he welcomed him as his *syncoenobiote*, and began to tell him many, many stories about Euthymius and Sabas.³²

.   .   .   .   .

The Origenists continued to have their own way in Jerusalem, and at last the Fathers of the Great Lavra persuaded their hegumen Gelasius to go up to Constantinople and report the state of things to the emperor.³³ He went with no great hope, conscious that he had compromised himself with Justinian by signing the *libellus* against anathematizing Theodore of Mopsuestia. Sure enough, when he arrived at the capital, he found every door closed against him, sensed plots of Theodore Ascidas all round him, and was soon starting back on foot for Jerusalem, but died at Amorium in Phrygia in October, A.D. 546, about fifty years after his arrival at the Great Lavra.

Hearing the news of his death, the fathers of the Lavra went up to Jerusalem to ask the Patriarch for a hegumen, but were driven out of the city, and returned to their lavra with nothing accomplished. The Origenists seemed triumphant on all sides. In February, A.D. 547, they went down and installed an Origenist, George, in Sabas' seat, and the fathers were scattered at the coming of the wolf. Bishop John himself left his enclosure, and came up with many others to the Mount of Olives, while others were scattered up and down the countries. But on that same day Nonnus, the arch-Origenist, died suddenly. George after only seven months was found unsatisfactory even by those who had installed him, and was deposed.[34] His successor, Cyril's fellow-townsman from Scythopolis, Cassian, had been brought up in the monastic life by Sabas, and had been for eight years head of Souka. He died after only ten months, on 20th July, A.D. 548. His successor, the Lycian Conon, a monk in his home country from boyhood,[35] though he had only come to Palestine after Sabas' death, was a wise and gentle man, who soon began to restore the fortunes of the Lavra, and gather back to it the fathers who were scattered. The Origenists began to be weakened by divisions among themselves. Bishop John does not seem to have remained long away from his cell. Cyriac, pestered by people at the Cave of St. Chariton, and assured that the battle against Origenism was already virtually won, had withdrawn once more, in his ninety-ninth year, the nine miles down from Souka to his old haunt of Sousakim.[36]

Hither came Cyril to visit him,[37] going first to Souka and collecting Cyriac's disciple John for a guide. As they drew near the place a great and fearful lion met them. But John told Cyril not to be afraid; and sure enough, when the lion saw they were going to the Old Man, he made way for them. The Old Man was full of joy on seeing them. 'Why!' says he, 'it is my *syncoenobiote*, Cyril'. 'Father', says John, 'he was greatly frightened when he saw the lion.' Says Cyriac, 'Do not be afraid, my child: for this lion stays with me here to guard my little vegetables from the wild goats'. After many stories of Euthymius and the other Fathers of the Wilderness, he invited them to a meal. As they ate, the lion came and stood in front of them, and the Old Man got up, gave him a piece of bread, and sent him off to guard the vegetables. Cyril and John spent the night with the Old Man, and next day he sent them off with a blessing and a prayer. As they went, there was the lion lying across their path munching a wild goat: but when he saw they were not daring to go on, he left his prey and withdrew till they were past.

. . . . . .

The division among the Origenists was between the *Isochrists* who taught that in the 'Restoration of all things' (*Apocatastasis*) all would be equal to Christ, and the *Protoctists* of the Lavra of St. Firminus near Michmash, who, holding to the pre-existence of the soul, taught that the pre-existent human soul of Christ was the First-born of All Creation.[38] It ended in an alliance between the latter and the Anti-Origenists, Isidore of St. Firminus' promising to keep quiet about pre-existence. He and Conon of the Great Lavra went up to Constantinople at the end of A.D. 551 to bide their time.[39] They did not have to wait long. Peter of Jerusalem died soon after, and the Neolavrites aroused the emperor's fury by installing their nominee, Macarius, by force as Patriarch without waiting for the emperor's approval.[40] Conon and his company, with all the more freedom now since Isidore had died, seized the opportunity to present the emperor with a *libellus* exposing the Origenists, and put forward a nominee of their own, Eustochius, who was then in Constantinople, for the Patriarchate of Jerusalem. Justinian accepted their proposal. Eustochius was sent as Patriarch to Jerusalem: and the Fifth Oecumenical Council was summoned to Constantinople, for the condemnation both of the Three Chapters and of Origenism.[41] The last session of the Council was on 2nd June, A.D. 553. The Origenists were finally expelled from the New Lavra, and a hundred and twenty monks, half from the Great Lavra and half from other monasteries of the wilderness, were installed in their place, on 21st February, A.D. 555. Among these was Cyril of Scythopolis, coming with the approval of Bishop John.[42] From his early days at the Coenobium of St. Euthymius, he had been inspired by repeated experience of the wonder-working power connected with the saint's tomb, to seek out what kind of a life lay behind this.[43] Cyriac could give him first-hand accounts of events of Euthymius' last years. Others could repeat to him what they had been told of that saint by those who had known him, and what they themselves had experienced of Sabas and Theodosius, etc. Like a busy bee he had gone up and down the wilderness gathering these reminiscences while they were still fresh, jotting them down on odd sheets, and storing them up without any order. Now for two years at the New Lavra he toiled over his notes, seeking in vain to make a beginning of setting them in order, conscious of his lack of secular education, his inexperience in Scripture, and his slowness of speech. At last, when he was almost despairing, there came a day when about the second hour, sitting in his usual seat with the sheets in his hands, he was borne down with sleep, and saw the holy Fathers Euthymius and Sabas in their customary sacred attire, and heard Sabas saying to Euthymius, 'Look, your Cyril has the sheets in his hands, and is showing most fervent zeal, and with all this toil and labour he has not strength to make a beginning of the composition'. The great Euthymius answered, 'Yes, for how shall he be able to make his composition about us when he has not yet received the grace of the uttered word in the opening of his mouth?' When Sabas said, 'Then give him the grace, father', Euthymius nodded, and took out of his bosom a silver ointment-box with a probe, dipped the probe in the box, and put it three times in Cyril's mouth, with something that was like oil in appearance, but in taste sweeter than honey, a true demonstration of the word of Scripture, 'How sweet are thy words unto my throat, yea, sweeter than honey into my mouth!' The ineffable sweetness woke him up, and with that spiritual fragrance still on his lips and in his mouth he began at once to write the preface to his *Life of Euthymius*. This first biography was quickly followed by the *Life of Sabas*. But before that was completed, he was being urged both by Bishop John and by his first master, George of Scythopolis, to whom he was dedicating his works, to move from the New Lavra to the Great Lavra of St. Sabas, and was preparing to build himself a cell there.[44] By the time that he wrote his *Life of Bishop John the Hesychast*, some time in A.D. 557, he was already installed there,[45] and able more frequently to visit John, who was now in his 104th year preparing for death.[46] Meanwhile in A.D. 556 Cyril had paid another visit to St. Cyriac in the Cave of St. Chariton, whither the fathers of Souka had brought him back the year before, after eight years in Sousakim.[47] Cyriac was now aged 107, yet would still stand for the office, and would serve with his own hands those who came to him. The next year he died. Cyril describes him as 'a man meek and approachable, prophetic, given to teaching, most orthodox, large and noble in body, and with all his limbs sound: and he was truly full of grace and of Holy Spirit'.[48] He is the most absolute, and perhaps the most attractive, of all Cyril's heroes. In him we seem to be returning to St. Antony.

. . . . .

Schwartz's publication, in 1939, of all the assured works of Cyril of Scythopolis in a single volume, while its text and its conclusions may be criticized, did us a very great service in helping scholars to realize what a valuable and remarkable historian we have here. Occasional errors in Cyril's dating are only troublesome because of his normal care and accuracy. Topographical details can again and again be confirmed on the spot. It was, for instance, from what he tells us that we were led to find the Cemetery of St. Euthymius, and the line of the walls of the church of his lavra in the vault under the church of the coenobium; to place the New Lavra, with the remains of two churches, on the hill south-east of Tekoa;[49] and to go down deep into the wilderness to find St. Cyriac's secret place of Sousakim—the stark cave with its rock-ledge for a bed, walled along its front, and with a square domed cell built without mortar at its mouth, looking down on the meeting of the two wadis.[50] While Cyril is a typical Palestinian of his day, full of naïve superstition (which makes his work of all the more value to the modern scholar), he never gives us the impression that he is embroidering or enlarging on what he himself has heard or seen. Nor does anything he tells us seem irrelevant to the picture that he is building up, as he brings to life for us both a series of remarkable characters and a century and a half of the history of an unforgettable stretch of country.

We have little impression of originality in Cyril's personal religion. But his works have yet to be fully explored as a mine of quotations from earlier works—the Vita Antonii,[51] the Vita Pachomii, the Apophthegmata Patrum, etc. Here we are reminded that Cyril is roughly contemporary with the early Latin versions of the Apophthegmata, while the earliest dated Syriac MS. of a collection of these comes from the year of St. Sabas' death. In the first generation in the fourth century we were conscious how all reading is of Holy Scripture—to which soon the Vita Antonii was added. By the end of that century, the library of the monks was growing. By Cyril's time it had reached considerable proportions—a corpus of 'case-law' of the desert which, because it dealt with the world the monks knew, might often seem a safer guide than Holy Scripture itself, subject as that is to such a variety of personal interpretations. The same impression of this age is confirmed in the literature of the Gaza region, to which we must now turn.

.   .   .   .   .

After the consecration of Severus as Patriarch of Antioch, the curtain falls on his anti-Chalcedonian monastery at Maiuma. It rises again on a remarkable community at Thavatha,[52] the birthplace of Hilarion, where Peter the Iberian had spent some time before his flight to Phoenicia in A.D. 487. This community comes into view under Justin, or possibly in the last years of Anastasius. Its *floruit* covers a period of at least eighteen years, including Justinian's Edict of A.D. 529 against the Pagans, and the Great Plague of A.D. 542-3. During this period it certainly accepted Chalcedon: but its spirituality is in the succession of the Abba Esaias; and we have no indication that adherence to the Council had occasioned any upheaval. We do not know how early the Egyptian monk Varsanuphius enclosed himself in his cell, and set his attendant Seridus as abbot over the ascetics who were gathering round him. The Great Old Man would normally never emerge from his cell, communicating with the outside world only by means of Abba Seridus who waited upon him and gave him absolute obedience (we remember the same pattern followed by Abba Esaias and his disciple Peter the Egyptian). Some time not earlier than A.D. 525 or later than A.D. 527, the Great Old Man moved to a new cell, giving over his first cell to the Other Old Man, John, who followed the same way of life there, with a monk for his attendant and mouthpiece, for the next eighteen years. The community took the form of a coenobium with the cells of anchorites in varying degrees of enclosure clustered around it. A written correspondence of fifty-four letters from Varsanuphius (one short letter is from the Other Old Man) in answer to questions from a monk John of Beersheba opens a series of well over eight hundred answers of the two Old Men to a great variety of questions and questioners. These were edited by a monk of the community whose identity is never revealed, but who tells us that he was present on the one occasion when Varsanuphius did come out and wash the feet of the brethren, to allay the doubts of one questioner who had begun to suspect that the unseen Old Man was just a figment of the Abba Seridus. When I gave these lectures, the only printed edition in the original Greek (there have been Russian translations) was that prepared by St. Nicodemus of the Holy Mountain, who died before its publication in Venice in 1816.[53] This is very hard to come by, in Western Europe at least: after long search, the indefatigable Marcel Richard found a copy of it with the Assumptionists in Paris, and procured me a microfilm. Since these lectures were given, it has been re-edited, at Volos in 1960, by Soterios N. Schoinas—practically a reprint of the earlier edition, but with the numbering of the Questions and Answers rationalized, and with some gaps in the MS. used by Nicodemus filled in from the kindred MS. Iviron 1307. I am engaged on a critical edition.

The John of Beersheba[54] correspondence seems, in fact, to have opened the series, as in the end of the first letter Seridus himself breaks in to explain the doubts he had had of his capacity to write down from memory all that Varsanuphius told him—he regretted not having paper and ink to take it down by dictation. But the Great Old Man assured him that the Holy Spirit would enable him to remember it all. The story that then unfolds itself is that of John's coming down, after some years' delay, from Beersheba to Thavatha, and of his gradual progress to the life of a recluse—in which we leave him. It would be tempting to identify John of Beersheba with the Other Old Man but for two mentions of a distinct Other Old Man John in the course of these same letters.[55]

The next letter is a solitary one to an Egyptian old man Abramius, who had written his question in Coptic.[56] Varsanuphius, himself of course a Copt, explained that he had set himself the rule never to write with his own hand, but always by way of Seridus, who did not know Coptic, and so must write in Greek.

It is impossible here to give more than a brief suggestion of the character of the whole collection. There are answers to monks of very varied calibre, often so many to one man that the whole story of his spiritual development is revealed to us, with all its ups and downs. There are letters to devout laymen. And there are letters to bishops. On the whole, while the two fathers are very much of one mind, Varsanuphius takes a wider sweep and goes deeper, while John is more occupied with practical detail, and is sometimes found interpreting Varsanuphius' answers to a questioner who finds them a little beyond him. One set of thirteen questions and answers is between Varsanuphius and an old man Euthymius whose mind is extremely active with allegorical interpretation of Scripture.[57] Varsanuphius pays him back in his own coin, sometimes in a highly fantastic manner, and finally tells him to enter into quiet and not to worry him with any more questions. But when the same Euthymius died, the Great Old Man seems to have reverenced his relics as those of a saint.[58] Then there is a moving correspondence of about fifty letters from the two Old Men to the old sick monk Andrew,[59] who is worried at not being able to keep the ordinary rule of the community, and who finds it hard to get on with the brother appointed to wait on him. It is, incidentally, worth noting how often the Great Old Man is asked to give a monk a personal Rule of Life, and refuses to do so—'for I want you to live not under the Law but under Grace'.

There are answers about how to distinguish between thoughts that come from God, from our nature, and from the demons.[60] There is a rebuke to some monks asking who gave the devil his rule and power[61]—'you should not be meddling with unnecessary questions'—and then the Old Man himself reasons about it quite a bit, and finishes up, 'Forgive me, who have been drawn down by childish questions, and left the search for perfection: my children, may the Lord Jesus Christ bless and increase your fruits unto the ages of ages'. There is an answer of the Great Old Man to a question which might follow on a reading of a passage of Cassian, whether the Lord's Prayer is only for the perfect:[62] 'It was set both for the perfect and for sinners, that the perfect knowing whose sons they have become may be zealous not to fall away from Him, and the sinners may be ashamed, calling Him Father whom they have often treated with insult, and may come to repentance. But as I suppose, it befits rather the sinners: for to say "Forgive us our debts" belongs to sinners.'

An answer to one who, after a long correspondence, asks about the final quiet, deserves quotation:[63] 'May the Lord Jesus, the Son of the blessed God most high, empower and strengthen you for the receiving of His Holy Spirit, that He may come and by His good presence teach you about all things, and enlighten your hearts and guide you in all truth: and may I see you flourishing as palm-trees in the paradise of my Father and God: and may you be found as a fruit-laden olive-tree in the midst of the Saints, and as a fruitful vine in the divine place, all true. And may the Lord count you worthy to drink of the Well of Wisdom. For already as many as have drunk thereof have forgotten themselves, becoming all outside the old man: and from the Well of Wisdom they have been guided to another Well, of Love which never faileth. And coming to this rank, they have attained to the unwandering and undistracted measure, becoming all mind, all eye, all living, all light, all perfect, all gods. They have toiled, they have been magnified, they have been glorified, they have been clarified, they have lived, since first they died. They are gladdened and make glad. They are gladdened in the Indivisible Trinity, and they make glad the Heavenly Powers. Desire their rank, run their race, be zealous for their faith, obtain their humility, their endurance in all things, that you may win their inheritance. Hold to their Love which fails not, that you may be found with them in the good things that none can utter, where eye hath not seen nor ear heard, neither hath entered into the heart of man, what God hath prepared for those that love Him. But as to quiet—for the present train thyself yet a little, and God works His mercy. God will enlighten your hearts to understand the meanings herein contained. For they are hard of understanding to him who has not come to their measure. Forgive me, and pray for me, that I may not fall short of this measure, unworthy though I be.'

The Other Old Man is more apt to be the one to give answers on liturgical questions, and questions about measure in food and wine and clothing and sleep and times of prayer. One illuminating answer about Hours of Prayer expounds the old Egyptian tradition:[64] 'Hours and Canticles are Church traditions, and good for the concert of all the people, and likewise in coenobia for the concert of the multitude. But the Scetiotes have no Hours and say no Canticles, but in solitude have their handiwork and meditation, and a little prayer. And standing to prayer you should entreat to be ransomed and set free from the old man, or say the *Our Father which art in heaven*, or both, and sit down to your handiwork. But as to extending the prayer when you stand up, if you *pray without ceasing* according to the Apostle, you should not extend it when you rise up: for all through the day your mind is at prayer. But if you are sitting to your handiwork, you should be learning by heart or saying psalms, and at the end of each psalm pray sitting down, "God have mercy upon wretched me", or if thoughts are troubling you, add, "God, Thou seest my affliction; help me". So when you have worked three rows in your net, rise up to pray, and bow the knee, and do likewise, and stand up and make the prayer aforesaid. As to Vespers, the Scetiotes say twelve psalms, at the end of each in place of the doxology saying *Alleluia*, and making one prayer: and likewise also at night twelve psalms. But after the Psalms, they sit down to their handiwork, and whoever wishes recites by heart, and whoever wishes searches out his own thoughts and the *Lives of the Fathers*. And when reading, he reads five or eight leaves, then turns to his handiwork. But when singing psalms, or learning by heart, he ought to recite them through his lips, unless anyone else is near and he wants to take care that no-one should learn what he is doing.' Much here is reminiscent of Cassian, whose works may well have been known to the Old Men—they were early translated into Greek.

About a hundred answers[65] are to a certain Dorotheus, showing us his growth from his first coming to the coenobium, asking how to divide his possessions between it and the poor. We are shown very fully his temptations of fornication, accidie, forgetfulness, etc., all dealt with very understandingly by both Old Men—mostly by John, whose attendant he became. In the course of time he was put in charge of the Hospital, and there come questions whether he is to read and depend on medical books, how he is to adjust himself between the needs of the Hospital and the regular hours of psalmody, etc.

One of the most revealing pictures of the life at Thavatha is contained, not in this collection, but in MSS. of the works of this Dorotheus. It is the story of the first disciple entrusted to his care[66]— the boy Dositheus, who had been a general's favourite, then went up to Jerusalem and had a vision in Gethsemane of the Mother of God telling him to leave that life and become a monk. He came down to Thavatha, still in a soldier's uniform, and was accepted by Seridus with some hesitation lest he should be a runaway, but became a pattern of obedience in the hospital service, though apparently never quite getting over his volubility and loud voice—'shouting like a Goth', he was told. He learned by a gradual process to reduce his daily ration of bread from six pounds to eight ounces. It is perhaps not surprising to find the boy dying of consumption after five years. But therein again he showed his obedience, waiting for the permission of the Great Old Man before dying. There are questions and answers in the Varsanuphius collection which seem to belong to this same story.

But we must pass on. An extremely interesting correspondence with an intellectual monk who has been reading Origen, Didymus, and the *Centuries of Evagrius* (from which he quotes) takes us right into the Origenist controversy then going on.[67] Part of this has been published in Migne (*P.G.* LXXXVI. i, 891–902), but only from a single Paris MS.[68] which breaks off in the middle. After Varsanuphius' condemnation of the errors, John qualifies this by saying that there are parts of Evagrius' works which can be read for the soul's profit. When it is asked how Gregory of Nyssa could seem to countenance some of the errors, the Great Old Man answers that the Saints were infallible when they spoke after praying about the question at issue; but often they would speak without thinking, in the tradition in which they had grown up—and then they might take over mistakes from their teachers.

Correspondence with bishops includes some about ordinations. For instance, the point is made that not more clergy should be ordained for a village than the village needs, even though the candidates proposed are worthy.[69] One set of letters apparently shows us the Patriarch Peter of Jerusalem in correspondence with the Great Old Man: and in one of these the question is what to do about the number of pagans coming in to seek baptism, as a result of Justinian's Edict, after Easter in A.D. 529.[70] The Patriarch is told to baptize them 'on the Holy Fortieth Day at the Holy Ascension' (i.e. on Ascension Day on the Mount of Olives), so that they will still have a week of feasting before Pentecost. Preparation for baptism must have been whittled down a lot since the days of St. Cyril of Jerusalem.

The next question concerns a pagan who has been caught at the Liturgy of the Faithful:[71] many say that he ought to be put to death, perhaps burnt. The saint naturally answers that that would not be Christian behaviour: but he should be given a hiding and fined— for these are things that touch a man—and be handed over to a God-fearing man to be taught the way of God, and so be baptized.

Another letter of which the question is missing from the printed edition is illuminating; in the course of some trouble with the Duke, there comes the question beginning, 'Since the Duke has lately become a Christian by zeal of the Christ-loving Emperor . . .'.[72]

Questions from laymen are of great variety, and we can hardly touch on them here—questions about working on Sunday,[73] talking in church,[74] slaves,[75] debts,[76] locusts:[77] can I let a Jew tread out my wine-press?[78] What shall I do when my father *will* talk unedifyingly about fleshly things?[79] Is it wrong to get somebody to put a spell on my horse when it is sick?[80] (Certainly, that is forbidden by God: get the vet to prescribe; and pour holy water on the beast.) I have rich relations near at hand, and some poor relations from a distance are coming to stay with me: it will offend my rich relations if I proclaim the relationship: need I?[81] If somebody tells me to anathematize Nestorius and his fellow-heretics, shall I?[82] (He deserves it: but your job is to mourn for your sins. But if after explanations your inquisitor still persists, anathematize Nestorius for his conscience's sake). If I am asked to anathematize someone when I do not know whether he is a heretic, what shall I do?[83] (Say, 'I cannot anathematize anyone without knowing what he teaches: but I can assure you that I know no other Faith than that of the 318, and whosoever thinks otherwise than that has cast himself under anathema').

When the Plague came ravaging the Roman Empire in A.D. 542–3, the Abbot and the Fathers of the coenobium appealed to the Old Man to stand like Aaron between the living and the dead, and received the answer[84] that there were only three in the world who had exceeded human measure, and for the sake of whose prayers God was joining mercy to His chastisement—John in Rome, Elias in Corinth, and another in the Province of Jerusalem.

.   .   .   .   .

Among the laymen who were in constant touch with the Old Men, and to whom questions are attributed in our collection, was one Aelianus. At last he was wanting to become a monk, but was hesitant about the disposal of his property and of his old mother and his slaves—Should he send her to live with her nephews, and hand over a property to them to pay for her keep?[85] While he was still delaying, Abba Seridus died, bequeathing the headship of the monastery to all the brethren in succession—when the first died, the second should succeed him, and so on. At the end of the list he added the name of the Christ-loving Aelianus if he should become a monk. One after another, the brethren humbly declined the office, until only Aelianus was left. He meanwhile, knowing nothing of this, was afflicted with despondency, and wrote to Abba John about that—but the answer he received was all about absolute obedience.[86] Aelianus could not see the relevance of this, though he found himself relieved of his despondency. Thereupon the Old Man wrote to him clearly, telling him to accept the office of Abbot. He replied, 'Abba, the Spirit of God that dwells in you knows me better than I know myself. And I am in fear and trembling because of the danger of the matter. If you know that I am able to find mercy in this, having your protection in Christ, I will not gainsay you. For you have authority over me, and I am in God's hands and yours.' Receiving once more assurance and command from the Old Man, he replied, 'Behold your servant. *Be it unto me according to thy word.*'

At the bidding of the Fathers, he was clothed in the monastic habit. Then there was a request from all the Community to the Bishop, and he was ordained priest, and so was made hegumen of the monastery, and for the first time was allowed to come to Abba

John himself. The Old Man, who was not a priest, received him
as he had been used to receive the late abbot, saying to him, 'Pray,
Abba'. Aelianus stood in embarrassment, not daring to pray over
him. When the Old Man said it a second time, Aelianus, not to
gainsay him, prayed, and, being bidden, sat down. The Old Man
said to him, 'Brother, a long time ago the Holy Old Man foretold
about you that you were going to become a monk, and hegumen of
the coenobium. Therefore *take heed to thyself*, and may thy heart
be made firm in the Lord which strengtheneth thee. Amen.'[87]

Now John in his turn announced that he would complete his life
a week after Seridus.[88] As the Great Old Man was no longer giving
answers, the brethren begged John not to leave them orphans. But
he replied: 'If Abba Seridus had remained, I could have stayed
another five years. But since God hid it from me, and took him,
I shall stay no longer.' Abba Aelianus with prayers and tears
worried the Great Old Man to let them have John longer. Hearing
of this, John forestalled Aelianus next day, when they came down to
entreat him, with the words, 'Why do you go on troubling the
Old Man about me? Do not put yourself out, for I am not staying.'
At last Aelianus begged him to remain two weeks, so that he might
question him about the monastery and its administration: and the
Old Man had compassion, and was moved by the Holy Spirit in-
dwelling in him to say, 'Well, then, you can have me for the two
weeks'. So Aelianus stayed, questioning him about everything.

Some of these questions and answers are found in our collection.[89]
They include one about Aelianus' old mother, who had refused his
proposal that she should go and live with her nephews.[90] He was
told that it was his duty to speak with her from time to time, and to
look after her needs, whether she chose to stay in the village of
Thavatha or in the city. So long as she lived, he was to look after
the material needs of his slaves, as well as their training. On her
death, he was to emancipate them, making reasonable provision for
their keep either in Thavatha village or elsewhere as he might
think fit.

When the fortnight drew to its close, the Old Man, having bidden
them not to make known his falling asleep until the day, called
together the brethren and all who happened to be in the coenobium,
greeted each one, and blessed them, then having dismissed them, he
gave up his spirit in peace to God.[91]

Varsanuphius at the same time shut himself up completely from
the world. Fifty years or so later, the historian Evagrius[92] wrote

that he was still believed to be alive there, though during all that time he had received no food and been seen by no-one: when Eustochius, who was Patriarch of Jerusalem from A.D. 552 to A.D. 563, would not believe this, and ordered the Great Old Man's cell to be opened up, fire came out and almost consumed the whole assembled company.

History tells us no more of Aelianus. Survival of the monastery into the seventh century is indicated by the mention in the *Life of St. John the Almoner* of a monastery of Abba Seridon (*sic*) by Gaza.[93] Dorotheus, who may perhaps be the editor of the *Questions and Answers*, went off to found his own monastery elsewhere.[94]

Dorotheus also appears to have been responsible for the surviving collection of sayings of the *Abba Zosimas*,[95] a monk from Phoenicia who settled near Caesarea after some time in the Lavra of St. Gerasimus in the Jordan Plain. We learn from the historian Evagrius[96] that Zosimas while at Caesarea had clairvoyant knowledge of the great earthquake at Antioch at the time of its occurrence in A.D. 526.

Evagrius also tells us of the occasion when Zosimas was travelling with a donkey laden with his possessions, and a lion came and ate the donkey. When the lion had had enough, the saint explained to him that he was an old man, and had not strength to carry the donkey's burden. So the lion obediently let the saint load the burden onto his back, and carried it for him to the gates of Caesarea.

One saying of Zosimas is worth quoting for its balanced appreciation of the human body:[97] 'It is not having a thing that harms us, but being attached to it. Who does not know that the body is the most precious of all our possessions? How then are we bidden, when occasion demands, to despise it? And if the body itself, so much more also the things that are external to us.'

Abba Dorotheus has himself left us a body of ascetical works in the tradition of his masters, Varsanuphius and John, but in fact far better known in the West, appearing in Migne's Patrology (*P.G.* LXXXVIII, 1611–1844). This, as has recently been pointed out in the article on Dorotheus in the *Dictionnaire de Spiritualité*, and at greater length by Dom Lucien Régnault of Solesmes in the *Revue d'Ascétique et de Mystique* (No. 130, April-June, 1957; pp. 141–9) is due to their discovery and use by the first generation of Jesuits, on whom they seem to have had considerable influence, being among the short list of books approved to be read by novices entering the Society.

NOTES TO CHAPTER VII

[1] *V.S.* c. 75 (180. 2–6): for the controversial date, see ch. VI, n. 153.

[2] c. 63 (164. 20–4).

[3] c. 75 (180. 9–181. 2).

[4] ibid. (181. 14–18).

[5] *V.E.* c. 49 (71. 11–20): *V.J.H.* 216. 8–17.

[6] *V.J.H.* 217. 12–21.

[7] *V.E.* c. 49 (71. 20–7): *V.J.H.* 216. 10–15.

[8] *V.S.* c. 36 (124. 21–125. 15).

[9] A. L. Frothingham, Jr., *Stephen Bar-Sudaili the Syrian Mystic*, Leyden, 1886.

[10] Ed. F. S. Marsh, for the Text and Translation Society, Williams & Norgate, 1927. See Guillaumont, *Évagre le Pontique*, II. 4 (pp. 302–32).

[11] *V.S.* c. 36 (125. 15–23).

[12] c. 72 (176. 7–20). Leontius appears already as apocrisiarius of the Judaean monks in conversations with the Monophysites in A.D. 532 (*Act. Conc.* IV. 2, p. 170. 5), and again five times in those of May–June, A.D. 536—see Schwartz, *K. von Sk.*, 388–91. The question of his identity with the writer—or one of the writers—bearing his name is not yet finally answered.

[13] *V.S.* c. 83.

[14] c. 84 (189. 10–14). The Palestinian-Georgian Calendar (3rd Jan., p. 124), together with Cyril's somewhat ambiguous phraseology, make it most probable that Melitas died in January, and was succeeded immediately by the other Isaurian brother, Theodulus, then on his death, perhaps in September, by Gelasius. If Cyril is right in stating that Melitas' rule had extended into a fifth year, his death must fall in A.D. 537, and Gelasius' accession in the autumn of that year—which would put Cyril's indictional dating (beginning of the 15th Indiction), as usual for this period, just one year out.

[15] *V.S.* c. 84.

[16] c. 85. Justinian's edict against Origen, *P.G.* 86. 1, 945–94. The date (A.D. 542 or 543) is in dispute, for the usual reason.

[17] *V.S.* c. 86.

[18] *V.E.* c. 49: *V.J.H.* c. 20 (216. 20–217. 13). For the date, see Stein, *A.B.* 62, pp. 172–4.

[19] *V. Cyr.* c. 11.

[20] *V.S.* c. 86 (193. 21–194. 12).

[21] *V. Cyr.* 3 (224. 3–12).

[22] 6 (225. 25–226. 3).

[23] 6–7 (226. 3–22).

[24] 7 (226. 22–5).

[25] 7–8 (226. 26–227. 6).

[26] 8 (227. 6–17).

[27] 8–9 (227. 18–228. 8).

[28] 9–10 (228. 9–19).

[29] 10 (228. 20–30).

[30] 10 (228. 30–229. 6).

[31] 11–14 (229. 7–231. 19).

[32] 15 (231. 20–26): cf. *V.E.* cc. 19, 21, 22, 28.

[33] *V.S.* c. 87.

[34] c. 88.

[35] c. 89.

[36] *V. Cyr.* 15 (231. 27–232. 2).

[37] 15–16 (232. 3–25).

[38] *V.S.* c. 89 (197. 7–18).

[39] Ibid. (197. 24–198. 6). See Stein, *A.B.* 62, pp. 176–7.

[40] c. 90 (198. 7–14).

[41] Ibid. (198. 14–199. 6).

[42] Ibid. (199. 6–200. 3). See Stein, *A.B.* 62, pp. 174–6: but in this case his arguments (for A.D. 555 as against 554) are perhaps not quite so conclusive: the eight months' delay before the expulsion of the Origenists from the Nea Lavra does correspond very suggestively with the interval between the end of the Council and February, A.D. 554.

[43] *V.E.* c. 60.

[44] *V.S.* cc. 75 (181. 3–18) and 82 (187. 22–4): *V.J.H.* 217. 21–3.

[45] *V.J.H.* 217. 2–23.

[46] 222. 8–12.

[47] *V. Cyr.* 20 (234. 24–30).

[48] 21 (235. 9–16).

[49] *P.E.F.Q.S.*, July 1929, M. Marcoff and D. J. Chitty, *Monastic Research in the Judaean Wilderness*, pp. 171–5.

[50] Ibid. pp. 175–6. On a subsequent visit in October 1930, Mr. Marcoff and I obtained photographs of the cell.

[51] See Garitte, *Réminiscences de la Vie d'Antoine dans Cyrille de Scythopolis*—Silloge bizantina in onore di Silvio G. Mercati (Rome 1957), pp. 117–22.

[52] Thavatha is named as the site of the monastery of Seridos in, e.g., MS. Par. gr. 1596, p. 609—published by Nau in *P.O.* IV, p. 176. This story shows it to have been beyond a river, clearly the River of Gaza, and fits well with its identification with Et Tût, marked on Bartholomew's Quarter-Inch Map of Palestine a mile and a half south-west of the river, and half a mile from the sea.

[53] QR 61.

[54] The printed text, and some late MSS., have Μηρωσάβης—probably representing that the monastery of Mar Saba was meant. In older MSS. the B is quite indubitable.

[55] QR 3 and 9.

[56] QR 55.

[57] QR 151–67.

[58] R 174.

[59] QR 168–216.

[60] QR 60.

[61] QR 63.

[62] QR 71: cf. Cassian, *Coll.* IX. 18.

[63] QR 120. Hausherr quotes this in his article on 'Barsanuphe' in *Dictionnaire de Spiritualité*.

[64] QR 74.

[65] QR 252–338 and a number of others.

[66] Text in *Orientalia Christiana*, XXVI (1932), pp. 89–123; *Dorothée de Gaza* (*Sources Chrétiennes* 92), pp. 122–43. English translation in *The Christian East*, Vol. II New Series, no. 2, pp. 57–64.

[67] QR 600–7.

[68] MS. Coislinianus 281.

[69] QR 815.

[70] QR 821.

[71] QR 822 (reading ὥρᾳ τῶν πιστῶν, not χώρᾳ).

[72] QR 839.

[73] QR 751.

[74] QR 737–8.

[75] QR 765, 649, 653–7.

[76] QR 620, 672–4.

[77] QR 685.

[78] QR 687.

[79] QR 767.

[80] QR 753.

[81] QR 764.

[82] QR 700–1.

[83] QR 702.

[84] QR 569.

[85] QR 571–3.

[86] QR 574 and preceding narrative.

[87] QR 575.

[88] QR 224.

[89] QR 576–98.

[90] QR 595.

[91] QR 224.

[92] Evagr. *H.E.* IV. 33.

[93] *V. Joh. El.* c. 36 (69. 21 and 75. 13).

[94] *Dorothée* (*SC* 92), pp. 146 (Instr. 1, tit.), 288 (§80 = *P.G.* 88, 1697b): J. Moschus, c. 166 (*P.G.* 87, 3033a).

[95] Published incomplete in *P.G.* 78 (1680–1701). The only complete edition is that published in Jerusalem by the monk Avgoustinos in 1913.

[96] Evagr. *H.E.* IV. 7.

[97] *P.G.* 78, 1681ab.

VIII

THE END OF THE PAX ROMANA

WHEN Cyril of Scythopolis wrote his *Life of St. John the Hesychast* in A.D. 557, while John was still alive at the Great Lavra, he inspired a monk whose links were with an older foundation—the Old Lavra of St. Chariton—to write the Life of its founder, who had come to Palestine over a century before Euthymius. We have entered on a retrospective age—and one in which legend has a larger part. The writer of this *Life of St. Chariton* might be identical with a St. John of the Old Lavra of whom we only know the name. The only MS. that is known to name the writer identifies him with 'John the son of Xenophon and brother of Arcadius'.[1] These saints are the heroes of a monastic novel of the two brothers going by sea from Constantinople to study law at Beirut, being shipwrecked on the way and parted and becoming monks independently—John is, in fact, said to have gone to Souka. In the end, father and sons are miraculously brought together on Calvary, recognize each other, and all settle down as hermits—and 'live happily ever after'. The best MSS., though not those that have been used in publication, begin the story with 'A certain great old man related to me'.[2]

This opening at once takes us into the world of John Moschus, the great anthologist of the Deserts, whose *Leimonarion*—'Spiritual Meadow'—is characterized with stories beginning with such a formula. John Moschus went out from the Judaean monasteries to travel widely through Palestine, Egypt, Sinai, Syria, and at last westwards to Samos and to Rome. The work is, indeed, an anthology such as he describes in his preface[3]—roses, lilies and violets gathered at random, and woven into a garland with little semblance of order; pedigree stories in large measure, going back in some cases over a century and a half, and only rarely relating the writer's own experiences. Here we find the earliest version of the story of Gerasimus' lion[4]—surely another monastic novel, most of the details of which could have been drawn from other better authenticated stories about lions in Cyril of Scythopolis. Two other chapters at least give independent but less reliable versions of anecdotes related also by Cyril.[5] Six chapters of the printed text belong rightly to the collection of anecdotes of the Abba Zosimas.[6] To others, Anastasius of Sinai has some claim.[7] On the other hand, it seems probable that a critical edition may be able considerably to increase the number of anecdotes that can reasonably be attributed to Moschus.[8] In such a collection, it is not easy to piece together Moschus' own story.

The earliest definite autobiographical information he gives us shows him spending ten years at the Lavra of Fara about A.D. 570.[9] The interval since the events described by Cyril of Scythopolis is not a long one. Conon was still hegumen of Mar Saba.[10] Eustace, whom Moschus met as hegumen of the coenobium of the Cave of St. Sabas,[11] had entered on that office a few days before Cyril wrote the *Life of St. John the Hesychast*.[12] Leontius, hegumen of St. Theodosius, told Moschus that he had gone to the New Lavra on the expulsion of the Origenists[13]—therefore in Cyril's company. Eustochius had been ousted from the Patriarchate in A.D. 563-4, and his rival Macarius restored to his throne on renouncing his Origenism.[14] It seems that, even so, not all the Judaean monks were ready to accept Macarius[15]—though their reasons were not always doctrinal. In one case, Julian the blind monk of St. Theodosius was reassured on consulting St. Symeon the New Stylite of the Wonderful Mountain near Antioch. Macarius retained his throne for close on twenty years.

Fara had had for hegumen one Gregory, who in the year A.D. 564 was insistent on visiting an anchorite Sergius, recently come from Sinai to the desert of Rouba by the Dead Sea.[16] Sergius' Armenian disciple, another Sergius, was scandalized to see the unique marks of respect paid to Gregory by his master. But the latter assured him that he had seen the visitor accoutred as a Patriarch, with omophorion and Gospel. Sure enough, six years later, after a brief period as hegumen of Sinai,[17] Gregory became Patriarch of Antioch, and held that office until his death in A.D. 593.[18]

By A.D. 578—the beginning of the reign of Tiberius—Moschus was in Egypt, and visiting the Oasis (of Khargah).[19] He met there a Cappadocian monk Leo, who told him, 'I am going to be a king'. Not long afterwards, the Mazices raided the Oasis, and took captive three monks, none of them in good condition. When the authorities could not raise the ransom demanded, Leo offered himself in place of part of the money, saying he was in good health. He was accepted, and the three released. But soon his health gave way, and he was beheaded—and so earned, indeed, his crown.

It must have been not long before or after this that the Mazices once more invaded Scetis, and its four monastic centres (they are now called 'lavras' like the Palestinian monasteries) were practically abandoned for a generation.[20] When Moschus came to Terenuthis, an Alexandrian Abba Theodore told him, 'Indeed, my child, the monks have lost Scetis, as the Old Men foretold'.[21] He went on to speak of the charity, asceticism, and discernment of the Scetiotes, and of old men there who would never eat anything except to comply with the law of hospitality. One such, Ammonius, had been a neighbour of his: so, knowing this practice, he had made a point of calling on him every Saturday, to ensure his eating. Clearly the old character of Scetis had remained little changed. Its abandonment was recent enough for the exploits of its Old Men still to fill the stories told to Moschus. John of Petra told him how, when he had been there as a young man, one of the fathers had trouble in his spleen, and no vinegar could be found in all the four lavras: he gave the number of the fathers in those days as about 3,500.[22] As of old, they would take their wares up to sell at Alexandria or Terenuthis.[23] As of old, at harvest time they would go up to work in the fields of the Delta for a daily wage.[24] One day Abba David, at noon in the heat of the sirocco, went into a hut for a short siesta. The farmer found him there and was angry: 'Why aren't you working, old man? Don't you know that I pay you?' The old man explained that in the great heat the grains were falling out of the ears, and he was waiting a bit, so that the farmer should not suffer loss. The farmer would not listen: 'Get up and work, even if it is all burnt up'. 'Do you want it all burnt up?' says the old man. 'Yes', says the farmer in anger, 'I told you so'. The old man got up, and at once the field caught fire. The farmer in a fright went and begged the other old men to plead for him with David, who answered, 'He said himself it should be burnt up'. Nevertheless, he gave way, and went and stood between the burnt and the unburnt in prayer, and the fire was quenched.

Another anecdote related by John of Petra tells of a visit of Abba Daniel the Egyptian to Terenuthis with his wares.[25] This turns us aside from Moschus to a whole cycle of stories, in Greek, Coptic, and Syriac,[26] in which Daniel appears as the central figure in Scetis—the 'hegumen' of the whole valley.[27] The Greek stories would seem to be the original: they are pieced together in the Coptic, with additions, into a continuous Life. In the Greek, Daniel is assumed to be Chalcedonian: the Coptic additions show him suffering persecution for his opposition to the Council.[28] We cannot say for certain which is correct—but it may be surmised that later

presuppositions have assumed a sharper cleavage than was always
to be found at this stage. There is, however, strong reason to doubt
the historical veracity of several of the stories, though the picture
they give of the life in Egypt and the Egyptian deserts at this time
seems firsthand and reliable. The earliest story shows Daniel in
Scetis from boyhood, but three times in his early years taken captive
in barbarian raids.[29] The first time, he was ransomed after two years
by a sea captain; the second time, he escaped after six months; the
third time, his escape involved his throwing a stone and killing one
of his captors. Penitent for the murder, he confessed it to Timothy
the Pope of Alexandria (the only possible Timothy seems to be
Timothy III, 519–36, an opponent of Chalcedon), who told him
he need not worry—he had only slain a wild beast. Unsatisfied, he
went in turn to the Pope of Rome, the Patriarch of Constantinople,
the Archbishop of Ephesus, the Patriarchs of Antioch and Jerusalem,
only to receive the same answer. Finally, he returned to Alexandria,
and gave himself up to the civil authorities as a murderer. After
thirty days in prison, he was brought before the governor. But
when he gave the facts truthfully, the governor dismissed the case:
'Go away and pray for me, Abba. I wish you had killed seven more
of them.' Deciding that after all God in His goodness was not going
to reckon the murder against him, he vowed all the days of his life
from henceforth to have one cripple in his care.

The next story involving precise dates shows Daniel telling how,
when he was a young man in the reign of Justin I, forty years ago,
he had prayed for wealth for a hospitable quarry-man, Eulogius, in
a village up the Nile.[30] Eulogius had then found a cave full of
treasure, had gone with the treasure to Constantinople, and become
patrician and praefect—but became involved with Hypatius and
Pompeius in the Nika Revolt, and fled back to his Egyptian village
with his wealth confiscated and a price on his head. Pretending that
the proscribed praefect was quite a different Eulogius, he returned to
his quarrying and his old hospitality, and lived on to be over a
hundred when Daniel revisited him, about A.D. 565. The story is
full of vivid and edifying detail—but falls to the ground historically,
as the careers and names of the praefects at Constantinople, both
urban and praetorian, are known, and do not include Eulogius.

Yet another story with indications of date shows Daniel going
eighteen miles out beyond Scetis to the death and burial of an
anchorite, the 'eunuch' Anastasius[31]—and revealing to his disciple,
on his discovering that it was a woman, that this was the patrician

lady Anastasia, who had fled from the jealousy of Theodora to found a monastery 'of the Patrician Lady' at the Fifth Mile from Alexandria. When Theodora died, and Justinian sought to bring Anastasia back to the palace, she had appealed to Daniel, who had dressed her as a monk, and placed her in the cell where, after twenty-eight years, she died. As Theodora died in A.D. 548, this would bring us at earliest to A.D. 576—which cannot have been long before the abandonment of Scetis. But it is difficult not to link the patrician lady Anastasia with the lady of that name otherwise known to history—the wife of Pompeius, who had frequented Sabas on his visit to Constantinople in A.D. 511-12, and retired after her husband's execution to the religious life on Olivet, where Cyril of Scythopolis consulted her, about A.D. 554, for facts for his life of St. Sabas.[32] The theme of the eunuch ascetic who proved on death to be a woman was a favourite theme at this time: the legend of Hilaria the daughter of the Emperor Zeno is one example among many.[33]

Another instance is found in the Daniel cycle—that of the Antiochene silversmith Andronicus and his wife Athanasia,[34] who betake themselves after the death of their two children to the religious life, he in Scetis, she in a Tabennesiote convent. Twelve years later, on the way to the Holy Places, he meets her as the monk Athanasius making the same pilgrimage, and fails to recognize her, though she knows him. They settle together at the Eighteenth Mile (from Alexandria) for another twelve years: and only at her death does Andronicus discover that Athanasius was his wife Athanasia.

For a picture of life (and not only monastic life) in Egypt and her deserts in the sixth century, the collection of stories is invaluable, and surely reliable, and written by a contemporary. If even for that time it cannot be regarded as strictly historical, we have just to note again that the fictional character seems to be a mark of the period. We may perhaps notice that the least reliable stories are those told to the disciple by the Old Man himself, not those told about him. The geographical setting is well brought out—Nitria and the Cells mentioned just once,[35] Scetis the great centre; but the centres along the road westward from Alexandria, at the Fifth,[36] Ninth,[37] and Eighteenth[38] Mile, much more in the limelight, and the way to Scetis not so much by Nitria or Terenuthis as the western route by the City of St. Menas,[39] whence they would leave with donkeys in the late afternoon, and travel through the night, to reach their destination by eight o'clock in the morning, before the heat of the day.

Some of Moschus' informants he met on a much later visit to Egypt. But their memories of Scetis were still vivid. At the lavra of Monidia, Marcellus,[40] a native of Apamea in Syria, told how back at his home a charioteer named Phileremus had been defeated, and his supporters cried out at him, 'Phileremus (the Desert-lover) in the city wins no palm'. Coming to Scetis, Marcellus had taken this as his motto, and it had kept him from leaving Scetis for thirty-five years, until the barbarians came and took him captive, and sold him in the Pentapolis. It was the same Marcellus who told how nothing so exasperates the demons, and Satan himself, against us as our constantly meditating the Psalms. On somewhat the same note, the Abba Irenaeus[41] told how an old man in Scetis had seen the devil in the night providing the brethren with hoes and baskets—'I am providing distraction for the brethren, thereby making them more careless in glorifying God'. He told how, when the barbarians came to Scetis, he himself had retired to the Gaza region (perhaps his home country) and taken a cell in a lavra. The hegumen gave him a *Gerontikon* (is it significant for us that this was in the Gaza region?), and he had opened it at the story of a brother asking an old man to pray for him, and being told, 'When you were with us, I used to pray for you: but now you have gone off to your own place, and I pray for you no longer'. Taking it to heart, he had returned the book to the hegumen, and himself to the Cells.

Old memories were not dead at the Cells. The story was told of a foreign monk coming there, and insisting on being given the cell of Evagrius.[42] The priest had warned him that the demon who had misled Evagrius was still there. But the brother had still insisted—and before a second Sunday came, he had hanged himself.

A story about the Cells in the *Apophthegmata*[43] takes us back before the abandonment of Scetis, when the narrator, Phocas, was still there—he subsequently went to the coenobium of St. Theognius in Judaea. It tells how there were then two churches at the Cells, one of the Chalcedonians and one of the Monophysites. A young man James, who was there with his natural father for his spiritual father (subsequently moved to Scetis),[44] was torn by the appeals of both parties. At a loss, he withdrew to a cell outside the lavra, and lay on the ground in prayer and fasting, until at the end of forty days the boy Christ appeared to him and told him, 'Where you are you are well', and immediately he found himself before the doors of the Chalcedonian Church.

The story suggests a comparatively peaceful condition, with the two parties able to live side by side. It is difficult not to conjecture that the same condition explains the rise of twin monasteries in all the four settlements in Scetis—though, of course, in later centuries all eight were monophysite. One such pair survives, the Monastery of the Syrians being the 'Theotokos' twin of the monastery of Psois. At one time all three other monasteries—that of Macarius, that of the Roman Brethren, and the now extinct monastery of John the Short—had 'Theotokos' monasteries beside them.[45]

As we have said, most of the stories of Egypt were probably told to Moschus on a longer visit later. He was certainly on Sinai by A.D. 590,[46] probably not long after A.D. 580. If the Lavra of the Aeliotes,[47] where he spent ten years,[48] was a Jerusalem colony on Sinai—this cannot be called certain—we may suppose he was there from A.D. 584 to A.D. 594, when he went with his hegumen to Jerusalem for the enthronement of the Patriarch Amos.[49] John, the Patriarch who had succeeded Macarius in A.D. 583, and was dead, with his successor not yet appointed, when the historian Evagrius was writing in A.D. 593, had been an 'acoemete' monk (perhaps in Constantinople).[50] Moschus tells of his making a cistern near the Aeliote Lavra[51]—on Sinai, if the Greek text is correct: but the Latin has 'Sigma' for Sinai, and in that case we might look for the site somewhere nearer Jerusalem. John's successor had also been a monk —perhaps on Sinai, as Moschus speaks of his coming *down* to Jerusalem. But he underwent a reaction against monasticism.[52] When a monk who had fallen to temptation was brought before him, he publicly stripped him of his angelic habit, which he put on a pig, and let the pig loose in the streets of the city. That night St. John the Baptist appeared to him: 'Man, why have you so treated my habit? I will make my suit against you in the dreadful Day of Judgment.' In a fright, the Patriarch quickly built a Church of St. John the Forerunner outside the City, to the east of St. Stephen's. But when it was completed and adorned, the Forerunner appeared to him again: 'I tell you the truth, though you build five churches for me greater than this one, I will still be against you in the dreadful Day of Judgment'. When he died, in A.D. 601, the fathers judged that his name should be erased from the diptychs of Jerusalem.

These closing years of the century would seem to have been Moschus' chief period for gathering his flowers in Palestine—in Jerusalem itself, in the Wilderness of Judaea, and in the Jordan Valley. His retrospective stories often bear evidence of having been told him during these years. With him was his younger friend Sophronius, a native of Damascus,[53] who after a sophist's training which included some knowledge of medicine,[54] had been with Moschus in Egypt, when he had not yet actually taken the monk's habit;[55] then probably on Sinai;[56] but settled down at this time to the monastic life in the coenobium of St. Theodosius.[57]

That great coenobium over the Cave of the Magi, and the Lavra of St. Sabas in the gorge of the Cedron beyond it, continue to dominate the mountainous wilderness. But, while most of the monasteries mentioned by Cyril of Scythopolis can be identified with reasonable certainty, Moschus' stories, fully confirmed by modern exploration, show that wilderness and the Jordan Valley pullulating with other unidentified monasteries. In the Jordan Valley, the lavras of the Reed-bed (Calamon)[58] and the Turrets (Pyrgia)[59] are prominent. For this half-century, by contrast with the years preceding and following, our monastic world seems free to build up its own soul-history, while the events of the outside world are recorded, but do not pierce deep into it. One monastery of which we learn much during this period is that of Choziba—the monastery hanging, within sight from one point on the Roman road to Jericho, on the precipitous northern side of the gorge of the Wadi Qelt (the one tenuous perennial stream in the wilderness) where, flowing down from Fara, it draws near to its debouchment into the Jordan Plain just south of Jericho. Along the sheer cliff-face behind it, precarious paths lead to anchorite cells. One great cave above the monastery is shown to-day as the place where Joachim came to pray for a child, and (but this is later tradition) where Elijah was fed by the ravens. At a lower level is the cave-cemetery of the monks, with very many ancient smoked graffiti upon its walls and roof, helping to indicate once more the international character of Judaean monasticism.[60] The Egyptian John was regarded as founder of its community. But we are told of five Syrians occupying the place in succession before him—the last of the five, at least, had been disciple there to his predecessor.[61] John was certainly head of the community in the 490s, when a monk expelled by St. Theodosius appealed to him, and was sent by him to St. Sabas.[62] There is a story also which suggests that he had been in relationship with Marcian of Bethlehem. Another story tells that he had been an opponent of Chalcedon, but was converted by discovering his inability to enter the Holy Sepulchre until he had accepted the Council.[63] He was metropolitan of Palestinian Caesarea by A.D. 518, when he was there to welcome

Sabas coming to announce the restoration of Chalcedon to the diptychs.[64]

To Choziba later in the century came the young Galatian pilgrim, Theodore of Sykeon, to be clothed in the monastic habit before returning to his own country[65] (after he became bishop, we find him again in Palestine on pilgrimage, then spending Lent at Mar Saba, and hoping to abandon his bishopric: but he was peremptorily ordered back in vision by St. George the Martyr).[66] Moschus has a story[67] of an old monk at Choziba who made it his task to wait on the road for travellers labouring up to Jerusalem, and to carry their burdens, sometimes their children, for them up to the Mount of Olives; or to sit down (he had a cobbler's outfit with him) and mend their worn-out shoes. But our most illuminating evidence is the *Life of St. George of Choziba*, written by his disciple Antony, with an appendix giving an account of other miracles at this monastery of the Mother of God, and some points in its history.[68] George was younger son of a small landowner in Cyprus.[69] On the death of his parents, finding himself the subject of contention between one uncle who wanted him to marry and another, to whom he had turned, who was an abbot,[70] he fled away to his elder brother Heraclides, who was already established as a monk in the Lavra of Calamon. As his beard was not yet grown, Heraclides entrusted him to the hegumen of Choziba, who in due course tonsured and clothed him,[71] and put him under a rough old Mesopotamian monk as assistant gardener. When the old man struck his apprentice for a supposed fault, the hand that struck was dried up, but was healed at the young man's prayers. This becoming known, George made haste to escape back to his brother at Calamon.[72] Here he stayed until his brother died at the age of seventy,[73] after which when strife arose over the election of a new hegumen, he returned to Choziba, asking the hegumen Leontius for lodging in the cells.[74] Being accepted, he left Calamon. Every Saturday night the cell-dwellers would come into the coenobium for the Sunday liturgy and the common meal. George would then be given by the storeman the sweepings of the tables, which he would take to his cell, pound them up, make them into balls and dry them in the sun, to eat them at two or three days' intervals as he found need.[75] Before he returned to his cell on Sunday night, brethren would take him round to bless their various works, and sometimes hold him in conversation. But he would never spend Sunday night in the coenobium. Once, when the porter, protesting, had let him out after the doors were locked for the night, an evil spirit molested him on the cliff-path to his cell, trying to throw him over, until he ordered it in the name of the Lord to carry him to his cell, and it had to obey.[76] When a brother asked what would happen if a leopard hurt him, he said that only once had anyone been hurt there by a leopard: a brother had met one on the cliff-path where there was no room to pass; as neither would make way, the brother adjured the beast in the name of the Lord Jesus Christ to give place, and at once the leopard leaped twelve feet down the cliff; the brother, showing no fear of God, threw great stones at the leopard, which, enraged, ran up another way and gave the brother two or three blows with its paw, not touching him with its teeth, and left him to be found by the brethren and taken to the hospital, where he was healed in a few days.[77]

Some time towards the end of this period, two aspirants to the monastic life, warned that the route to Rhaithou was infested with Saracen robbers, were advised to come to Choziba, where the hegumen Dorotheus received them, and tonsured them in due course. But one of them, going up with the hegumen to the Holy City, slipped off unbeknown and made his way after all to Rhaithou. His companion Antony, much distressed, contemplated following him thither.[78] Dorotheus, failing to dissuade him, appealed to George, who proved more persuasive, and from this time Antony became George's disciple and constant attendant.[79] To him we owe the saint's *Life*, written some twenty years later, when Modestus was Patriarch (i.e. in A.D. 631), and Dorotheus had become Cross-warden.[80] While historically reliable, he is not primarily a historian as Cyril of Scythopolis may be said to be. But he is more con-cerned than Cyril to enter into the spirituality of his master and convey it to us. Herein is his great value, for this is the generation which had known the old Roman security and survived its shattering by the Persians. The besetting sins of his generation he sees in pride, shown especially as ἀφοβία—lack of fear of God—and a 'contemplation falsely so called'; and judgment of our neighbour. Love and respect for God and for our neighbour are constantly urged. In a world which certainly did not undervalue dogmatic orthodoxy, we are glad to find his master's words quoted: 'For I tell you, brethren, that there is not a Greek, or a Jew, or a Samaritan, who has genuine piety and gentleness, who is not loved and found acceptable with God and with man.'[82]

. . . . .

Jerusalem continued to be established in the top of the mountains, and many nations flowed unto it. There was peace between the Roman and Persian Empires in the last years of the Emperor Maurice, giving an additional sense of security. Churches and monasteries grew in number, in wealth and adornment, with gifts and pilgrims from all over the Christian world. Typical is the Abramius who, from his own monastery in Constantinople, came to found that 'of the Byzantines' on Olivet, then was hegumen of Justinian's New Church of the Mother of God, and finally Archbishop of Ephesus.[83] The New Church, with the monastery attached to it, enjoyed something of a privileged position, became much absorbed in worldly wealth, and was apt to be a thorn in the side of the Patriarch. Its hegumen Anastasius received in A.D. 596-7 a letter of admonition from St. Gregory of Rome.[84] When Isaac succeeded Amos as Patriarch in A.D. 601, St. Gregory in replying to his synodical spoke again of this strife, as well as appealing to him to put an end to simoniacal practices.[85] It is reported that St. Gregory sent a monk to found a hostelry in Jerusalem.[86]

The September feast of the Encaenia, and the Exaltation of the Holy Cross, was the great annual proclamation of the Christian Empire, not outdone by Easter itself as a time of pilgrimage. To it belongs the story in which Sophronius (if ancient tradition is right in naming him the author) characterizes his time and place—the story of the Egyptian harlot Mary,[87] joining the pilgrimage out of curiosity, then finding herself unable to enter the place of the Cross until she has confessed and renounced her sin—and going off over Jordan, beyond sight of man, to be found after forty-seven years twenty days' journey east of Jordan by the old monk Zosimas spending Lent in the desert, and to be buried there by him, with the help of a lion, two years later. The writer claims to have put down the story as he received it from monks of Zosimas' coenobium by Jordan, to whom it had come down over generations as unwritten tradition. It is a true ikon. A whole Sunday in Lent is devoted to it in the Eastern Church. But it is hardly history.

In A.D. 602 the centurion Phocas seized the throne, executing the Emperor Maurice and his family, and instituting a period of tyranny and growing insecurity. Chosroes the Persian king was quickly on the warpath to avenge his benefactor Maurice. Rumours were rife of the survival of different members of the slaughtered family—a son in Alexandria,[88] perhaps a sister and a daughter in Jerusalem[89]—and Phocas and his henchmen were hot in pursuit. Perhaps this lies behind the report that the general Bonosus—who became hardly less hated than Phocas himself—had plotted to murder the Patriarch Isaac.[90] Meanwhile the circus factions, the Blues and the Greens, were coming in to disturb the peace of Jerusalem itself.[91] Magic in various forms was rife. Jews and monophysites were growing in hostility to the Empire. And Faith was in danger of losing its roots. The Sabaite Antiochus, of whom we shall hear more presently, tells as a warning against trust in dreams the story of a solitary on Sinai of many years' standing, who had a series of dreams that came true, and then one which showed him the people of the martyrs and apostles and all the Christians dark and filled with shame, while Moses, the prophets, and the Jews were enveloped in light, living in joy and gladness. He left the Holy Mountain, came to the Jewish settlements at Noara and Livias, on the two sides of the Jordan Valley (Noara was only three or four miles from Choziba), was circumcised, married a wife, and conducted open propaganda on behalf of the Jews against the Christians. Antiochus had seen him there, greatly venerated by the Jews as a second Abraham, not more than a year or two before the Persian invasion.[92] The story reminds us not very happily of that told by Moschus of the Mesopotamian monk on pilgrimage to Palestine, persuaded to accept Orthodox communion by a dream in which he saw Nestorius and Theodore and other heresiarchs in the flames of hell.[93]

It was probably in the early years of Phocas that Moschus and Sophronius moved out once more from Palestine to travel up to Antioch and the monasteries of Syria and Cilicia.[94] But the threat of Persian invasion soon sent them south again, to reach Egypt[95] probably some time before Heraclius overthrew Phocas, and Nicetas raised the Cypriote layman John (who became known as the Alms-giver) to the patriarchal throne of Alexandria, in A.D. 610.[96] With their learning and their counsel, the two were a great support to the new pope in his remarkably (if only temporarily) successful efforts to reconcile the Egyptians to Chalcedon.[97] Sophronius was now afflicted with a blindness which the doctors failed either to diagnose consistently or to treat. Then he appealed successfully to St. Cyrus and St. John at their shrine at Canopus,[98] and wrote in thankfulness a great collection of seventy long stories of healings at the shrine, finishing up with his own. In this extraordinary document there is much that looks like credulity, a great deal of detailed observation, medical and other, and very little that is distinctively Christian. But it shows the same rhythmical style (every sentence ending in a dactyl) which marks all the prose works of this versatile writer—alike the sermons, the *Life of St. Mary of Egypt*, and the *Synodical* in which, twenty years later, he was to make his authoritative exposition of the Faith in Christ.

The confusions of counter-revolution in which Heraclius took over the Empire from Phocas opened to Chosroes his opportunity, while depriving him of his pretext of vengeance for Maurice. Edessa had already succumbed before Phocas' death. In A.D. 611 it was the turn of Antioch. In A.D. 613 Damascus surrendered, and Palestine began to be in terror and confusion.[99] But still it seemed incredible that Jerusalem itself should be in danger. Advancing along the Phoenician coast towards Caesarea, the Persians captured two monks and led them on with the army, daily asking them what would happen to Jerusalem. Daily they answered that the Lord would defend His Holy City.[100]

When the army had reached Diospolis (Lydda) at the foot of the road up through the hills to Jerusalem, the monk Antony at Choziba came to his master George, and told him that the hegumen Dorotheus was fleeing to Arabia and wanted him (Antony) to go with him. But George insisted that it was right to stick in life or in death to the land of their renunciation: 'Though the Lord may chasten us for our sins as a compassionate and loving Father, He will not forsake His Holy City, but His eyes ever watch over it and over this land as the Land of Promise, unto the end of the world, according to His promises'. So Antony stayed on, going out to the caves with the brethren when they abandoned the monastery, and frequently in danger from Hebrews and from Saracens, but never taken, protected by the Old Man's prayers because he had obeyed his word.[101]

As the Persians approached the Holy City, they were ready to offer terms of surrender, and the Patriarch Zacharias (he had succeeded Isaac in A.D. 609, when it is said that Isaac resigned[102]) strongly urged their acceptance, to save the city from massacre and the Holy Places from destruction. But the secular authorities would not hear of it. Having failed of that, he called the hegumen of St. Theodosius, Modestus, and sent him down to Jericho to summon up the imperial forces there to help.[103] They came up, but found the city already invested, and were put to flight. Left alone, Modestus took refuge in a rock in a valley. The Persians came all round it and on top of it, but did not see him, and at last he was able to go down peacefully to Jericho.[104]

For three weeks the Persian army invested the city.[105] At the news, all the enemies of the Roman order, Saracen or Hebrew, began to roam the country in search of plunder. Dorotheus of Choziba, and Nicomedes, hegumen of St. Sabas, fled with most of their monks to Arabia.[106] Others from Choziba hid in the caves; others, among them St. George, at Calamon. The Saracens combed the valleys, pressed the old men they caught to reveal to them hidden treasure, killed one Syrian monk, a centenarian, and took others off into captivity—but something in George's bearing made them let him go, giving him a basket of bread and a pitcher of water, and telling him to save himself where he chose. So to Jericho he went.[107]

At the Great Lavra of St. Sabas, the Saracen marauders arrived a week before the fall of the city. The forty-four monks who had insisted on remaining were tortured many days to reveal hidden treasure, then slaughtered to a man.[108] A mile and a half to the north, at the dependent lavra of Heptastomus, an old man John was pressed by his disciple to tell him whether the Holy City would be delivered into the hands of the enemy. At last he told him the dream he had had five days before. He had been rapt away to find himself before Golgotha, with all the clergy and people crying 'Kyrie eleison'. The Mother of God was entreating her Son for the people, and He was rejecting them, saying, 'I will not hear them; for they have defiled my sanctuary'. Still crying 'Kyrie eleison', the people went into Constantine's Church, and John went in with the clergy. But when he went down to worship at the place of the Finding of the Cross, he saw mud coming out from it into the church. Seeing two venerable old men standing by, he asked them, 'Do you not fear God, that we cannot even pray because of the mud? Whence is this evil smell lying here?' They answered, 'From the iniquities of the clergy of this place'. Again he said, 'And can you not cleanse it, so that we may be permitted to pray?' But they told him, 'What is here will not be cleansed save by fire'. So far the vision: and the old man went on with tears, 'This also I tell thee, my child, that the sentence has gone forth that I should be beheaded; and I besought God that I might be reprieved, and He revealed to me that certainly it must be: and He alone knows that I have never shed blood upon the earth'. As they were speaking, the barbarians came upon them. The disciple fled; but they took and slew the old man, and quickly went off. The disciple returned and took him up and buried him in the cemetery of the fathers.[109]

Meanwhile the two Phoenician monks persisted in their precarious optimism. On every tower and turret of the besieged city they seemed to see an angel with shield and spear of flame. But three days before the end, an angel came down from heaven to tell those angels, 'Depart hence and withdraw: for this Holy City is delivered by the Lord into the hands of the enemy'.[110]

When at length the Persians broke in, the city was given over to massacre for three days.[111] Then the fugitives were called out of their hiding-places with a general promise of their lives.[112] Those skilled in any craft were collected together to be taken away to Persia. The rest were crowded into a concentration camp by the Pool of Mamilla—many of them to die of overcrowding, hunger and thirst, in the May heat, others to be bought by the Jews (who were in favour with the Persians as a fifth column), and offered the alternative of apostasy or death.[113] The aged Patriarch Zacharias, after being tortured with the Cross-Warden to reveal where the Cross was hidden,[114] was brought in chains to Sion to join the company for transportation. Out from the gates of Jerusalem he went like Adam out of Eden—over the Cedron, and up to Olivet. Awaiting their escort there, the company looked back to see the flames pouring heavenwards from the Church of the Resurrection, from Holy Sion, the Mother of all Churches, and from the other shrines[115]—three centuries of the best that man's wealth and skill could offer, three centuries of the aspiration of a Christian Empire, going up in smoke. Then the escorting army came to hustle them eastwards out of sight of the city, Zacharias still repeating his farewell words of peace to his home and to the sanctuaries of the Faith.[116] The captive Cross was in their company as they went down through the wilderness, past the spot which commands the first view of St. Euthymius' monastery (the spot where Eudocia had set her latest foundation); past Choziba, hanging at the foot of its cliff in the gorge deep down to the left of the road, then out onto the Plain at Jericho, across Jordan, and away to Damascus. In Jericho, one of the monks of Choziba had a vision of the Mother of God calling to the saints to hasten with her to escort the Cross upon its way.[117]

The Faith of the Cross, which took them confident in penitence on the road to captivity, had not lost the resilience of Easter. Among the survivors in Jerusalem, one Thomas was quickly undertaking the burial of the dead, in caves and tombs and mounds as best they could;[118] first seven found dead upon the altar of the Church of St. George outside the city; then 28 in the hall of the governors; 275

in cisterns; 2,270 before the gates of Holy Sion—and so on. The number at each place is given, and the total estimated in one version at 66,509, and at the lowest at 33,877. The Armenian Sebeos[119] speaks of 57,000 dead and 35,000 captives. He says also that the counting and burial of the dead was ordered by the Persians, who seem to have been wise and generous in encouraging a return to such normality as was possible. Fugitives quickly began to return, including some escaped from the Persian captivity, among them the Sabaite monk Strategius to whom we owe our main account of these events.[120] From Jericho came Modestus, to be installed as *locum tenens* of the bereaved church for the ensuing years.[121] Thence also came George, the Great Old Man of Choziba.[122] Dorotheus the hegumen and his monks stayed huddled together in the hostelry at Jericho, where George's disciple Antony was appointed cellarer (storeman). Unable to put up with the temptations and distractions of this work if they stayed in Jericho, Antony appealed in vain to Dorotheus for a return to the monastery; then went up secretly to Jerusalem to seek counsel of the Old Man. Next day, as the Old Man had foretold, two priests and a deacon came in search of Antony, reporting that Dorotheus had been persuaded, and they had returned to the monastery. So he went down with them;[123] and a few days later the Old Man himself followed.[124] But even George returned only to the coenobium, not to the outer cells.[125] For one would hardly dare now to venture into the gorge alone: since the Persians, it had become all savage with wild beasts and unclean spirits.[126]

It was the same all over the wilderness. At the Great Lavra—Mar Saba—the Abbot Nicomedes, returning with his monks from Arabia, fell down in a dead faint at the sight of the unburied bodies of the slain. Modestus came down to see to their honourable burial, and persuaded the monks not to leave the lavra. But two months later, another rumour of barbarian attack took them in flight up to the monastery of Abba Anastasius, two miles out of Jerusalem, which was then empty. There for two years they stayed. Then at Modestus' persuasion there was a return to the lavra. But some remained at the monastery of Anastasius, under its abbot Justin, himself a Sabaite of many years' standing, who gathered round him a large company keeping unchanged the rule of the lavra, so that the Sabaites rejoiced that the seed of their holy father was shining like luminaries in every country.[127] The monastery of St. Sabas on the

Aventine in Rome appears to have been founded before the end of the sixth century.[128]

Among those who returned to settle in the Great Lavra under its new hegumen Thomas[129] was a monk Antiochus. To him came an appeal from an abbot Eustace, of a monastery near Ancyra, driven similarly into wandering flight before the Persian invaders, and needing an abstract of Scriptural teaching on the religious life, in a form which he could carry about with him.[130] Antiochus replied with a letter which is our source of information for the events at Mar Saba, and a collection of 130 homilies, known as the *Pandect*, which is in fact a compendium of extracts from the Old and the New Testaments, with not a little from Ignatius of Antioch and other fathers, and a minimum of personal comment, culminating[131] in a statement of full Chalcedonian faith (in view specially of the abandonment of the throne of Antioch to the Jacobite Athanasius), anathema on a long list of heretics, and a summons to seek the Kingdom of Heaven. Gibbon in a scornful footnote speaks of the work as 'extant, if what no-one reads may be said to be extant'.[132] But it is not negligible.

The *Exomologesis*, or confession, which is appended to the work as published in Migne,[133] seems to have been written slightly earlier, when the Holy Places were still desolate. Antiochus' *Letter to Eustace* speaks of Modestus as already restoring them, like a new Zerubbabel, as well as bringing the monasteries of the wilderness back to life.[134] The Armenian Sebeos[135] shows that the work of restoration had in fact been ordered by Chosroes, who had never intended the destruction. Sebeos tells of Chosroes' expulsion of the Jews from Jerusalem at this time, which confirms the statement of Strategius making them responsible for the fires.[136] The expulsion of the Jews and their responsibility for the fires is also recorded by Modestus in his friendly exchange of letters (their text is given by Sebeos)[137] with the Armenian Patriarch Kumitas, wherein he gives thanks for the appearance of an Armenian pilgrimage, which the inclusion of both countries under the sway of Persia now made possible again as of old. Neither of the letters mentions dogma.

From another quarter of the Christian world Modestus could look for encouragement, and something more, in his remarkable work. St. John the Alms-giver not only welcomed refugees in Alexandria, and made provision for them. He appointed Ctesippus, abbot of the Enaton, to go up to Jerusalem to inspect the damage, and sent Modestus 1,000 *nomismata*, all kinds of supplies, and a thousand

Egyptian workmen—while expressly desiring that his name should not be recorded.[138] He is said to have written one of the laments for the Holy City, of which there were many at this time. We have already mentioned the *Exomologesis* of Antiochus. Another appears among the Anacreontic poems of Sophronius[139], a series of poems in the old quantitative classical metres in which this retrospective writer shows considerable competence. Sophronius and Moschus were still with the Pope John in Alexandria. But it was not long before the Persian armies were advancing into Egypt. Before they took Alexandria, the Pope John had withdrawn across the sea, to die in his native Cyprus, probably on 11th November, A.D. 617.[140] Moschus and Sophronius went with him[141]—then, on his death, westward again, to Samos,[142] and at last, it seems, to Rome. Short, summary *Lives* of John Moschus,[143] not wholly reliable, tell us that he died in Rome, and that his body was taken back by Sophronius to Jerusalem, and buried at St. Theodosius, in the Cave of the Magi, when it proved impossible to fulfil his desire that it should be taken to Sinai. As this is attributed to the 8th Indiction, it is assumed that Sophronius returned in A.D. 619–20, and settled once more at St. Theodosius.[144] But it is more probable that he remained for the present in the West, and that his return to Palestine in the 8th Indiction was in A.D. 634 and not before. We shall come back to this. But many things fall into place if our Sophronius was, indeed, he under whose direction St. Maximus was living at a monastery of the Eucratades in Africa, some time after A.D. 626.[145]

.   .   .   .   .

Meanwhile, after the arrival of the captives in Persia, the influence of the Christian (Nestorian) queen had soon gained for the Patriarch and for the Cross (its precious case remained sealed) an honourable captivity in her palace,[146] whence the Patriarch wrote an Epistle to the Church in Jerusalem.[147] But the influence of the Cross was at work in unexpected ways. Magundat, the young son of a magian priest, was fired with curiosity on being told that the captive Cross was the god of the Christians.[148] When he learned of Christ the Son of God crucified thereon, he went and attached himself to a Christian silversmith at Hierapolis (Mabbug); then to another silversmith at Jerusalem, who brought him to Elias, priest of the Anastasis. With another convert (who suffered martyrdom afterwards at Edessa) he was baptized by the *locum tenens*, and given the name of Anastasius. On expressing desire for the monastic life, he was taken by Elias to the monastery of Abba Anastasius, where the abbot Justin received him, in the tenth year of Heraclius (A.D. 620–21), giving him a master who taught him Greek and the Psalter; and in due course he was tonsured and clothed. He was there seven years, serving in the kitchen and the garden, but especially excelling in the Divine Office. His concentration on the Lives of the Martyrs seemed already to indicate a desire growing in him. At last a dream caused him to go out into the sacristy during the night office, and open his heart to the Abbot. With his understanding, he received Communion at the Liturgy, breakfasted with the fathers, and after a short sleep went out with nothing but the clothes he had on, down to the shrine of St. George at Lydda (Diospolis), then to Garizim and the other Holy Places, then to Caesarea, where he spent two days in the house of the Theotokos before finding his opportunity to court arrest and confess his conversion. He was kept waiting for three days until the arrival of the marzban, who decided to send him to the king. During the next five days before his escort was ready, he was allowed to go to church on Holy Cross Day. Abbot Justin sent two monks to visit and encourage him, and one of these accompanied him on his journey, with two other accused Christians. Twice on the journey he wrote to the abbot, asking for his prayers. He was imprisoned at Bethsaloe, six miles from Discartha (Dastgard) where the king was staying, and finally put to death on 22nd January, A.D. 628. The monk who had accompanied him, with the son of his host, secured the body, and took it to the shrine of St. Sergius, a mile away. Ten days later, on 1st February, Heraclius' army arrived. Before March was out, Chosroes, as Anastasius had predicted, had been slain by order of his son Siroes.[149] The monk went with Heraclius' army through Armenia, and returned next year to his monastery with the martyr's colobium. One more year, and Razmiozdan, the conqueror of Jerusalem, made peace with Heraclius, and restored the Cross, which Heraclius brought back in great triumph to Jerusalem in March, A.D. 631.[150] Zacharias having died in captivity, Modestus was consecrated Patriarch on the emperor's insistence,[151] while Dorotheus, the hegumen of Choziba, became Cross-warden.[152]

But the old imperial security was not recovered. Morally, there was the shock of seeing Heraclius bring with him his first-cousin Martina for wife.[153] In dogma, he was planning compromise with the Monophysites, for political reasons.[154] And the empire had already had its first clash with the new power coming out of Arabia.[155]

Modestus survived but a few months in the position which he had so richly deserved. Setting out on a mission to the emperor to make some appeal for the churches, he died (rumour said, by poison) at Sozousa on the coast of Palestine on 17th December in that same year.[156] It was, it seems, nearly three years before his successor was appointed.

At some time before or early in A.D. 633, Sophronius appears to have gone from Africa to Alexandria, having with him a sufficient library to imply the purpose of a fairly long stay—Maximus, writing to Peter the Illustrious, who had been transferred from Numidia to Egypt during this year, refers him to 'my blessed master and father and teacher, lord Abba Sophronius', and speaks of Sophronius' wealth of books as against his own poverty in them.[157] Sophronius was shocked to find Cyrus, the Pope of Alexandria, patching up (in June of that year) a reunion with the Monophysites on the basis of 'a single operation (ἐνέργεια)'. Having pleaded against this in vain with Cyrus,[158] he went to Constantinople to appeal to the Patriarch Sergius, little thinking that Sergius himself (who had been Patriarch since A.D. 610) had for years been brewing this very compromise.[159] Sophronius' vehemence seems at least to have made Sergius think again: he wrote to Pope Honorius of Rome urging an agreement to refrain from speaking of either one operation or two, and saying that Sophronius, having failed to find patristic support for speaking of two operations, had assented to this.[160] Sophronius returned at last to the Holy City, and was quickly raised to the patriarchal throne—probably at the beginning of the 8th Indiction, September, A.D. 634;[161] certainly before the end of A.D. 634.[162] Immediately he sent out his *Synodical*,[163] with a full exposition of doctrine, including a long section dealing with the 'operations' of the Incarnate Word. Here the doctrine of 'two operations' is so clearly implied again and again, that we are surprised to realize that the actual phrase is avoided. 'One only operation' is directly denied; and the 'common and theandric operation' spoken of by the Pseudo-Denys is interpreted as not really meaning a single undifferentiated operation. The *Synodical* as we have it is addressed to Sergius. It is couched in terms of trust and humility, asking for correction where it might be necessary, and showing no suspicion that Sergius would find it embarrassing. But it was, in fact, to prove a decisive document, and was quickly recognized as such on both sides. It seems finally to have convinced Maximus that

clear thinking could not allow the compromise either of 'one operation' or of 'one will' (though the latter phrase is not mentioned in
the *Synodical*), thus setting him upon the path which was to lead to
his long confessorship and his virtual martyrdom.[164]

Already in his *Synodical*, Sophronius speaks of the unforeseen
Saracen inroads.[165] By Christmas of that year, their raids were
making the five-mile journey to Bethlehem unfeasible, and Sophronius preached his Nativity sermon in Justinian's New Church in
Jerusalem.[166] He would have little time or opportunity from now
on to take part in the dogmatic controversy. Even so, it is said that
when he saw Cyrus was not observing the pact of silence, he put
together in two books six hundred patristic testimonies in support
of his own position. Knowing he could not himself leave Jerusalem,
he sent Stephen, Bishop of Dor, to the West, adjuring him on
Calvary to go to the ends of the earth, and to Rome, insisting on
the full faith. More than ten years later, at the Lateran Council of
A.D. 649,[167] Stephen told how he had carried out his master's commands, though orders were out that he should be put in chains
wherever found, and taken to Constantinople.

The Saracen threat became ever more intense and closer. Damascus fell. Heraclius' forces were routed at the Yarmuk. At last
Jerusalem was cut off for many months—and no help was coming.
Sophronius was not going to allow another massacre. In February,
A.D. 638, he sought for terms of surrender, insisting that it should
be made to no subordinate general, but to the Caliph Omar himself.
The terms were generous. The imperial forces were allowed to
withdraw. The Christians could keep their churches, only paying
the inevitable poll-tax. After twenty-four years of confusion, peace
returned to the Holy Places—but a peace imposed by the missionaries
of a new religion.

Against the demands of such a time, those whose kingdom is not
of this world had been building for three hundred years. Would it
indeed prove that 'the rain descended, and the floods came, and the
winds blew, and beat upon that house; and it fell not, for it was
founded upon a rock'? Those who have heard, after thirteen
centuries, the bell of Mar Saba clanging out at night over the
wilderness, have recognized there, in spite of all vicissitudes and
shortcomings of man who still needs his Saviour, the abiding triumph
of Easter.

NOTES TO CHAPTER VIII

[1] MS. Ottobonianus 373, f. 14ʳ.

[2] See Halkin, *Bibl. Hag. Gr.*, 1877 u–y: Ehrhard, *Überlieferung*—I. 149, 157, 237, 243.

[3] *P.G.* 87. 3, 2852.

[4] c. 107: 2965–70.

[5] c. 53 echoes the story in *Vita Sabae*, c. 26: c. 99, that of Anthus in *V.S.* c. 14.

[6] cc. 203, 211, 212, 216, 218, 219 (cf. Zos. cc. 6, 15, 12, 8, 13, 14).

[7] cc. 126, 192 (cf. Anast. Sin. 18, 57).

[8] See Bousset, *Apophthegmata*, §5 (pp. 13–15): Th. Nissen in *B.Z.* 38, pp. 351–76.

[9] c. 40: 2893D.

[10] c. 42.

[11] c. 186: 3061D.

[12] *V.J.H.* c. 22 (218. 10).

[13] *J.M.* c. 4.

[14] Evagr. *H.E.* IV. 39.

[15] *J.M.* cc. 19, 96.

[16] c. 139.

[17] Evagr. *H.E.* V. 6: he was made hegumen of Sinai by order of Justin, therefore not earlier than A.D. 566.

[18] Evagr. *H.E.* VI. 24.

[19] *J.M.* c. 112.

[20] Evelyn White, *History*, pp. 249–56, 268–78: Severus, *Hist. Patr.*, p. 209.

[21] *J.M.* c. 54.

[22] c. 113.

[23] cc. 114, 194.

[24] c. 183.

[25] c. 114.

[26] *Vie (et Récits) de l'abbé Daniel le Scétiote*, ed. L. Clugnet (Bibliothèque hagiographique orientale), Paris, 1901.

[27] *V. et R.* c. 3 (p. 12, l. 5–6): ὁ τῆς Σκήτεως πρῶτος, c. 5B (19. 27): ὁ πρεσβύτερος τῆς Σ, c. 9 (30. 1).

[28] *V. et R.* pp. 96–7 (= 109).

[29] c. 8.

[30] c. 9.

[31] c. 2.

[32] *V.S.* c. 53 (145. 8) and c. 54 (147. 6–9).

[33] *Legends of Eastern Saints*, ed. A. J. Wensinck, Vol. II, *The Legend of Hilaria*—Leyden, 1913. The legend, which probably goes back in the Coptic to the sixth century, is valuable for the picture of Scetis that it gives us.

[34] *V. et R.* c. 10.

[35] c. 3 (14. 5–6).

[36] c. 2 (4. 6 = 7. 9 = 8. 18).

[37] c. 3 (14. 5).

[38] cc. 5, 6, 10. The last chapter ends with an illuminating account of strife between the Scetiotes and the monks of the Eighteenth over the body of Andronicus, settled in favour of the Eighteenth by Daniel who threatens to remain at the Eighteenth himself.

[39] c. 10 (50. 8–23 = 54. 27–55. 8: 51. 25 = 56. 8).

[40] *J.M.* c. 152.

[41] c. 55.

[42] c. 177.

[43] G Phocas 1.

[44] G Phocas 2.

[45] Evelyn White, *History*, pp. 232–5, where it is suggested that the twin monasteries had their origin in the schism between the Gaianites and Theodosians within the Monophysite body: but the view I have put forward seems at least as plausible—if, in fact, the twin monasteries were already in existence before the devastation of Scetis at this time. This is not improbable: but positive evidence for it—and that slender—can only be produced in the case of the Monastery of the Syrians.

[46] *J.M.* cc. 123, 124: the latter chapter shows that its narrator, Zosimus the Cilician, had become Bishop of Egyptian Babylon not more than twenty years before his meeting with

Moschus on Sinai, being consecrated by Apollinarius, who was Pope of Alexandria A.D. 551–70. He had since abandoned his bishopric and returned to Sinai.

[47] *J.M.* cc. 62–8, 134.
[48] c. 67.
[49] c. 149.
[50] Evagr. *H.E.* V. 16, VI. 24.
[51] *J.M.* c. 134.
[52] *Recits du moine Anastase* (ed. Nau), c. lix, Oriens Christianus, t. 3, pp. 87–8.
[53] Sophronius, *SS. Cyri et Joannis Miracula,* 70 (*P.G.* 87. 3, 3665AB: cf. 3421C).
[54] This is clear from the contents of the last mentioned work, and borne out by the description of him as 'iatrosophist' in the title of *Anacreontic XXIII* (3855A).
[55] *J.M.* cc. 69–77, 110.
[56] The Sinai chapters in the Meadow use the first person plural: but this is not in itself conclusive evidence that Sophronius' presence is implied where he is not named. But another Sinai story, of great importance for the history of the nightly office, and published by Pitra in *Juris eccl. graec. historia et monumenta,* II. 220, opens Διηγήσατο ἡμῖν ὁ ἀββᾶς Ἰωάννης καὶ ὁ ἀββᾶς Σωφρόνιος, and tells of their visit (surely our John Moschus and Sophronius are meant) to Abba Nilus, on the peak of Sinai, with two disciples. The exact historicity of this story is, however, not completely above suspicion.
[57] Sophr., *SS. C. et J.M.* 70 (3665B: cf. 3421C): *J.M.* c. 92. Moschus mentions three archimandrites of St. Theodosius: Leontius (c. 4), George or Gregory (cc. 92–4 and 109), and Strategius (c. 103).
[53] *J.M.,* cc. 26, 46, 157, 163.
[59] cc. 5–10, 100.
[60] See A. M. Schneider in *Römische Quartalschrift* XXXIX (1931), pp. 316–32.
[61] *Miracula B. Mariae in Choziba,* 5. *J.M.,* c. 25, gives another less authentic version of the same story about the words of the Anaphora, as concerning an unnamed boy and John, instead of John's last predecessor Zeno and his master Aian.
[62] *V.S.* c. 44.
[63] See S. Vailhé, *Jean le Khozibite et Jean de Césarée,* in *Echos d'Orient,* 6 (1903), pp. 107–13.
[64] *V.S.* c. 61. Evagr. *H.E.* IV. 7 (157. 20–158. 21) has a story bringing him at Caesarea into relation with Zosimas.
[65] *V. Theod. Syk.* c. 24 (Dawes and Baynes, *Three Byzantine Saints,* p. 104).
[66] Ibid. c. 63 (Dawes and Baynes, p. 132).
[67] *J.M.* c. 24.
[68] *Anal. Boll.,* 7 (1888)—also published as an *excerptum.*
[69] *V.G.C.* I. 1.
[70] Ibid. I. 2.
[71] I. 3.
[72] I. 4–5.
[73] II. 6–10.
[74] III. 11.
[75] III. 12.
[76] V. 20.
[77] V. 21.
[78] VIII. 32.
[79] VIII. 32–3.
[80] IV. 16 (115. 5–7).
[81] See especially III. 14, and X (discourses of the saint).
[82] III. 14 (113. 10–14).
[83] *J.M.,* cc 68, 97, 187.
[84] Greg. *Ep.* 7. 32.
[85] *Ep.* 11. 46.
[86] *V. Greg.* II. 52 (*P.L.* 75. 110A).
[87] *P.G.* 87. 3. 3697–3726.
[88] Sophr. *Anacreont.* XXI (ibid. 3823–30).
[89] Couret, *La Palestine sous les Empereurs grecs,* p. 213: Abel, *Revue Biblique,* 34 (1925), pp. 575–7. The evidence appears tenuous.
[90] *Prise de Jérusalem* (ed. Garitte) IV—C.S.C.O. Scr. Iber. 12, p. 7.
[91] Ibid. II. (pp. 4–5).
[92] Antiochus, *Pandect* 84 (*P.G.* 89, 1689D–1692B).

[93] *J.M.* c. 26.

[94] cc. 27–9, 31–4, 36–7, 39, 51, 57, 78–91. Intercourse between the various monasteries seems to have been frequent, and it is by no means necessary to assume that Moschus' Syrian and Cilician visits were confined to a single journey. It is interesting to note the specially close connection implied between the monastery of St. Theodosius in Palestine and that of his namesake on the borders between Syria and Cilicia, near Rhossus, of the origins of which we learn in Theodoret, *Hist. Rel.* X (cf. *J.M.*, cc. 80–7, 90–104).

[95] *J.M.* cc. 146–7, tell stories related to the travellers by Menas, coenobiarch of Enaton, about Pope Eulogius of Alexandria, probably after his death in A.D. 607. But Sophronius' *Anacreontic* XXI celebrates the clearing of the same Menas (called oeconomos of Enaton) before Phocas of a charge of harbouring Maurice's son Theodosius. So we may assume they reached Enaton before the fall of Phocas.

[96] *V. Joh. El.* (ed. Delehaye, *Anal. Boll.* 45) c. 4.

[97] *V. Joh. El.* (ed Gelzer) c. 32.

[98] *SS. C. et J.M.* c. 70.

[99] *V.G.C.* VII. 30.

[100] *P. de J.* V. 1–6.

[101] *V.G.C.* VIII. 34.

[102] *Chron. Pasch.* A.D. 609 (*P.G.* 92, 977B): 'παύεται 2ὲ καὶ Ἰσαάκιος ἀπὸ Ἱεροσολύμων καὶ γίνεται ἀντ' αὐτοῦ Ζαχαρίας ἀπό πρεσβυτέρων καὶ σκευοφυλάκων τῆς ἐκκλησίας Κωνσταντινουπόλεως.'

[103] *P. de J.* V. 7–20.

[104] *P. de J.* VII.

[105] Ibid. VIII. 5.

[106] *V.G.C.* VII. 31; Antiochus, *Ep. ad Eust.* 1424B.

[107] *V.G.C.* loc. cit.

[108] Ant., *Ep. ad E.* 1424BC.

[109] *P. de J.* VI: this chapter survives in Greek in MS. collections of Apophthegmata. It was published by Avgoustinos in *Nea Sion*, 1914, pp. 427–8, from MS. Sin. 448 (eleventh century).

[110] *P. de J.* V. 28–32.

[111] Sebeos c. XXIV (trad. Macler, pp. 68 ff.): *P. de J.* VIII.

[112] *P. de J.* IX.

[113] Ibid. X.

[114] Sebeos, loc. cit.

[115] *P. de J.* XIII–XIV.

[116] Ibid. XV.

[117] *V.G.C.* VI. 29.

[118] *P. de J.* XXIII.

[119] Loc. cit.

[120] *P. de J.* XX. 1.

[121] Sebeos, loc. cit.

[122] *V.G.C.* VII. 31.

[123] Ibid. VIII. 35.

[124] Ibid. 36.

[125] Ibid. IX. 38.

[126] Ibid. IX. 42.

[127] Ant., *Ep. ad E.* 1424C–1425C.

[128] See P. Styger, *Die Malereien in der Basilika des hl. Sabas auf den Kl. Aventin in Rom* (*Römische Quartalschrift* 28 (1914), pp. 49–96). The *Life of St. Gregory of Acragas* (*P.G.* 98, 549–716) seems to prove that the monastery in Rome must go back to the times of St. Gregory of Rome. It was written by Leontius, an abbot of this monastery, in which its hero had himself occupied a cell on coming from Constantinople to Rome.

[129] *Ep. ad E.* 1425D.

[130] Ibid. 1421A–D.

[131] *Hom.* 130, 1841–50.

[132] *Decline and Fall*, c. 46, n. 73 (ed. Bury, Vol. V, p. 70).

[133] *P.G.* 89, 1849–56.

[134] *Ep. ad E.*, 1428AB.

[135] Sebeos, loc. cit.

[136] *P. de J.* X. 9.

[137] c. XXV.

[138] *V. Joh. El.* (ed. Delehaye) c. 9; (ed. Gelzer) c. 20.

[139] *Anacr.* XIV. Migne (3800B) has the title only. The text was published by Couret in *Revue de l'Orient Chrétien,* 2 (1897), pp. 125–64.

[140] *V. Joh. El.* (ed. Delehaye) cc. 13 and 15; (ed. Gelzer) cc. 44–6.

[141] Cf. *J.M.* c. 30.

[142] *J.M.* cc. 108, 185: Sophron. *Anacreont.* XXII tells of the death of Mary, the narrator of the latter chapter, in the form of a lament by her son Paul the Candidate.

[143] *P.L.* 74, 119–22: Photius, *Bibliotheca,* cod. 199 (*P.G.* 103, 668). The *Meadow* itself contains no direct evidence of a visit to Rome.

[144] The George of whom the Lives speak as hegumen of St. Theodosius on Sophronius' return is surely intended to be the same spoken of in the *Meadow,* cc. 92–4 and 109, who is assumed dead in the latter chapter, and must have preceded Modestus as hegumen. The Life has probably found these chapters attributed to Sophronius, and has then placed them wrongly in his life. Moschus and Sophronius were responsible for a lost Life of St. John the Almsgiver. It is hardly likely that they would have completed it by A.D. 619 if Moschus died that year.

[145] The name *Eucratades* for the monastery is found in Maximus, *Ep.* 12. John Moschus is called Eucratas in the title of the *Meadow,* and Sophronius is so called in some MSS. in the title of Maximus, *Ep.* 8—see Delehaye in *Anal. Boll.* 45 (1927), p. 6; Devreesse in *Rev. S. R.* 17 (1937). Is it possible that Moschus died here in Africa, and not in Rome? For Sophronius' meeting with Maximus in Africa, see *P.G.* 91, 142A.

[146] *P. de J.* XX.

[147] *P. de J.* XXII.

[148] The story I here summarize is found in the Life of St. Anastasius the Persian, written by a contemporary, and published by Usener, *Acta M. Anastasii Persae,* Universitätschrift von Bonn, 1894. Usener also argues that the panegyric on the saint attributed to George the Pisidian (*P.G.* 92, 1680–1729) is based on this Life, and is really the work of Sophronius.

[149] *P. de J.* XXIV. 1.

[150] Ibid. 6–9.

[151] Ibid. 10–11.

[152] *V.G.C.* IV. 16.

[153] *P. de J.* XXIV. 8.

[154] See Bréhier in Fliche et Martin, *Histoire de l'Eglise,* Vol. V, c. iv, § 3.

[155] At the Battle of Muta in A.D. 629.

[156] *P. de J.* XXIV. 12–14.

[157] Maximus, *Ep.* 13 (*P.G.* 91, 533A).

[158] Maximus, *Op. Theol. et Pol.* 12 (*P.G.* 91, 142–3).

[159] Maximus, *Disput. c. Pyrrho* (*P.G.* 91, 332).

[160] Ibid., and letter from Sergius to Pope Honorius in Mansi, XI. 533–8.

[161] See the Life of Moschus already referred to, n. 143, 144.

[162] His Christmas sermon in Jerusalem was preached in a year when Christmas Day fell on a Sunday (*P.G.* 87. 3, 3201). This fixes the date at A.D. 634.

[163] *P.G.* 87. 3, 3147–3200.

[164] See von Balthasar, *Liturgie Cosmique,* pp. 36–7, 40: P. Sherwood's introduction to *St. Maximus the Confessor* (Ancient Christian Writers, 21), pp. 10–11, 14–15.

[165] *P.G.* 87. 3, 3197D.

[166] Ibid. 3201–3212—the Latin translation. The Greek original was published by Usener in *Rheinisches Museum für Philologie,* Frankfurt am Main, 1886, pp. 501–16.

[167] Mansi X. 892–902. A letter of protest against the Monothelete compromise was brought forward at this Council with the signatures of thirty-seven representatives of Greek monasteries in Rome, Africa and Palestine, including those of John, abba and priest of the monastery of St. Sabas, near Jerusalem, and of Theodore from another monastery of St. Sabas in Africa—ibid. 903–10.

IX

A HIGH MOUNTAIN APART

THE high mountain system of Sinai stands ever somewhat apart from the rest of the world, yet near enough to Egypt and Palestine for it to be impossible to treat of the monasticism of those countries without reference to it. Hither from Egypt Moses had come to meet with God at the Burning Bush, and again in the cloud upon the peak. Hither Elijah had come forty days' journey from Beersheba, to hear the Still Small Voice upon Horeb, the Mount of God. Hither the generations of the Church have come upon the same quest, but with a new understanding. In the apse mosaic of Justinian's Church beside the Bush, Moses and Elijah are shown speaking with the Lord Incarnate, Jesus transfigured before His three Apostles—His Uncreated Light shining for those whose hearts are opened.

It is perhaps rather typical of Sinai that its earliest recorded Christian monasticism should be neither from Egypt nor from Palestine. Some time about the middle of the fourth century, the great Syrian ascetic Julian Saba came there, and founded the Church upon the peak of the Mountain of Moses—Gebel Musa—which has continued ever since to be a focus of pilgrimage. Both Ephraim and Theodoret attest the visit:[1] and the latter speaks of at least one other Syrian pilgrim to the mountain in the fourth century—Symeon the Ancient.[2] The picture given us by the Western pilgrim Aetheria[3] about the end of the century would be consistent with a purely Syrian monasticism—*monasteria*, in the sense primarily of solitary cells, clustered about the neighbourhood of the mountain, with the little Church and cave on the top of Gebel Musa—where no-one spends the night—the Church and cave of Elijah, and the Church beside the Bush, with its garden and spring, at the foot of the mountain. But the ascetics were certainly not then exclusively Syrian. Well before the end of the century, as we have seen, the Palestinian Silvanus had come with his followers from Scetis to establish some kind of community life on Sinai before moving again, northward, to the Gaza region.[4] A disciple of his on Sinai, Netras, became Bishop of Paran[5]—the episcopal see of the whole region, in the great valley oasis some thirty miles away. Down on the coast, Rhaithou—traditionally identified with the little port of Tor[6]—was a monastic centre at least from early in the fifth century, when Amoun of Rhaithou is met with in connection with Sisoes who was then at St. Antony's Interior Mountain and at Clysma.[7]

We know little more of Sinai or Rhaithou through the fifth century. Three of St. Euthymius' first twelve disciples at his lavra were from Rhaithou.[8] The Emperor Marcian wrote after Chalcedon to Macarius, bishop and archimandrite, and the other venerable monks of Mt. Sinai,[9] to warn them against Theodosius the Jerusalem intruder. A monk Zosimus, who had been a solitary at Rhaithou and on Sinai, came some time after Chalcedon to Jerusalem and Bethel, and finally settled with Peter the Iberian on the Coastal Plain.[10] In the Constantinople conversations in A.D. 536, the monks of Sinai, the Church of Paran, and the Lavra of Rhaithou, shared an apocrisiarius.[11] Moschus gives us an account[12] of the miraculous appearance in Jerusalem at Easter, A.D. 551 (or 552?), of George, hegumen of Sinai, who died six months later at the same time as the Patriarch Peter of Jerusalem. Peter's letter to Bishop Photius of Paran in connection with this indicates both the subjection of the Sinai monks to the see of Paran, and the subjection of that see to the Patriarchate of Jerusalem. We are told that George had not left Sinai for some seventy years—which takes us back to about A.D. 480.

One of George's envoys to the Patriarch Peter, a priest Zosimus,[13] subsequently went with his disciple to spend two years in the Porphyrite Mountain west of the Red Sea. Returning to Sinai, he was sent with two other envoys to Alexandria, where the Pope Apollinarius (A.D. 551–70) laid hands on all three and made them bishops. Zosimus later withdrew from his bishopric of Babylon (to-day 'Old Cairo') and returned to Sinai, where he told the story to John Moschus about twenty years after his consecration. Some time before A.D. 564, another anchorite, Sergius,[14] with his Armenian disciple, another Sergius, left Sinai for the region of Rouba by the Dead Sea: there he washed the feet of Gregory, hegumen of Fara, foreseeing that he was going to be a patriarch.

Meanwhile Justinian had done in Sinai what Sabas had asked him to do in the Judaean Wilderness, and built a fortress ('Castrum') by the Holy Bush,[15] completed, it is said, in the thirtieth year of his reign—A.D. 556–7—when Doulas was hegumen.[16] Within its walls was the Church of the Mother of God (the Burning Bush was ever seen as a type of Her); its great apse mosaic of the Transfiguration[17] is dated nearly ten years later, in the 14th Indiction (A.D. 565–6), when Longinus was hegumen and Theodore his second; it contains portraits of Longinus and his deacon John. Longinus must have died soon after, and Justin II, who had succeeded Justinian in November, A.D. 565, brought Gregory of Fara from Palestine to be hegumen of Sinai, where he had to withstand a siege by the tent-dwelling tribes, but won through to peace before he was called in A.D. 570 to the patriarchal throne of Antioch.[18] He remained there for twenty-three years, until his death in A.D. 593, playing a very positive role in the history of his time. The historian Evagrius, writing just after his death, speaks of him with great admiration.

Justinian built his fort—but our records seem to say nothing of soldiers there, even when Gregory and his monks were besieged. Soldiers there certainly were at the other fort, in the oasis of Paran.[19] But it cannot have been long before the Castrum by the Bush became simply the enclosing wall of the coenobitic centre of the eremitic life of the mountain, and the focal point of the Sinaitic cycle of stories added over the next century and a half to the collection of *Gerontika*. Sinai was always the goal of pilgrimage when the times allowed, with an international character no less marked than that of Jerusalem. An anonymous pilgrim from Placentia, who visited the Holy Mountain in A.D. 570, speaks of three fathers who knew Latin, Greek, Syriac, Coptic and Bessic, and many interpreters of single languages.[20] The monastery library tells the same tale— Greek, Syriac (Edessene and Palestinian), Georgian and Arabic, all represented among its manuscripts. From Moschus, Anastasius (of whom more presently) and elsewhere we learn of Byzantines, Cappadocians, Isaurians, Cilicians, Armenians and Iberians (Georgians) among the monks. The Lavra of the Aeliotes, at which Moschus spent ten years (A.D. 584–94?), may well have been a monastic colony from Jerusalem (Aelia) on Sinai.[21] A letter of St. Gregory of Rome,[22] dated 1st September, A.D. 600, to John, Abbot of Sinai, congratulates him on his quiet, and tells how 'our son Simplicius' has reported the shortage of equipment in the hospital for old men founded on Sinai by a certain Isaurian, and announces that he is sending 15 cloaks, 30 'rachanae', and 15 beds.

It would be tempting to identify this Abbot John with the great ascetic writer, John 'Climacus', also hegumen of Sinai. But, as we shall see later, the temptation has almost certainly to be resisted.

While travellers like John Moschus keep us near to history, Sinai in the sixth century was in the mood of its time. Two of its major contributions to hagiographical literature—the account by 'Ammonius' of the Martyrs of Sinai and Rhaithou,[23] and the narratives of

Nilus[24]—have long confused our picture by being taken as strict history. The first, with its claim to be a Greek translation of a Coptic document found in a monk's cell in Egypt, instantly awakes our suspicion. Its atmosphere is surely that of the sixth century—the monks of Sinai retreating into a fortress and a tower, and even the name, Doulas, of the hegumen identical with that of the hegumen in whose time, it seems, the fort was built in A.D. 556–7. Its claim to come from the time of a Patriarch Peter of Alexandria in flight from persecution—we suppose Peter II (A.D. 373–80) is intended—is surely an anachronism. As for the Nilus of the *Narratives*, he is certainly not to be identified with the early fifth-century Nilus of Ancyra, whom no other evidence would link with Sinai.[25] Both documents are valuable for the picture they give of monastic life and outlook, and of the 'barbarian' world around, but are to be taken otherwise as romance. Even in connection with John Moschus and Sophronius—a story of the greatest value for the history of the development of the Night Office tells of their visit to Nilus and two disciples on the Holy Peak, and their all-night vigil there.[26] But the story comes down as told 'to us' by the two travellers, not as written by them. Elsewhere we are constantly told that it was not permitted to spend the night on the peak: and the name of Nilus adds to our suspicion that the story may perhaps after all be a fabrication of a puritanical monastic party seeking support for its objection to the embellishment of the long and starkly scriptural office with liturgical singing and hymnody. But the order it gives is undoubtedly of early date, and may well be genuinely Sinaitic. The early date of the Ammonius narrative is also proved by the translation into Palestinian Syriac, surviving in a palimpsest which cannot be much later than the seventh century.

St. Gregory may have been right in thinking of Sinai in A.D. 600 as a haven of peace. But within the next decade, the routes which linked it and Rhaithou with Palestine had become 'barbarized' and hardly passable.[27] It would seem that only with the Arab conquest did the journey again become comparatively secure. But the eremitic life of the mountain region itself was little disturbed. Of this seventh-century world of Sinai a vivid picture is given in the collection of forty stories attributed to *Anastasius of Sinai*, published by Nau.[28] Other Sinaitic stories still unpublished may well prove to come from the same source. If all these stories belong to a single collection, they were not written earlier than the second half of the century, well after the Arab conquest.[29] But their atmosphere is largely retrospective, and we still feel ourselves in the world of the Christian Empire. They belong to a country of high mountains, with an ethos of its own, distinct from that of Palestine (where the mountain tops are inhabited) or of Egypt. One of the first stories[30] tells how one Pentecost, when the Liturgy was being celebrated on the Holy Peak, and the priest in the Anaphora raised the triumphal hymn of majestic glory, the surrounding mountains answered 'Holy, holy, holy' for half an hour, but only those who had ears to hear could hear it. Another[31] tells how, during one August drought, a thirsty herd of wild goats went up with one accord to the top of the highest mountain, and looked up to heaven bleating until the rain came down, there and there only, from God 'Who giveth fodder unto the cattle, and feedeth the young ravens that call upon Him'.

A number of these stories[32] concern one John the Sabaite, who used to tell how once,[33] when he was in the extreme wilderness, he asked a visitor about a brother with a bad reputation: on being told the brother had not yet set himself free from that reputation, he said 'Ouph!' Immediately he was rapt away to find himself standing before Calvary, and the Lord hanging upon the Cross between the two thieves. Making to draw near and worship Him, he heard the Lord ordering the attendant angels to cast him out, 'for he is an antichrist unto me: for before I have judged, he was condemning his brother'. As John was being driven out, his cloak was caught in the door as it closed, and he left it there—and woke up. He told his visitor, and said, 'Believe me, my cloak is God's protection over me, and I have been deprived of it'. From that day, he spent seven years in the deserts neither eating bread nor coming under a roof nor meeting a man, until he saw the Lord ordering His cloak to be restored to him.

One day an Abba Martyrius took his twenty-year-old disciple John and tonsured him, as was customary, on the Holy Peak. Coming down, they met the hegumen Anastasius, who did not know the lad, but prophesied that he would be hegumen of Sinai.[34] Then they went to John the Sabaite, fifteen miles away in the wilderness of Goudda.[35] He also did not know the lad, but washed his feet, and assured his disciple that he had washed the feet of the hegumen of Sinai. Forty years later, the prophecy was fulfilled. The writer of the stories, writing apparently a year after the younger John's death,[36] honours him as 'our new Moses', and has other stories about him.[37] We can be certain that this is indeed John the 'scholasticus' who, in answer to a request from John, hegumen of

Rhaithou, wrote that *Ladder of Divine Ascent*[38] for which he is commonly known as St. John Climacus, and which every Orthodox monk is supposed to read every Lent. The appearance in the *Meadow* of a chapter of sayings of John the Cilician, hegumen of Rhaithou (which also appears in the *Alphabetical Gerontikon*)[39] might encourage us to place John Climacus a little earlier, and make him the correspondent of St. Gregory. But we cannot be sure either that this chapter really belongs to the *Meadow*, or that its John the Cilician is, in fact, the addressee of the *Ladder*. In any case, all doubt is removed as to the identity of Climacus with the John of our stories when we find the *Ladder* itself to contain several new stories of John the Sabaite (of his origins in Asia Minor, and of his time at Mar Saba before he came to Sinai),[40] and a teaching of George ot Arselaum, an old man whom John of Rhaithou is stated certainly to have known:[41] George of Arselaum also figures prominently in the Anastasius stories, which describe his death.[42]

Writers of this generation seem to have had an instinct that they were at the end of an epoch. They are summing up the teaching of the preceding centuries. They are also called to look wide. Before he can settle down to his teaching which is specifically for monks, John Climacus must proclaim the universality of the Creator God— 'God is for all those who make choice, life for all, salvation for all— faithful, unfaithful; just, unjust; religious, irreligious; passionless, passionful; monks, secular; wise, foolish; healthy, sick; young, advanced in age; even as the outpouring of light and the sight of the sun and the changes of the air—so, and no otherwise; for there is no respect of persons with God'.[43] He goes on to insist that marriage does not prevent salvation[44]—though the married man must not expect to reach the attainments of the monk.[45] To the married man he says:[46] 'Do all the good things you can. Revile no-one, rob no-one, lie to no-one, be uplifted against no-one, hate no-one, don't stay away from the services of the Church, show sympathy to those who need it, cause offence to no-one, don't meddle in other people's matters, and be content with the food your wives provide for you. If you do thus, you are not far from the Kingdom of Heaven.' In another passage, he is insistent that chastity is not the monopoly of those who have never been married—and he quotes St. Peter for his example.[47] Later in the work[48] we read that, while vices and passions are not in us by nature, the virtues, including Faith, Hope and Love, are set in us from God by nature— are even to be seen in the animals. Prayer is listed among the things which are above nature: and yet Love, which is in us by nature, is greater than prayer.

After the first four *Steps* of the *Ladder*, on renunciation, impartiality, exile and obedience, we come to that on penitence: and herein comes a fearful account of a monastic penitentiary,[49] or prison—called 'Metanoea' (a different use of the term from that in which it was applied to the Tabennesiote monastery at Canopus). One may suppose that the writer intended those who were not ready for his work to be put off by this chapter. Certainly I knew a young Russian layman (now a reverend archimandrite) who got as far as this step, and decided that the *Ladder* was not for him.

One notices how in this ascetic work there is extremely little talk of dogma—which is taken for granted. Only once do I remember a directly dogmatic statement, of considerable importance—in the *Step* on *Remembrance of Death*, where it is stated that 'Christ dreads death, but does not tremble at it, that He may clearly manifest the properties of the Two Natures'[50]—an implied reference to Gethsemane, in language reminiscent of St. Maximus, which reminds us that this was the generation of the stand for the Two Wills and Two Operations, and that Theodore, Bishop of Paran (in whose episcopal jurisdiction Sinai came), was one of the champions of the heretical compromise.

In another passage, the connection between right faith and right ascetic practice is emphasized, where what John regards as an error of Evagrius in matters of fasting (the keeping to bread only, which is found also in Cassian) is laid at the door of Evagrius' aberrations in doctrine.[51]

At last the thirtieth *Step* brings us to the inevitable Figure at the head of the Ladder.[52] 'And she (Agape)—but I think it is fitter to say "He" (Christ)—as if appearing to me from Heaven, this Queen speaking in the ears of my soul, was saying, "If thou be not loosed, O lover, from the grossness, thou canst not learn my beauty as it is. But let the Ladder teach thee the spiritual synthesis of the virtues. And at its very summit am I set, even as my great initiate said— And now abideth Faith, Hope, Love, these three: but the greatest of these is LOVE." '

Written, as we suppose, when the convulsions of the time were near their highest, the work still vindicates St. Gregory's picture of Sinai as a haven of calm. Towering above the deluge like the Ark upon Ararat, it gives no hint of the political cataclysm, and speaks as for all time. But the doors of Sinai were not shut. Pilgrimages were not interrupted for long—we read of a party of 800 Armenians, apparently very soon after the Arab conquest.[53] And individuals from diverse origins still came to seek salvation there. Our stories tell us[54] how old men remembered a lad coming, probably about A.D. 620, not revealing his name or origin, and dying after about two years—when the report spread that this was the son of the Emperor Maurice, rescued from Phocas' massacre of his family by his nurse who put her own son in his place: discovering the facts as he grew up, he came to Sinai to make an offering of himself in reparation. Then after the disaster of the Yarmuk, one source tells us[55] that the Roman general Vahan, whose insubordination had contributed to the defeat, did not dare to face Heraclius, and fled to Sinai, where he took the name of Anastasius, and that one at least of the writings which have come down to us under the name of Anastasius Sinaita—the deeply penitential homily on the *Sixth Psalm*[56]—was in fact his work.

Research is needed to sort out how many writers pass under this name—often with the title of Patriarch of Antioch added. It seems probable that Anastasius I of Antioch (A.D. 559–70 and 593–9) had been a monk on Sinai, perhaps in Palestine as well. We have already seen that an Anastasius was hegumen of Sinai forty years before the hegumenate of John Climacus. But the writings which most concern us come from after the Arab Conquest. This appears to be true of both the collections of stories published by Nau, even if they come, as he thinks, from different hands. One or other of these may well be identical with the writer of the Ὁδηγός (*Viae Dux—P.G.* 89, 35–310)—an exposition of the Faith which seems dated[57] from the sixth or seventh year of the Monophysite Pope of Alexandria, John III (*c.* 683 A.D.), but perplexes us with accounts of debates in Alexandria in the presence of the Augustal Praefect[58]—and so, we suppose, before A.D. 642. The work shows us the writer as a priest and monk of Sinai active in controversy with Monophysites in Alexandria and elsewhere in Egypt, at a stage when the language of Two Energies and Two Wills has already been thrashed out, and the teaching of Islam is known. He shows, like Sophronius and Maximus, great learning, unflinching Chalcedonian faith, and often ruthlessness in castigating heresy—but from time to time also an attractive restraint in debate. He urges us, for instance,[59] in arguing with Monophysites, always to use pre-Chalcedonian authorities; and in debate with 'Arabs' to start by anathematizing him who says that there are two Gods, or that God begat a Son carnally, or who worships as God any creature whatever in heaven or on earth.

The nucleus of a large collection of *Questions and Answers*[60] may well be due to the same writer and certainly goes back to the seventh century, though it has been added to greatly later. We cannot resist giving the story it quotes[61] as from old tradition of the lawyer (*scholasticus*) who was always cursing Plato, until one night Plato appeared to him in a dream: 'Man, stop cursing me: for you are only hurting yourself. I do not deny that I was a sinful man: but when the Christ came down into hell, truly no-one believed on Him before I did.'

There was an adverse account also. We have told in the last chapter[62] of the apostate monk of Sinai who became a propagandist for Judaism. According to John of Nikiou, another renegade monk from Sinai was one of the earliest Islamic persecutors of the Church.[63] But individual failures could not break the continuity of the life on the Holy Mountain. Still attracting recruits, no doubt, from all over the Christian world, and at the same time surrounded by Christian tribes in the Peninsula—whether native Semites, or peoples brought in from elsewhere by Justinian for the service of the monastery—it must soon have begun to appear as a danger to the Islamic authorities, who were content to leave the monastery in peace, but at last decided that the tribes must accept Islam.[64] Those of Paran and the region of the monastery prepared to resist, and gathered on the Holy Peak with this intent—but in the end gave way to numbers, and renounced their Faith. Only one perfervid Christian would not submit, and prepared to throw himself over the southern cliff of the peak. His wife clutched hold of his garments, and adjured him not to leave her and their children to their souls' destruction, but to slay them if he could not take them with him. Finally he consented, drew his sword and slew them, then leaped over the cliff—and survived. For many years he wandered about in mountains and holes and caves of the earth—living with the wild beasts, having escaped from evil human beasts—entering neither house nor city nor village, until his journey to the Heavenly City; at once an eremite and citizen of God. Some wondered whether God accepted such a sacrifice as his. But, for their reassurance, when he knew his end was approaching, he came to the Holy Bush, prayed and received Communion with the monks, then lay sick in the hostelry. The fathers who visited him there would tell how they found him, at the hour of his departure, welcoming the holy fathers who here had been slain as martyrs of God by the barbarians—greeting them by name as friends, and embracing them, then going gladly with them as if he were called to some fair or festival.

Was it, indeed, the holy fathers themselves whom he saw then, or as the writer thought, angelic powers appearing in the form of those who had fought the good fight and put on the crown of victory, to escort him who in their place had followed in their ways, and shown love and faith to God above the righteous who were before?

NOTES ON CHAPTER IX

[1] St. Ephraim, *Hymni de Juliano Saba*, XIX and XX (ed. Lamy, *Hymni et Sermones*, III 907–14): Theodoret, *Hist. Rel.* II (*P.G.* 82, 1316 BC).

[2] *Hist. Rel.* VI (1360D–1364C). See above, c. IV, n. 85.

[3] *Itinerarium Aetheriae* 1–5 (*Sources Chrétiennes* 21, pp. 97–119). See above, c. III, n. 57, and c. IV, n. 85).

[4] See above, c. IV, nn. 86–90.

[5] G Netras (*P.G.* 65, 312A): above, c. IV, n. 89.

[6] See above, c. IV, n. 84.

[7] Ibid., nn. 81–3.

[8] *V.E.* c. 16 (ed. Schwartz, 26. 10).

[9] *Acta Conc. Oec.* (ed. Schwartz) II. 1, p. 491.

[10] *Pleroph.* XXX.

[11] Mansi IX, 911c, Labbe V. 969D.

[12] *J.M.* c. 127 (2988–9).

[13] cc. 123- 4 (2985–8).

[14] cc. 125, 138, 139 (2988, 3001–4).

[15] Procopius, *De Aedificiis*, V. 8: Eutychius of Alexandria, *P.G.* 111, 1071–2.

[16] Eutychius, loc. cit. The inscription over the door of the monastery (C.I.G. IV, 8634) is not original, and has some incompatibilities in its dating, but may well be an inaccurate copy of the original. See Grégoire, *Chronologie byzantine*, in *Byzantinische Zeitschrift*, 1909, p. 500; Beneševič in *Byzantion*, 1924, p. 147.

[17] The mosaic is reproduced in Soteriou, *Icones du Mont Sinai*, II (Text), Pll. 6 and 7—see also pp. 4–5, and Beneševič, op. cit., pp. 145–72.

[18] Evagr. *H.E.* V. 6.

[19] Anonymus Placentiae, c. 40 (ed. Geyer, *Itinera Hierosolymitana*, p. 186).

[20] Ibid. c. 37 (ed. Geyer, p. 184).

[21] *J.M.* cc. 62–6 and 134.

[22] *Ep.* XI. 1: cf. Anastasius, *Récits* (ed. Nau) XXXIX.

[23] Ammonii monachi relatio de sanctis Patribus barbarorum incursione in monte Sina et Raithu peremptis (ed. Combefis, *Illustrium Christi martyrum lecti triumphi*, Paris, 1660, pp. 88–122): Palestinian Syriac version published with English translation (completed from the Greek) by Mrs. Lewis, 'The Forty Martyrs of the Sinai Desert', in *Horae Semiticae*, IX (1912).

[24] *P.G.* 79, 589–603.

[25] Throughout this section I am greatly indebted to the article of Mgr. Devreesse, 'Le Christianisme dans la péninsule sinaïtique, des origines à l'arrivée des Musulmans'—*Revue Biblique*, April 1940, pp. 205–23.

[26] Ed. Pitra, *Juris eccles. graec. historia et monumenta*, II, p. 220.

[27] *V. Georg. Choz.* c. VIII, 32 (*Anal. Boll.* VII, p. 131): cf. Anastasius, *Récits* IX.

[28] *Oriens Christianus*, II (1902), pp. 58–89: the second collection of stories attributed to Anastasius Sinaita—O.C. III (1903), pp. 56–90—are not directly concerned with Sinai, and may be from a different writer, though they also date from the middle seventh century.

[29] c. II speaks of the Peak of Elias 'before it was defiled by the present nation'. C. XX describes the death of Stephen the Byzantine, who had been 'chartularius' of the general Maurianus—who is known as a general in A.D. 653 (Theophanes, *P.G.* 108. 70–A.M. 6145).

The writer's 'Abba', who had died two years before the writing, was a companion of this Stephen (c. XXI). One of the old fathers gave as a memory of his youth the coming (c. A.D. 620?) of the supposed son of the Emperor Maurice (c. XXIX).

³⁰ c. III.

³¹ c. XVI.

³² cc. VI, XIV, XV, XVII: XXXII?

³³ c. XVII.

³⁴ c. XXXIV. If this Anastasius could be identified with him who became Patriarch of Antioch in A.D. 559, and his hegumenate placed before this and not during his exile from Antioch (A.D. 570–93), Climacus could be identified with St. Gregory's correspondent. But it would be hard to adapt other evidence in our *Récits* to this.

³⁵ c. VI. On any reckoning, it would be hard on chronological grounds to identify the disciple, Stephen the Cappadocian, with the monk of the same name of whom we read in the *Meadow*, cc. 122 and 127, who was already a priest, and sent to represent the hegumen in Jerusalem, in A.D. 551–2.

³⁶ c. XXXII. But here, if the MSS. are reliable, he is called the Sabaite—so there is some doubt whether Climacus is intended. It can hardly mean the John the Sabaite of the other stories, unless they were written at different dates. It is unlikely to mean the John who was hegumen of Mar Saba in A.D. 649, and signed the Letter to the Lateran Council of that year.

³⁷ cc. V, VII, XXXIX (a story which may be reminiscent of St. Gregory's interest in the Mountain: John the hegumen of Sinai told the writer how a few years ago a Pope of Rome learned that the monastery needed a hospital, and sent money and letters and built the hospital—of which either John or the writer became hospitaller: we do not get the impression that this had happened when the John here spoken of was already hegumen).

³⁸ P.G. 88, 623–1164.

³⁹ J.M. c. 115: G John the Eunuch 3–6 (P.G. 65, 233AB). Moschus adds two extra sayings, in one of which the old man says he has been in his place seventy-six years. Is it the same John the Cilician who, in c. 177, tells the story of the monk in the cell of Evagrius as from a time when he himself was at Enaton?

⁴⁰ 720A–724B.

⁴¹ 1112B.

⁴² Récits IX and XII.

⁴³ 633A.

⁴⁴ 656B.

⁴⁵ 657B.

⁴⁶ 640C.

⁴⁷ 893D–896A.

⁴⁸ 1028AB.

⁴⁹ 764D–777B.

⁵⁰ 793BC.

⁵¹ 865AB.

⁵² 1160CD. The translation I give of the first sentence was based on a text restored with the help of the early Syriac version—'Η Ͻὲ, οἶμαι Ͻὲ λέγειν οἰκειότερον, 'ὁ Ͻὲ,' ἐξ οὐρανοῦ μο φανεῖσα . . . This text has now been confirmed from a microfilm of the Greek Moscow MS. Bibl. Syn. 145 (Vladimir 184).

⁵³ Anastasius, Récits c. XXXVIII.

⁵⁴ c. XXIX.

⁵⁵ Eutychius of Alexandria, P.G. 111, 1097C.

⁵⁶ P.G. 89, 1077–1184.

⁵⁷ c. XV—P.G. 89, 257AB.

⁵⁸ c. X—185C.

⁵⁹ c. I—41AB.

⁶⁰ P.G. 89, 311–824.

⁶¹ Q. 111—764CD.

⁶² c. VIII, p. 154—Antiochus, Pandect, 84 (P.G. 89, 1689D–1692B).

⁶³ John of Nikiou, c. CXXI. 11.

⁶⁴ Anastasius, Récits XLI (published here by Nau appended to the Anastasius stories, but with no opinion expressed as to the writer). Eutychius places the submission of the servants of the monastery to Islam under the caliphate of Abd-el-Malik ibn Marwan (A.D. 685–705)—P.G. 111, 1072CD.

EPILOGUE

JOHN MOSCHUS at least, if not his pupil Sophronius, was born before the death of St. Cyriac, and conversed with those, like Conon, hegumen of Mar Saba, who must have known him. Cyriac as a young man had spent Lent in the Utter Desert with Euthymius. Euthymius had been baptized by Otreius of Melitene, the correspondent of St. Basil, at a time when the two Macarii, who had known St. Anthony, and themselves were born before the Peace of the Church, were still alive in Scetis and the Cells. So four, or at most five, overlapping lifetimes cover our period from the Conversion of Constantine to the Arab Conquest. At the beginning of that period, the monastic movement was a new enterprise, a lay movement with no literature but Holy Scripture—a determination, in renunciation of the world, to live the full evangelical life, whether in solitude or community. Egypt was not alone in these beginnings: and yet her inspiration can be felt from Mesopotamia to the Celtic lands.

The heart of the movement was ever true to the Church: and it was quickly harnessed to the Church order—sometimes a mixed blessing. But as the focus of our attention moves from Egypt to Palestine, we find how the Holy Places can hold the Church and the Monks to a true balance of Historical Faith which is more easily lost sight of elsewhere. Nor do we forget here the international character, both in giving and taking, which belongs to the Church of the Holy Places as the centre of pilgrimage from the utmost bounds of the Christian world.

At the end of our period, we find monasticism an institution, with a vast tradition and literature of its own, integrated into the organization, ecclesiastical and civil, of the Christian Οἰκουμένη—Christendom.

In the testing centuries that followed, when all around them Christendom was swamped by Islam, the monasteries of Sinai and of Mar Saba, with other of the great Palestinian foundations only less enduring, stood as rocks of the Faith to which all Christians could turn in time of spiritual need, fortresses of that quest for Perfection without which Christianity could not have survived in Islamic lands. And there they stand.

It would take another book to tell how these monasteries continued for several hundred years to be the central formative influence in the development of Orthodox monasticism. In liturgical order, the *Typikon* of Mar Saba provided the basic pattern for the year's worship: and rubrics reprinted to this day in the service-books have frequent reference to the practices found in the great Judaean monasteries. A Sabaite, St. Andrew of Crete, introduced in his *Great Canon* a new type of church poetry, taken up in the next generation by two other Sabaites, St. John of Damascus and St. Cosmas of Maiuma, around whose work, in *Octoechos* and *Triodion*, the structure of Byzantine hymnody is largely built—completed, in the main, in the next century (the ninth) by the Studites under the influence of another Sabaite, Theophanes the Branded, who suffered in Constantinople for the faith of the Ikons. For it was in the face of Islam that Christians could see the need of the Ikons for proclaiming the Incarnation: and was not Jerusalem itself an abiding Ikon? So in both bouts of iconoclasm Sabaites stood for the full Faith—St. John of Damascus against the Isaurian emperors; three Sabaite envoys to Constantinople, Michael Syncellus and the two Branded Brothers, Theodore and Theophanes, against Leo the Armenian and the Amorians. Nor do we forget how independence of Constantinople enabled Sinai to preserve through these times an unbroken succession of Ikons, from the sixth century onwards, which must be unique—for the fortress walls of the Sinai monastery made it less vulnerable than Mar Saba, which was again and again ravaged by Bedouin inroads. Through all this, the intellectual life of the monasteries went on—by no means confined to St. John of Damascus, whose *Fountain of Knowledge* has earned him in some quarters the misleading title of 'the St. Thomas Aquinas of the Eastern Church'. In particular, in these international monasteries, translation went on from and into a number of languages, including, of course, Arabic. It was at Mar Saba that the ascetic works of the 'Nestorian' bishop, Isaac of Nineveh, were translated from Syriac into Greek, adapted to Orthodox use—so that St. Isaac is recognized as a great saint of the Orthodox Church. A document of uncertain date tells of a time at Mar Saba when Iberians, Syrians, and *Franks*, had the Liturgy of the Catechumens in their own chapels, joining with the Greeks for the Liturgy of the Faithful. More important for us are those lives of saints, and stories of martyrs, sometimes directly historical, sometimes with an admixture of legend, which show us, changing from age to age and yet ever the same, the spiritual life of the monasteries going on—with indications from time to time to suggest to us how each new spurt of monastic life within the empire received stimulus from Judaea, until first Athos and then the Caves of Kiev grew not only upon the inspiration of the old days of Egypt and Judaea, but on the still living example and contact of Sinai and Mar Saba. It is fitting to conclude the story with the memory of another St. Sabas—or Sava—the great Serbian archbishop, coming on pilgrimage about A.D. 1230, to carry back to his home country the Staff of Sabas the Sanctified, and to his monastery of Khilandari on Athos that Ikon of the Mother of God named 'of the Three Hands', to which St. John of Damascus had, it was said, attached a silver hand in thankfulness for his healing.

The by-products of monasticism have been many, and full of life and interest. But one thread alone can give our story its true meaning—the search for personal holiness, the following of the Lord Jesus, whether in the solitary cell or on the abbot's seat, or in all the menial works of the monastery. This imperfectly told tale will not have failed completely if somewhere in the course of it can be found illustrated each point of the unchanging Gospel pattern:

Blessed are the poor in spirit: for theirs is the Kingdom of Heaven.

Blessed are they that mourn: for they shall be comforted.

Blessed are the meek: for they shall inherit the earth.

Blessed are they which do hunger and thirst after righteousness: for they shall be filled.

Blessed are the merciful: for they shall obtain mercy.

Blessed are the pure in heart: for they shall see God.

Blessed are the peace-makers: for they shall be called the children of God.

Blessed are they which are persecuted for righteousness' sake: for theirs is the Kingdom of Heaven.

Blessed are ye, when men shall revile you, and persecute you, and shall say all manner of evil against you falsely for My sake. Rejoice and be exceeding glad; for great is your reward in Heaven.

—Remember me, O Lord, when Thou comest in Thy Kingdom!

INDEX OF PERSONS

INDEX OF PLACES

SUBJECT INDEX

CHRONOLOGICAL TABLE

Emperors, etc.	Egypt	Palestine
249–51 DECIUS. Persecution.	c. 251 Antony born. Paul of Thebes flees into the desert.	
270–5 AURELIAN.	c. 271 Antony enters ascetic life.	c. 275 Chariton from Iconium settles at Fara?
285–305 DIOCLETIAN.	c. 285 Antony to desert fort. c. 292 Pachomius born.	
293 1st Tetrarchy.	c. 293 Macarius the Alexandrian born. c. 300 Macarius the Egyptian born.	Hilarion born at Thavatha.
303 Edict of Persecution.	c. 304 Pambo born.	
305 2nd TETRARCHY.	Antony emerges. Monks join him.	Hilarion in Egypt, visits Antony.
306 CONSTANTINE proclaimed at York.		
		c. 308 Hilarion returns to ascetic life near Gaza.
312 Battle of Milvian Bridge.	c. 311 Antony in Alexandria to encourage martyrs. Pope Peter martyred. Amoun enters ascetic life.	
313 Maximin Daia defeated and dead.	313 Antony to Interior Mountain. Pachomius baptized. Athanasius in household of Pope Alexander. c. 320 Pachomius founds Community at Tabennesis. c. 321 Theodore joins him.	
324 CONSTANTINE sole Emperor. 325 Council of NICAEA (the Son consubstantial and co-eternal with the Father).		
	328 Athanasius Pope. Foundation of Faou?	
	330 Athanasius in Thebaid. Amoun moves to Nitria? Macarius the Egyptian to Scetis?	From c. 330 Monasteries spring up in Palestine: e.g. Epiphanius at Besandûk, near Eleutheropolis.
	333 Macarius the Alexandrian baptized.	
	335 Council of Tyre. Athanasius' first exile.	335 Consecration of Anastasis in Jerusalem.
337 Constantine dies baptized. CONSTANTIUS (Arianizing Emperor in East; CONSTANS in West.	337 Pachomius moves headquarters to Faou. Athanasius returns. 338 Antony visits Alexandria and Nitria. Foundation of Cells. 339–46 Athanasius' second exile.	

208

General	Egypt	Palestine
	340 Macarius the Egyptian ordained Priest? Athanasius in Rome with monks. Pachomian foundations round Panopolis. *c.* 341 Paul of Thebes, discovered by Antony, dies.	
343 Council of Sardica— East and West divided. *c.* 345 Rufinus and Jerome born.	345 Synod of Latopolis. 346 Pachomius dies.	
		c. 348 Cyril of Jerusalems' Catechetical Lectures.
350 Constans killed.	Athanasius returns. John of Lycopolis enclosed. 351 Orsiesius calls in Theodore to direct Tabennesiote Community.	*c.* 350 Cyril Bishop of Jerusalem.
353 Constantius sole emperor.		
357 Basil baptized, tours Egyptian and Palestinian monasteries.	356 Antony dies. Athanasius a fugitive. 357 Hilarion visits Interior Mountain. Saracens raid it. Sisoes settles there. Athanasius writes *Vita Antonii*. 360 Duke Artemius searches Faou for Athanasius.	356 Hilarion leaves Palestine.
361 JULIAN Emperor (apostate).	361 Athanasius emerges. 362 Athanasius exiled from Alexandria.	
363 JOVIAN Emperor.	363 Athanasius in Thebaid, then back in Alexandria.	
364 VALENS Emperor in East (baptized Arian, 366).		
		367 Epiphanius Bishop of Salamis in Cyprus.
	368 Theodore dies: Orsiesius resumes headship of Community.	
370 Basil Bishop of Caesarea Mazaca.		*c.* 370 Innocent on Olivet.
	373 Athanasius dies. Peter, succeeding, flees to Rome. 373–5 Rufinus and Melania in Egypt. Pambo dies. Bishops and monks in exile.	*c.* 375 Egyptian exiles at Diocaesarea. Melania in attendance. *c.* 376 Melania on Olivet.
376 Euthymius born at Melitene.		*c.* 377 Porphyry by Jordan.
378 Valens killed at Adrianople. 379 Basil dies. THEODOSIUS Emperor in East (Orthodox).		
	380 Timothy Pope.	*c.* 380 Rufinus joins Melania on Olivet.

General	Egypt	Palestine
381 Council of Constantinople (Nicaea reaffirmed: the Holy Ghost true God).		
		382 Evagrius Ponticus on Olivet. Porphyry in Jerusalem.
	383 Evagrius in Nitria.	
	385 Evagrius at Cells. Theophilus Pope.	385 Jerome and company at Bethlehem.
		386 John Bishop of Jerusalem.
	388 Palladius to Alexandria.	
	c. 390 Macarius the Egyptian dies. Palladius to Nitria.	
	391–2 Palladius to Cells. Destruction of Sarapeum. Temple at Canopus becomes Tabennesiote monastery ('Metanoea').	392 Porphyry Cross-Warden.
	393 Dioscorus Bishop of Damanhur. Macarius the Alexandrian dies.	393 Epiphanius visits Jerusalem. Jerome turns against Origen.
	394 Arsenius to Scetis? John of Lycopolis visited by Palladius and by author of *Historia Monachorum*.	394 Jerome and Epiphanius break with John and Rufinus.
395 Theodosius dies. ARCADIUS Emperor in East.	395 John of Lycopolis dies.	395 Porphyry Bishop of Gaza.
		397 Reconciliation in Jerusalem. Rufinus returns to the West.
398 John Chrysostom Bishop of Constantinople.		
	399 Evagrius dies. Theophilus' Paschal Letter against Anthropomorphism. Palladius and Cassian leave Egypt. Theophilus turns against Origen.	399 Palladius for a short time in Palestine.
400 Cassian deacon in Constantinople. Palladius Bishop of Helenopolis. Heraclides Bishop of Ephesus.	400 Synod at Alexandria condemns Origenism. Pilgrimage of Postumian.	400 Melania returns to the West. Tall Brothers, etc., exiled from Egypt, come to Scythopolis.
401 Tall Brothers in Constantinople.		
403 Epiphanius dies. Synod of the Oak.	Surviving exile monks return to their desert.	
404 Chrysostom exiled.		404 Paula dies. Jerome translates Pachomian Rule, etc. Rufinus translates *Historia Monachorum*.
405 Cassian in Rome.		405 Euthymius comes to Jerusalem, settles at Fara.
	406 Palladius in exile at Syene.	
407 Chrysostom dies.	407–8 First Devastation of Scetis.	
408 Arcadius dies. THEODOSIUS II (a boy).	408 Palladius at Antinoe.	

General	Egypt	Palestine
410 Alaric sacks Rome. Rufinus dies.		410 Melania returning dies in Jerusalem.
		411 Euthymius and Theoctistus settle in the Wadi Mukellik.
	412 Cyril Pope. Palladius leaves Egypt. 415 Murder of Hypatia.	415 Synod of Diospolis.
c. 417 Palladius Bishop of Aspuna.		417 Eustochium and Bishop John die. Praylius Bishop of Jerusalem. Melania the Younger comes to Jerusalem.
419–20 Palladius writes *Lausiac History.* c. 421 Cassian writes *Institutes* at Marseille.		
		c. 422 Conversion of Peter Aspebet. Euthymius leaves Theoctistus in Wadi Mukellik. 425 Juvenal Bishop of Jerusalem.
c. 426 Cassian writes *Collations.* 428 Nestorius Bishop of Constantinople.		c. 426 Euthymius settles at Khan-el-Ahmar. 428 Consecration of Church of Euthymius' Lavra. Nabarnugi (Peter the Iberian) comes to Jerusalem. Passarion dies.
c. 430 Theodosius the Coenobiarch born at Mogarissus. 431 Council of Ephesus (Christ indivisible: Mary *Theotokos*: Nestorius deposed).		
	c. 434 Second Devastation of Scetis. Arsenius to Troe.	
438 Bones of Chrysostom brought to Constantinople. Empress Eudocia and Cyril of Alexandria in Jerusalem for consecration of Churches. 439 Sabas born at Moutalaska.		439 Melania dies.
		443 Eudocia retires to Jerusalem.
449 Cyriac born at Corinth. Tome of Leo (two natures in Christ. Eutyches condemned). 'Latrocinium' of Ephesus (one nature). 450 MARCIAN Emperor. 451 Council of Chalcedon. (Tome of Leo accepted)	444 Cyril dies. Dioscorus Pope. c. 449 Arsenius dies.	444 Peter the Iberian withdraws to Maiuma.
	Dioscorus deposed. Proterius Pope.	Juvenal recognized as Patriarch; signs at Chalcedon.

General	*Egypt*	*Palestine*
		452 Monks in rebellion. Theodosius installed as bishop. Euthymius withdraws to Rouba. Peter the Iberian Bishop of Maiuma. 453 Juvenal restored. Peter withdraws to Egypt.
454 John the Hesychast born at Nicopolis. 455 Rome sacked by Vandals.	454 Dioscorus dies at Gangra.	
		456 Eudocia and Elpidius reconciled to Juvenal. Theodosius (Coenobiarch) and Sabas come to Jerusalem.
457 Marcian dies. LEO Emperor.	457 Proterius murdered. Timothy 'the Cat' consecrated by Peter the Iberian. Elias and Martyrius leave Nitria for Palestine.	457 Sabas to St. Theoctistus.
		458 Romanus returning from exile goes to Eleutheropolis.
459 Symeon the Stylite dies.		459 Juvenal dies. Anastasius Patriarch.
460 Daniel mounts pillar near Constantinople.	460 Timothy the Cat exiled. Timothy Salophaciolus Pope.	460 Eudocia dies.
461 Pope St. Leo dies.		
		466 Theoctistus dies. Cyriac comes to Jerusalem. 473 Euthymius dies.
474 ZENO Emperor.		474 Sabas in the Wilderness. Peter the Iberian back in Palestine.
475 BASILISCUS seizes power. *Encyclical* against Chalcedon. Peter the Fuller Patriarch of Antioch, ordains John Rufus. 476 End of Western Empire. *Antencyclical*. Zeno restored.	475 Timothy the Cat restored.	475 Gerasimus dies. Anastasius accepts Encyclical.
	478 Timothy the Cat dies. Salophaciolus restored.	478 Sabas at 'Mar Saba'. Martyrius Patriarch.
479 Calandion Patriarch of Antioch. John Rufus leaves Antioch.		479 Theodosius founds Coenobium. Martyrius compromises. Marcian of Bethlehem reconciled. John Rufus joins Peter the Iberian.
481 John Bishop of Colonia. 482 *Henotikon* of Zeno.	482 Salophaciolus dies. Peter Mongus Pope.	482 Coenobium of St. Euthymius consecrated. 483 Sabas establishes Lavra at Mar Saba. 485 Cyriac to Souka. 486 Sallust Patriarch. Marcian Archimandrite. 487 Peter Ib. flees to Phoenicia to escape summons to Constantinople.

General	Egypt	Palestine
		489 Esaias and Peter die.
	490 Athanasius Pope.	490 Sabas ordained priest. 'God-built' Church consecrated. Severus becomes a monk at Maiuma.
491 ANASTASIUS Emperor (favouring monophysites).		491 John Bishop of Colonia flees to Mar Saba.
		492 Foundation of Castellium. Marcian dies. Theodosius and Sabas Archimandrites.
		494 Elias Patriarch.
	497 John II Pope.	
498 Flavian Patriarch of Antioch.		
		501 *Theotokos* Church at Mar Saba consecrated.
	505 John III Pope.	
		507 Foundation of New Lavra.
508–11 Severus in Constantinople.		
		509 John enclosed in cell at Mar Saba.
511 Synod of Sidon.		
511–12 Sabas in Constantinople.		512 Sabas returns. Mamas of Eleutheropolis accepts Chalcedon.
512 Severus Patriarch of Antioch (Flavian deposed).		513 Elias refuses Severus' synodicals.
	516 Dioscorus Pope.	516 Elias banished to Aila. John Patriarch.
	517 Timothy Pope.	
518 Anastasius, Elias and Flavian die. JUSTIN Emperor. Chalcedon accepted. Severus flees to Egypt.		518 Synod at Jerusalem proclaims Four Councils. Sabas carries news round Palestine.
519 Reconciliation with Rome.		
		524 Peter Patriarch.
		525 Cyriac leaves Souks for desert of Natoupha.
526 Earthquake at Antioch.		
527 JUSTINIAN Emperor.		
529 Edict against Pagans.		529 Theodosius dies. Samaritan Revolt.
		530 Cyriac in desert of Rouba.
531 Sabas in Constantinople.		531–2 Sabas returning visits Caesarea and Scythopolis.
532 Nika Revolt. Dogmatic conversations at Constantinople.		532 Sabas dies.
	535 Theodosius Pope of Alexandria.	535 Cyriac to Sousakim.
536 Synod at Constantinople.	537 Paul Pope of Alexandria.	537 Gelasius hegumen of Mar Saba.
c. 537 Theodore Ascidas Bishop of Caesarea in Cappadocia.	538 Severus dies in Egypt.	

General	Egypt	Palestine
	540 Paul deposed by Synod at Gaza. Zoilus Pope.	
542–3 Plague.	Plague.	Plague. 542 Cyriac to Cave of St. Chariton.
543 Edict against Origen.		543 Sophronius successor of Theodosius dies. Consecration of *New Church*. Cyril of Scythopolis comes to Jerusalem. *c.* 543 Seridus, John and Varsanuphius die. 544 Cyril enters Coenobium of St. Euthymius. 546 Gelasius dies returning from vain visit to Constantinople. 547 George (Origenist) hegumen at Mar Saba, then deposed. Cassian installed. Cyriac back at Sousakim.
548 Theodora dies.		548 Cassian dies. Conon hegumen.
551 Conon in Constantinople.	551 Apollinarius Pope of Alexandria.	552 Patriarch Peter dies. Macarius installed, then replaced by Eustochius.
553 5th Council (Constantinople; Origenism and 'Three Chapters' condemned).		555 Origenists ousted from New Lavra. Cyriac back at Cave of St. Chariton.
556–7 Castrum built on Sinai. Doulas hegumen.		556–7 Cyril writing Lives. Cyriac dies. 557 Cyril moves to Mar Saba; writes Life of St. John the Hesychast not yet dead. 563–4 Eustochius ousted from patriarchate: Macarius restored. Gregory is hegumen of Fara. *c.* 564–74? Moschus at Fara.
565 Justinian dies. JUSTIN II Emperor. 565–6 Apse-mosaic in Sinai: Longinus hegumen. *c.* 567 Gregory hegumen of Sinai. 570 Gregory Patriarch of Antioch. (Anastasius ousted.)	570 John Pope.	
	574–84? Moschus in Egypt. *c.* 576? Death of Anastasia in Scetis?	

General	Egypt	Palestine
	577? Devastation of Scetis.	
578 TIBERIUS Emperor.	578 Moschus in Oasis.	
	581 Eulogius Pope.	
582 MAURICE Emperor.		
		583 Macarius dies. John III Patriarch.
584-94 Moschus at Lavra of Aeliotes on Sinai?		
590 Gregory Pope of Rome.		
593 Gregory of Antioch dies. Anastasius restored.		593 John III dies.
Evagrius completes History.		
		594 Amos Patriarch. Moschus and Sophronius in Palestine.
602 PHOCAS murders Maurice, seizes Empire.		601 Isaac Patriarch.
604 St. Gregory dies.		
	c. 608 Moschus and Sophronius in Egypt.	
		609 Isaac resigns.
610 HERACLIUS Emperor.	610 John the Almoner Pope of Alexandria.	Zacharias Patriarch.
611 Persians take Antioch.		
613 Persians take Damascus.		
		614 Persians take Jerusalem.
	617 Persians take Alexandria. Pope John dies. Moschus and Sophronius to Samos, then to Rome, where Moschus dies.	Zacharias a captive.
626 Maximus with Sophronius in Africa.		
628 Martyrdom of Anastasius. Death of Chosroes.		
629 Peace between Rome and Persia.		629 Battle of Muta.
		631 Heraclius restores the Cross to Jerusalem. Modestus Patriarch, then dies.
	633 Sophronius in Alexandria.	
		634 Sophronius Patriarch.
		636 Battle of the Yarmuk.
641 Heraclius dies.		638 Sophronius surrenders Jerusalem to Omar.
	642 Alexandria falls to Arabs.	
649 Stephen Bishop of Dor at Lateran Council against Monotheletes.		

BIBLIOGRAPHY

I. SOURCES AND RELATED STUDIES

AETHERIA. Éthérie, Journal de Voyage, ed. H. Pétré, S.C. 21.

AMMONAS. Epistulae, etc.—syriae, ed. Kmosko, P.O. X. 6; graece, ed. Nau, P.O. XI. 4.

AMMONIUS. Account of the Martyrs of Sinai and Rhaithou, ed. Combefis, *Illustrium Christi Martyrum lecti triumphi*, Paris, 1660, pp. 88–122; *The Forty Martyrs of the Sinai Desert*, ed. Mrs. Lewis, *Horae Semiticae* IX (1912)—Palestinian Syriac version and English translation.

ANASTASIUS PERSA. *Acta Martyris Anastasii Persae*, ed. Usener, Bonn, 1894—see also *P.G.* 92, 1680–1729.

ANASTASIUS SINAITA. *P.G.* 89—Ὁδηγός (*Viae Dux*), 35–310: *Quaestiones et Responsiones*, 311–824: *Homilia in Psalmum Sextum*, 1077–84: *Récits*, ed. Nau, *O.C.* II (1902), pp. 58–89; III (1903), pp. 56–90.

ANTIOCHUS SABAITA. *Pandect*, etc., *P.G.* 89, 1421–1856.

ANTONIUS MAGNUS. Seven *Letters*—Latin version, *P.G.* 40, 977–1000: Georgian version, with fragments of Coptic original, ed. Garitte, *C.S.C.O.*, Scr. Ib. t. 5 (Latine, t. 6): Syriac (1st letter only), ed. Nau, *R.O.C.* 14 (1909), pp. 282–97. *Vita Antonii*—see Athanasius. See also ANTONIUS MAGNUS EREMITA, *Studia Anselmiana* 38, ed. Steidle, Rome, 1956 (a centenary symposium: note bibliography on pp. 13–14).

ANTONIUS CHOZIBITA. *A.B.* 7 (1888)—Vita S. Georgii Chozibitae, pp. 97–144, 336–59: *Miracula B. V. Mariae in Choziba*, pp. 360–70.

APOPHTHEGMATA PATRUM. Essential for the study of the *Apophthegmata* are W. Bousset, *Apophthegmata*, Tübingen, 1923, and J.-C. Guy, S.J., *Recherches sur la tradition grecque des Apophthegmata Patrum* (Subsidia hagiographica, No. 36), Brussels, 1962.

   a. *Alphabetical Collection*—P.G. 65, 71–440, supplemented by Guy, pp. 19–36.

   b. *Anonymous Collection* (to accompany the Alphabetical), partially published by Nau (N 1–392) in R.O.C. 12–14, 17–18 (1907–9, 1912–13): the rest analysed by Guy, pp. 64–74—N (Guy) 393–670—and pp. 95–7—J *661–765*.

   c. *Systematic Collection*, still unpublished in Greek. Latin version made by Pelagius and John (PJ) is found in *P.L.* 73, 851–1052. Guy (pp. 126–81) gives tables of the much fuller form of this collection to be reconstructed from the Greek MSS. A fragmentary Coptic (Sahidic) version was prepared for the press by M. Chaine, and published after his death by A. Guillaumont—*Le Manuscrit de la version copte en dialecte sahidique des 'Apophthegmata Patrum'*—Bibliothèque d'Études coptes, VI (Cairo, 1960), of the Institut francais d'Archeologie orientale.

   d. *Syriac Systematic Collection* of 'Anân-Isho', published by Bedjan, A.M.S. VII, pp. 442 to end; and by Budge, with some variants, in various editions—most accessible in the English version, *The Wit and Wisdom of the Christian Fathers of Egypt* (O.U.P. 1934). This has no direct connection with the Greek Systematic Collection: and the older unpublished collections on which it is based (e.g. MS. Add. 17,176, dated A.D. 532) seem to show no clear relationship in their order to any of the known Greek or Latin collections.

At present, the Greek text of very many of the Apophthegmata is only to be found published in the Ascetic Anthology of Paul Evergetinos, Συναγωγὴ τῶν θεοφθόγγων ῥημάτων καὶ Διδασκαλιῶν τῶν ἁγίων καὶ θεοφόρων Πατέρων, 3rd edition, Athens, 1900.

ATHANASIUS. Opera Omnia, *P.G.* 25–8: *Vita Antonii, P.G.* 26, 835–976; tr. Meyer, *A.C.W.* 10 (1950): *Epistula ad Amunem monachum*, 26, 1169–76: *Epistula ad Dracontium*, 25, 523–34: *Festal Letters*, with preceding *Index* (Latin from Syriac, with Greek fragments), 26, 1351–1444; Syriac version, ed. Cureton, London, 1848; English, tr. Burgess, Oxford (Library of the Fathers), 1854.

BARSANUPHIUS—see VARSANUPHIUS.

BASIL OF CAESAREA. Opera Omnia, ed. Garnier, Paris, 1721–30, reprinted 1839 (3 vols): *P.G.* 29–32. *Ascetica* in Garnier, t. 2: tr. W. K. Lowther Clarke, *The Ascetic Works of St. Basil*, S.P.C.K. 1925. *Letters* in Garnier, t. 3: text and translation (by R. Deferrari) in Loeb edition (4 vols.). See also W. K. L. Clarke, *St. Basil the Great*, C.U.P., 1913.

BELL, H. Idris. *Jews and Christians in Egypt*, British Museum, 1924—Meletian and other fourth-century monastic papyri, Greek and Coptic, with translation.

CASSIAN. Opera Omnia, *P.L.* 49–50: ed. Petschenig, *C.S.E.L.* 13 and 17 (Vienna, 1886–8): Collations (*Conférences*) ed. and Tr. Pichery, S.C. 42, 54, 64: Institutes (*Institutions cénobitiques*) ed. and tr. Guy, S.C. 109. See also Owen Chadwick, *John Cassian*, C.U.P., 1950. S. Marsili, *Giovanni Cassiano ed Evagrio Pontico*, Studia Anselmiana 5, Rome, 1936.

CHARITON. *Vita Charitonis*, ed. Garitte, Bulletin de l'Institut historique belge de Rome, 1941, pp. 5–50.

CHRIST (W.) and PARANIKAS (M.). *Anthologia graeca Carminum Christianorum*, Leipzig, 1871.

CHRYSIPPUS. Encomium of St. Theodore, *A.S.* Nov. 4, 55–72: St. Michael, ed. Sigalas, Ἐπετηρὶς Βυζαντινῶν Σπουδῶν, 1926, 85–93: the Theotokos, P.O. XIX. 3 (1926), 336–43: St. John Baptist, ed. Sigalas, *Texte und Forschungen zur byzantinisch-neugriechischen Philologie*, Nr. 20 (Athens, 1937)—with a very full bibliography.

COLLECTIO AVELLANA—Letters of Popes and Emperors, C.S.E.L. 35 (1895–8).

CONSULTATIO ZACCHAEI ET APOLLONII, ed. Morin, *Florilegium Patristicum* 39 (1935).

COSMAS INDICOPLEUSTES, *Christian Topography*, P.G. 88, 51–470, ed. Winstedt, C.U.P., 1909.

CYRIL OF SCYTHOPOLIS. Vitae SS. Euthymii, Sabae, etc., ed. Schwartz, *Kyrillos von Skythopolis*, T. und U. 49. 2 (1939)—reviewed by Stein, *A.B.* 62 (1944), pp. 169–86: French translations by Festugière in *Les Moines d'Orient*, III. 1–3 (Paris, 1961–3).

DANIEL OF SCETIS. *Vie et récits de l'Abbé Daniel le Scétiote*, ed. Clugnet, Paris, 1901 (reprinted from *R.O.C.* 5: Greek, Coptic and Syriac).

DAWES (E.) and BAYNES (N. H.). *Three Byzantine Saints* (Oxford, Blackwell, 1948)—Translations of Lives of St. Daniel the Stylite, St. Theodore of Sykeon, and St. John the Almsgiver.

DIONYSIUS AREOPAGITA (PSEUDO-). *P.G.* 3–4. *La Hierarchie céleste*, ed. Roques and Heil, tr. de Gandillac, *S.C.* 58 (1958). *The Divine Names* and *The Mystical*

Theology, tr. C. E. Rolt, S.P.C.K., 1957 (1st ed. 1920). See also R. Roques, *L'univers dionysien*, Paris, 1954.

DOROTHEUS OF GAZA. *P.G.* 88, 1611–1842. *Dorothée de Gaza, Œuvres spirituelles*, ed. and tr. Regnault and de Préville, *S.C.* 92 (1963)

DRAGUET, R. *Les Pères du Désert*, Paris, 1949 (French translations with Introduction).

EPHRAIM SYRUS. 'Opera Omnia' (Syriac, Greek, Latin), 6 vols., ed. Assemani, Rome, 1732–46. *Hymni et Sermones*, 4 vols., ed. Lamy, Malines, 1882–1902. *Carmina Nisibena*, ed. Bickell, Leipzig, 1866, etc.

EPIPHANIUS OF SALAMIS. *P.G.* 41–3. G.C.S. 25, 31, 37 (ed. Holl), Berlin, 1915–33.

ESAIAS OF SCETIS. Τοῦ ὁσίου πατρὸς ἡμῶν ἀββᾶ 'Ησαΐυ λόγοι κθ', ed. Avgoustinos, Jerusalem, 1911. Latin version in *P.G.* 40, 1105–1206. *L'Ascéticon Copte de l'Abbé Isaïe*, fragments sahidiques, ed. and tr. A. Guillaumont, Cairo, 1956.

EUNAPIUS. *Vitae Sophistarum* (Philostratus and E.), ed. and tr. Wright, Loeb Classical Library, London, 1922.

EUSEBIUS OF CAESAREA. *Historia Ecclesiastica*, ed. Schwartz (with Rufinus' Latin version and continuation, ed. Mommsen), 3 vols., G.C.S. 9, 1903–9: English translation and Notes, Lawlor and Oulton, S.P.C.K., 1927–8. *Chronicle* (Jerome's version and continuation), ed. Helm, G.C.S. 24 and 34.

EUTYCHIUS OF ALEXANDRIA. *Annals* (Latin from Arabic), P.G. 111, 907–1156.

EVAGRIUS PONTICUS. *Opera, P.G.* 40, 1213–86. Works attributed to Nilus, *P.G.* 79, 1139–1245. *Opera syriace*, ed. W. Frankenberg, Abh. der Kgl. Gesellsch. der Wissensch. zu Göttingen, Phil. Hist. Klasse N.F. XIII. 2, Berlin, 1912. *Les Six Centuries des 'Kephalaia Gnostica' d'Évagre le Pontique* (two Syriac versions), ed. Guillaumont, P.O. XXVIII. 1 (1958). *Nonnenspiegel und Mönchspiegel des E.P.*, ed. Gressmann, T. und U. 39. 4 (Leipzig, 1913). See also Muyldermans, *À travers la tradition manuscrite d'E. le P.*, Bibliotheque du Muséon 3, Louvain 1932; *Evagriana Syriaca*, B. du M. 31, Louvain, 1952; and especially Guillaumont, *Les Kephalaia Gnostica d'Évagre le Pontique* (Patristica Sorbonensia 5), Paris, 1962, for a very full account and bibliography.

EVAGRIUS SCHOLASTICUS. *Historia Ecclesiastica*, ed. Bidez and Parmentier, London, 1898.

GARITTE, G. (ed.). *Le Calendrier Palestino-Georgien du Sinaiticus 34 (Xe siècle)*— Subsidia Hagiographica 30, Brussels, 1958.

GERONTIUS. *Vita S. Melaniae Junioris*: ed. Gorce, *Vie de Ste. Mélanie, S.C.* 90, Paris, 1962.

GEYER, P. *Itinera Hierosolymitana, C.S.E.L.* 39, Vienna, 1898.

GREGORY OF ACRAGAS—*Vita*, P.G. 98, 549–716.

GREGORY OF ROME, *Letters*, ed. Ewald and Hartmann (2 vols.), 1891–9. *Dialogues*, ed. Moricca, Rome, 1924.

HALKIN, F. *Bibliotheca hagiographica graeca* (3rd edition, 3 vols.), Subsidia hagiographica 8a, Brussels, 1957.

HESYCHIUS OF JERUSALEM. *Opera, P.G.* 93. But see K. Jussen, *Die dogmatischen Anschauungen des H. von J.* (2 vols.), 1931 and 1934.

HIEROTHEUS. *The Book of the Holy Hierotheus*, ed. and tr. Marsh, Text and Translation Society, 1928. See also A. L. Frothingham, *Stephen Bar-Sudaili, the Syrian Mystic*, Leyde, 1886.

HISTORIA ACEPHALA. P.G. 26, 1443–50.

HISTORIA MONACHORUM IN AEGYPTO: ed. E. Presuchen, *Palladius und Rufinus* (Giessen, 1897), pp. 1–97; A.-J. Festugière, Subsidia hagiographica 34, Brussels, 1961. Rufinus' Latin version, *P.L.* 21, 387–462.

JEROME. *P.L.* 22–30. Letters, *P.L.* 22; *C.S.E.L.* 54–6, 59, Vienna, 1910–18. Lives of Monks, Pachomian translations, polemical writings, *De Viris illustribus*, etc., *P.L.* 23. *De Viris illustribus*, ed. Richardson, *T. und U.* 14. 1, Leipzig, 1896. *Chronicle*, ed. Helm, *G.C.S.* 24 and 34 (1913, 1926). See F. Cavallera, *Saint Jerome, sa vie et son œuvre*, Louvain, 1922.

JOHN CLIMACUS. *P.G.* 88, 596–1210: ed. Trevisan (2 vols. with Italian translation), Corona Patrum Salesiana, ser. gr., 9, Turin, 1941; English translation, *The Ladder of Divine Ascent*, L. Moore and M. Heppell, Faber & Faber, 1959.

JOHN THE ALMONER. *Leontius von Neapolis, Leben des heiligen Johannes des barmherzigen, Erzbischofs von Alexandrien*, ed. Gelzer, 1893: *Une Vie inédite de S. Jean l'Aumonier*, ed. Delehaye, *A.B.* 45 (1927): English translation in Dawes and Baynes, *v. supra.*

JOHN MOSCHUS. *Pratum Spirituale*, *P.G.* 87. 3, 2851–3116: *P.L.* 74, 119–240: Th. Nissen, *Unbekannte Erzählungen aus dem P.S.*, *B.Z.* 38 (1938), 351–76: French translation by Rouet de Journel, *S.C.* 12, Paris, 1946.

JOHN OF NIKIU. *Chronicle*, tr. R. H. Charles, London, 1916, from Ethiopic version, ed. Zotenberg, Paris, 1883, reprinted 1935.

JOHN RUFUS OF MAIUMA. *Life of Peter the Iberian*, ed. Raabe, *Petrus der Iberer*, Leipzig, 1895 (Syriac text and German translation): English summarized version in D. M. Lang, *Lives and Legends of the Georgian Saints*, Allen & Unwin, 1956, pp. 57–80. *Plerophories*, ed. Nau, *P.O.* VIII. 1, Paris, 1911. *Narratio de obitu Theodosii Hierosolymorum et Romani monachi*, ed. Brooks, *C.S.C.O.*, Scr. Syr., ser. 3, t. 25, 18–27.

JUSTINIAN. Opera Dogmatica, *P.G.* 86. 1, 945–1152.

KEKELIDZE, K. *Ierusalimskij Kanonar' VII vjeka* (Georgian version), Tiflis, 1912 (a retranslation of this into Greek by Archimandrite Kallistos was being published in Νέα Σιων in 1914 (Year XI, tom. 14, pp. 35–59, 202–41, 310–42), but was interrupted by the war).

KOIKYLIDES, Kleopas M. Αἱ παρὰ τὸν 'Ιορδάνην Λαῦραι Καλαμῶνος καὶ ἁγίου Γερασίμου, καὶ οἱ βίοι τοῦ ἁγίου Γερασίμου καὶ Κυριακοῦ τοῦ ἀναχωρητοῦ, Jerusalem, 1902 (contains the text of the *Vita Gerasimi* attributed to Cyril of Scythopolis, and other Lives).

LEONTIUS OF BYZANTIUM. Works attributed to L., *P.G.* 86. 1–2, 1155–2100. See S. Rees in *J.T.S.* 40 (1939), 346–60, and 41 (1940), 263–80.

LEONTIUS OF NEAPOLIS. *Life of St. John the Almoner—v. supra. Vita Simeonis Sali*, *P.G.* 93, 1669–1748; ed. Rydén, Stockholm, 1963

LIBERATUS DIACONUS. *Breviarium*, *P.L.* 68: Schwartz, *A.C.* II. 5, 98–141.

MACARIUS AEGYPTIUS (Pseudo-). *P.G.* 34: *Macarii Anecdota*, ed. Marriott, Harvard, 1918: *Neue Homilien des Makarius-Symeon*. I: aus Typus III, ed. Klostermann and Berthold, *T. und U.* 72, Berlin, 1961: *Die 50 geistlichen Homilien des Makarios*, edd. Dorries, Klostermann and Kroeger, *Patristische Texte und Studien*, 4, Berlin, 1964.

MARCUS DIACONUS. *Vita S. Porphyrii Gazensis*, edd. Grégoire and Kügener, *Vie de Porphyre*, Paris, 1930: Tr. Lat., *P.G.* 65, 1211–54: Georgian, ed. Peeters, *A.B.* 1941, 65–216.

MARCUS MONACHUS (EREMITA). *P.G.* 65, 905–1140. We look forward to a much-needed critical edition being prepared by Dr. Kallistos Ware.

MARIUS MERCATOR. *P.L.* 48: Schwartz, *A.C.* I. 5, 5–70.

MAXIMUS CONFESSOR. *P.G.* 90–1. *The Ascetic Life: the Four Centuries on Charity,* tr. P. Sherwood, *A.C.W.* 21, 1955. See also Sherwood, *An annotated Date-List of the works of Maximus the Confessor,* Rome, 1952: H. U. von Balthasar, *Kosmische Liturgie* (2nd ed.), Einsiedeln, 1961; *Liturgie Cosmique* (French version of 1st ed.), Paris, 1947; L. Thunberg, *Microcosm and Mediator,* Lund, 1965, with a very full up-to-date bibliography.

NILUS OF ANCYRA. *P.G.* 79 (a number of works attributed to him belong to Evagrius Ponticus).

NILUS OF SINAI. *Narrationes de caede monachorum in Monte Sinai* (of very doubtful historicity), *P.G.* 79, 589–603.

PACHOMIUS, THEODORE AND HORSIESIUS. *Oeuvres de S. Pachôme et de ses Disciples,* ed. and tr. Lefort, *C.S.C.O.,* Scr. Copt., tt. 23–4, Louvain, 1956. *Pachomiana Latina,* ed. A. Boon, Louvain, 1932. *S. Pachomii Vitae graecae,* ed. Halkin, Subsidia hagiographica 19, Brussels, 1932. *S. Pachômii Vita bohairice scripta,* ed. Lefort, *C.S.C.O.* Scr. Copt., ser. 3, t. 7, Paris, 1925: *S.P. Vitae sahidice scriptae,* ed. Lefort, ibid., t. 8, Paris, 1933–4. *Les Vies coptes de S. Pachôme et de ses premiers successeurs* (French translation), ed. Lefort, Louvain, 1943 (I criticized some points in this in *J.E.H.,* V. 1 (1951), pp. 38–77, *Pachomian Sources reconsidered*). *Histoire de S. Pakhôme et de ses communautés,* documents coptes et arabes inédits, publiés et traduits par E. Amélineau, *A.M.G.* 17, Paris, 1889 (still important for the Arabic Life, pp. 337–711). *Der Papyruscodex saec. VI-VII der Phillippsbibliothek in Cheltenham,* Koptische theologische Scriften, ed. W. E. Crum, Strassburg, 1915. See also P. Ladeuze, *Étude sur le Cénobitisme Pachomien,* Louvain, 1898.

PALLADIUS. *Dialogus de Vita Chrysostomi,* ed. Coleman-Norton, C.U.P., 1928. *Lausiac History,* ed. Dom Cuthbert Butler, Texts and Studies 6, C.U.P.— Vol. 1. Prolegomena, 1898: Vol. 2. Introduction and Text, 1904. Tr. Lowther Clarke, S.P.C.K., 1918.

PAULINUS OF NOLA. Ed. Hartel, *C.S.E.L.* 29–30, Vienna, 1894.

PAUL OF ELOUSA. Vita Theognii, *A.B.* 10, pp. 72–118.

PAULUS HELLADICUS. *Epistula*—Anecdota Byzantina, ed. V. Lundström, Upsala and Leipzig, 1902, pp. 15–23.

PHILOSTORGIUS. *Historia Ecclesiastica,* ed. Bidez, *G.C.S.* 21, Berlin, 1913.

PRISE DE JÉRUSALEM (Strategius). Georgian Version, ed. and tr. Garitte, *La prise de Jérusalem par les Perses en* 615, *C.S.C.O.,* Scr. Ib., 11–12, 1960.

PROCOPIUS OF CAESAREA. *Wars: Secret History: Buildings*: ed. and tr. Dewing and Downey, Loeb Classical Library (7 vols.), 1914–40.

RUFINUS OF AQUILEIA. *Opera, P.L.* 21. *Historia Ecclesiastica,* continuing Eusebius (bks. 10–11), ed. Mommsen, *G.C.S.* 9, vol. II, pp. 957–1040. See F. X. Murphy, *Rufinus of Aquileia* (345–411), *His Life and Works,* Catholic University of America, Studies in Mediaeval History, New Series, Vol. VI, Washington, D.C., 1945. *Historia Monachorum in Aegypto* (Latin version), *P.L.* 21, 387–462.

SARAPION OF THMUIS. *Epistula ad Monachos, P.G.* 40, 925–42: *Letter on the Death of St. Antony,* ed. Draguet, Le Muséon 64 (1951), pp. 1–25.

SEBEOS. *History of Heraclius*, Armenian text and Russian translation, ed. Patkanian, St. Petersburg, 1879: French translation, ed. Macler, Paris, 1904.

SEVERUS OF ANTIOCH. *The Sixth Book of the Select Letters of Severus*, ed. and tr. Brooks, Text and Translation Society, 1904: *A Collection of Letters of Severus of Antioch*, ed. and tr. Brooks, *P.O.* XII. 2: *Lives, P.O.* II: Homilies and other works in *P.O., O.C., R.O.C., C.S.C.O.*, etc. See J. Lebon, *Le Monophysisme sévérien*, Louvain, 1909.

SEVERUS OF ASHMUNEIN. *History of the Patriarchs of the Coptic Church*, ed. Evetts, *P.O.* I, 99–214, 381–518; V. 1–25; X. 357–552.

SOCRATES, *H.E.*, ed. Hussey (3 vols.), Oxford, 1853; *P.G.* 67, 29–872.

SOPHRONIUS OF JERUSALEM. *P.G.* 87. 3, 3147–4104: Christmas Sermon (A.D. 534), ed. graece Usener, *Kleine Schrifte* IV (1913), pp. 162–77: *De Praesentatione Domini*, Bonner Universitäts-Programm, 3rd. Aug., 1889: On the *Baptism*, ed. Papadopoulos-Keramevs, Ἀνάλεκτα Ἱεροσολυμιτικῆς Σταχυολογίας, 5 (1898), pp. 151–68.

SOZOMEN. *H.E.*, ed. Hussey (3 vols.), Oxford, 1860; *P.G.* 67, 844–1630.

SULPICIUS SEVERUS. Ed. Helm, *C.S.E.L.* 1, Vienna, 1866.

THEODORET. *H.E.*, ed. Gaisford, Oxford, 1854; ed. Parmentier, *G.C.S.* 19, 1911. *Historia Religiosa, P.G.* 82, 1283–1496. *Letters*, ed. Azéma, *S.C.* 40, 98, 111, Paris, 1954–65 (147 out of 232 surviving: the rest to follow).

THEODORUS LECTOR. *H.E., P.G.* 86, 165–228.

THEODORE OF PETRA. *Vita Theodosii Coenobiarchae*, ed. Usener, *Der heilige Theodosius*, Leipzig (Teubner), 1890: French translation in Festugière, *Les Moines d'Orient*, III. 3 (Paris, 1963), pp. 85–160.

VARSANUPHIUS AND JOHN. Βίβλος Βαρσανουφίου καὶ Ἰωάννου, ed. Nikodemos, Venice, 1816; S. Schoinas, Volos, 1960.

WADDELL, Helen. *The Desert Fathers*, translated from the Latin with an introduction by H.W., London, 1931.

WENSINCK, A. J. *Legends of Eastern Saints*: I. *Archelides*, Leyden, 1911: II. *Hilaria daughter of Zeno*, Leyden, 1913.

ZACHARIAS RHETOR. *Vita Esaiae*, ed. Brooks, *C.S.C.O.*, Scr. Syr. 3, t. 25, 1–16. *Vita Severi*, ed. Kugener, *P.O.* II, 1–115. *Chronicle*, ed. Land, *Anecdota Syriaca* 3, 2–340; tr. Hamilton and Brooks, *The Syriac Chronicle known as that of Zachariah of Mitylene*, London, 1899.

ZOSIMAS, Abba. Τοῦ ὁσίου πατρὸς ἡμῶν ἀββᾶ Ζωσιμᾶ κεφάλαια πάνυ ὠφέλιμα, ed. Avgoustinos, Jerusalem, 1913: less complete in *P.G.* 78, 1680–1701.

II. OTHER RELEVANT BOOKS

ABEL, F.-M. *Géographie de la Palestine* (2 vols.), Paris, 1933 and 1938.

CAUWENBERGH, P. VAN. *Étude sur les moines d'Égypte depuis le Concile de Chalcédoine jusqu'à l'invasion arabe*, Paris and Louvain, 1869–1914.

COURET, A. *La Palestine sous les Empereurs grecs*, 326–636, Grenoble.

DE COSSON, A. *Mareotis*, London, 1935.

DE VAUX, R. *L'Archéologie et les Manuscrits de la Mer Morte.* O.U.P., 1961

DIEKAMP, F. *Die Origenistischen Streitigkeiten im sechsten Jahrhundert*, Münster, 1899.

DORESSE, J. *Les livres secrets des gnostiques d'Égypte*, Paris, 1958.

EVELYN WHITE, H. G. *The Monasteries of the Wadi'n Natrnû*: Part II, *The History of the Monasteries of Nitria and Scetis*: Part III, *The Architecture and Archaeology*: New York, 1932–3.

FAVALE, A. *Teofilo d'Alessandria* (345c.–412), Turin, 1958.

FESTUGIÈRE, A.-J. *Antioche paienne et chrétienne*, Paris, 1959. *Les Moines d'Orient*, I. *Culture ou Sainteté*, Paris, 1961. II. Lives of Hypatius and of Daniel the Stylite, Paris, 1962. III. Cyril of Scythopolis' Lives, Paris, 1962–3. IV. Historia Monachorum and Vita Prima of Pachomius, 1965.—All these Lives in French translation with notes.

GÉNIER, R. *Vie de Saint Euthyme le Grand* (377–473), Paris, 1909.

HARDY, E. R. (Jr.). *Christian Egypt: Church and People*, O.U.P., 1962. *The Large Estates of Byzantine Egypt*, New York, 1931.

HAUSHERR, I. *Les leçons d'un contemplatif. Le traité de l'oraison d'Évagre le Pontique*, Paris, 1960.

HEUSSI, K. *Der Ursprung des Mönchtums*, Tübingen, 1936.

HOLL, K. *Enthusiasmus und Bussgewalt beim griechischen Mönchtum*, Leipzig, 1898. Gesammelte Aufsätze, 1928.

JONES, A. H. M. *The Later Roman Empire*, 284–602, Blackwell, 1964.

KOCH, H. *Quellen zur Geschichte der Askese und des Mönchtums in der alten Kirche*, Tübingen, 1931.

MAZZARINI. *Aspetti soziali del IV secolo*. 1951.

MONNERET DE VILLARD, U. *Les Couvents près de Sohag*, Paris, 1925. *Il Monastero di S. Simeone presso Aswan*, 1927.

ROSTOVTZEFF, M. *Social and Economic History of the Roman Empire*, Oxford, 1926.

SCHIWIETZ, S. *Das morgenländische Mönchtum*, Bd. 1, Mainz, 1904; Bd. 2, 1913; Bd. 3, 1939.

SEECK, O. *Geschichte des Untergangs der antiken Welt*, Berlin, 1895–1913.

SMITH, G. ADAM. *The Historical Geography of the Holy Land*, London, 1935 (26th edition).

SOTERIOU, G. and M. *Icones du Mont Sinai* (2 vols.), Athens, 1956–8.

STEIN, E. *Histoire du Bas-Empire*: I. 284–476 (in German), Vienna, 1928: 2nd edition (in French), Paris, 1959; II. 476–565 (in French), Paris, 1949.

VINCENT (L.-H.) and ABEL (F.-M.). *Jérusalem Nouvelle*, Paris, 1914–26.